GL🌐BAL
B®AND ©
INTEGRITY
MANAGEMENT ™

How to Protect Your Product in Today's Competitive Environment

RICHARD S. POST AND PENELOPE N. POST

New York   Chicago   San Francisco   Lisbon   London   Madrid   Mexico City
Milan   New Delhi   San Juan   Seoul   Singapore   Sydney   Toronto

1 2 3 4 5 6 7 8 9 0 DOC/DOC 0 9 8 7

ISBN 978-0-07-149444-1
MHID 0-07-149444-8

This publication is designed to provide accurate and authoritative information in regard to the subject matter covered. It is sold with the understanding that neither the author nor the publisher is engaged in rendering legal, accounting, futures/securities trading, or other professional service. If legal advice or other expert assistance is required, the services of a competent professional person should be sought.
—*From a Declaration of Principles jointly adopted by a Committee of the American Bar Association and a Committee of Publishers*

McGraw-Hill books are available at special quantity discounts to use as premiums and sales promotions, or for use in corporate training programs. For more information, please write to the Director of Special Sales, Professional Publishing, McGraw-Hill, Two Penn Plaza, New York, NY 10121-2298. Or contact your local bookstore.

This book is printed on acid-free paper.

Library of Congress Cataloging-in-Publication Data

Post, Richard S.
  Global brand integrity management : how to protect your product in today's competitive environment / Richard S. Post and Penelope N. Post.
      p. cm.
  ISBN-13: 978-0-07-149444-1 (hardcover : alk. paper)
  ISBN-10: 0-07-149444-8
  1. Brand name products.   2. Trademark infringement—Prevention.   3. Product counterfeiting—Prevention.   4. Product management.   I. Post, Penelope N.   II. Title.
HD69.B7R644   2007
658.8'27—dc22   2007009029

CONTENTS

FOREWORD

The global business landscape has undergone dramatic changes over the last 17 years. In many ways the changes have been the most rapid and dramatic in the history of the global economy.

Geopolitical blocks that at one time appeared to be formed in stone have reshaped themselves into open and competitive markets, starting with the demise of the Soviet Union in 1991, through the market reforms that the Chinese government began pushing in 1992, to the increased liberalization of the Indian economy beginning in 1994. In only a few years' time, a significant portion of the world's population went from toiling under state-controlled economies to jumping into the global capitalistic marketplace. The developed capitalistic societies suddenly had access to once-closed markets, teeming with individuals desiring access to their products and wanting to work in their stores and factories.

In a remarkable corollary, as the geopolitical world was undergoing this dramatic transformation, modern science and engineering were delivering rapid advancements in the areas of communications, data storage, access and analysis, manufacturing, printing, and transportation. One of the most significant changes was the opening of the Internet to commercial purposes. Within a few short years, we moved from a world where we communicated within our companies on private networks isolated from the rest of the world to instant global access 24/7 from just about any place we wanted. In our personal lives in 1990, we relied on paper catalogs and a phone tied to a wire to make purchases (most likely within the same country) when we didn't feel like going to a store. By 2000 most of the world had moved to wireless communications. We could now browse, shop, e-mail, or talk to a person anywhere in the world from almost anywhere else. The entertainment industry went from consumers having to purchase a CD, DVD, or videotape to a market that allowed consumers to download their entertainment digitally, directly into devices such as a computer, MP3 player, or cell phone.

The confluence of the changes in the geopolitical landscape, coupled with the significant advances in technologies, has, on an absolute scale, resulted in the largest and most rapid economic growth in global economic activity that the world has ever seen. Commercial enterprises large and small now have easy access to new, large, and growing markets for their products, as well as the ability to source material and finished goods from low-cost producers at the click of a mouse key. Consumers, with the ability to globally price, shop, and compare products without ever leaving their home, never had it so good.

However, there is a threat to commercial enterprises in this new global economy, a threat that has always existed, but never on the scale and intensity that we see today. That threat is to the economic viability and integrity of a company's products and brands posed by counterfeiters, diverters and parallel traders, and the thieves of intellectual property. It is a result of poor regulation and poor enforcement of trademarks and intellectual property rights in these rapidly developing markets; and, equally, it is a result of the ease of movement and communication in the twenty-first century, the low-cost and increased capability of packagers and photocopy technology, and—in the case of parallel traders and diverters—poor management by the brand owners.

We see the news stories often, almost daily it seems, about counterfeit copies of movies, designer clothing and accessories, pharmaceuticals—you name the type of product, and if it hasn't been copied, it probably isn't a successful brand. Go online to shop; you'll see many products with pricing too good to be true. Are the products genuine? Do you know what part of the world they are being supplied from? How often have we heard of and seen exact copies of well-known brands marketed under a different brand name?

From a brand integrity standpoint, many companies—whether they are large multinational corporations, regional enterprises, or small family-run businesses—still operate, control, and manage their business much as they had done before 1990. In the view of these companies, each market or country is unique, as if it were not tied into the wider, global market. As a result, the companies do a poor job handling their global pricing, distribution networks, and third-party supplier networks. Their focus is on the cost of trademark filings versus the concept of filing trademarks as a defensive effort. Overwhelmingly, most companies rely solely on legal protection.

The counterfeiters and diverters in the global marketplace understand this lack of focus on brand integrity. They intensely focus their efforts on how to take advantage of poor controls or sloppy management. In many cases, they actually have better information about a global enterprise's pricing and distribution than the managers of the enterprise themselves.

Richard and Penny Post are out to change that mindset, and in this book they provide you with valuable and timely advice on how to operate a business in the modern global economy in a way that protects the integrity of a company's brands and products. As Rich and Penny write, "Brand and product are the foundation of the financial success of an enterprise. Product integrity is the foundation of a successful product. If a product or brand cannot be protected, its useful revenue-producing life will be short. If the integrity of the product cannot be maintained in the marketplace, brand loyalty will fade quickly."

The concept of a brand integrity program is a fairly recent development in the business world. There isn't a wide and deep pool of experts concentrated in the area. And many companies still think of a brand integrity effort as an insurance policy, rather than a critical part of running an effective and profitable enterprise in this new global marketplace. In *Global Brand Integrity Management*, Penny and Rich provide a well-thought-out and comprehensive doctrine detailing how to prepare and manage an effective brand integrity program. In the numerous examples they provide throughout the book, they also give guidance to resourcing a brand integrity effort. Many companies do a poor job of funding and resourcing efforts that they feel are not directly tied to the bottom line. Rich and Penny demonstrate how that attitude, when it is directed at spending on brand integrity, is wrong and can damage the health of the enterprise.

Rich and Penny Post have spent years working across the globe on brand integrity with companies large and small. In this book, they bring that wealth of experience to you, taking you through the broad as well as in-depth requirements for a successful program. They reinforce their recommendations with well-chosen case studies emphasizing the reasoning behind their recommendations. In addition, they present useful and intelligent management policies, excellent enforcement and defensive strategies, and best practices.

The book also gives a broad and detailed view of brand integrity within an enterprise. Penny and Rich provide specific recommendations on the role of various departments in support of brand integrity and show how an enterprise should organize its effort from an oversight as well as an operational perspective to maximize its efforts. The authors offer excellent advice on the way brand integrity should be viewed—not just as a way to protect your brands from counterfeit or your intellectual property from theft but as a means of achieving the pure economic gain that will result from running your business more effectively when brand integrity becomes an integral part of every operation.

The book drives the point home in the discussion about diversion and parallel trade. In a meeting I attended, in which Rich was presenting to a number of executives, I clearly remember him saying, "Diversion is the result of a company shooting itself in the foot. It is a result of how you run your business." It is a point he and Penny make in this book, but they also tell you how to avoid that painful foot ache. Diversion and parallel trade can cost business a significant amount of profit loss and can even result in an enterprise competing against itself. However, diversion and parallel trade are not just economic concerns; they are the primary way that the counterfeit product is inserted into the legitimate supply chain. *Global Brand Integrity Management* gives excellent advice on how to minimize this threat and its corrosive effect on *your profits, your brand value, and your company's reputation.*

Larry Malloy
Worldwide Vice President
Brand Protection and Channel Management
Johnson & Johnson Health Care Systems, Inc.

PREFACE

"It is somebody else's problem, not mine." "If we take the risk and not add another level of protection to the package, we will save x dollars on each unit produced." "That's a security problem. Let the lawyers handle it." These are all excuses we have heard over the past 40 years of dealing with brand and product loss problems. Executives point the finger at each other, continue to count on luck when approving a questionable sales agreement, or move on to the next job before bad results from poor judgment multiply and losses mount.

We have seen billions of dollars in losses take place because executives do not take due care in handling key company assets. We often wonder if they would make the same decisions if it were their company or money at risk, not that of shareholders. Perhaps we have been involved in too many tragic situations in which companies have been destroyed, product reputations ruined, employee downsizing forced, and trade secrets stolen to trust that the best interests of "the company" is of concern to some executives. Otherwise, how could deals be made to sell products that will easily find their way into the gray market? Why are products designed in ways that make them easy to counterfeit? Why are enforcement measures so lax that both gray market and counterfeit products are allowed to flood a market? Why can't anyone watch what's happening?

It could be a lack of information about how to lower risk and protect products in the marketplace. It could be that executive leadership in the company is more interested in short-term profits. It could be that management is more interested in lining its own pockets at the expense of shareholders. It really does not matter, as we have seen examples of each of these reasons. The fact is that there are very few companies that have thought through the outcome of not managing their business with the goal of preserving brand reputation, product protection, and global competition. Those that have thought it through—that have determined that a process to manage product integrity is crucial to long-term market and financial success—make for successful and better competitors. And they will be the new global business leaders.

We have worked with all types of clients and learned "the good, the bad, and the ugly" from them. This book presents the lessons we have learned.

This book provides the key concepts of brand integrity as a tool for management to lower risks, improve profitability, and make product and brand protection an essential aspect of corporate management. We have identified best practices for those with day-to-day responsibilities to manage brands and products more effectively. We believe that this new approach will provide all levels of management with a blueprint for rethinking how they can manage the core assets of their company more profitability while protecting those assets in the global marketplace.

Richard S. Post
Penelope N. Post

ACKNOWLEDGMENTS

We would like to thank all the executives and companies that lost billions of dollars for their shareholders due to inadequate brand integrity. Without you, well, this book would not have been possible.

To those of you who labor in the fields of corporate management trying to make a difference by promoting product, brand, and information protection, we hope this book helps!

GL BAL
B®AND©
INTEGRITY
MANAGEMENT™

INTRODUCTION

This is a book dedicated to help you increase profits and better manage products. The lessons learned to write it have cost business and industry hundreds of billions of dollars. Theft of trade secrets, patent infringements, counterfeit goods, and product diversion are not normally taught in business school but are a regular part of day-to-day life in global business. The integrity of products and brands are at the core of global business: it drives profitability, marketing, supply chain, and legal strategies. Unfortunately there is little common definition about what constitutes a product or brand integrity program for a company. This book tries to fill that gap.

No CEO wakes up in the morning and asks himself (or herself), "I wonder how safe my products and brands are today?" But a CEO does ask, "Am I getting full value from the products in my global supply chain?" or "Are we getting the best margins in our markets?" or "How is the share price today?" Of the two sets of questions, the first, which does not get asked very often, is, however, almost more important. Ideas, products, and brands drive the business. How they are exploited, manufactured, distributed, marketed, and provided to end users is most often thought of as "the business of business." How they are protected is most often considered a problem for the lawyers or the security staff, not something that requires significant executive-level time or attention. Unfortunately this key premise of modern business is just not true.

The loss of intellectual property (IP) has reached staggering levels of cost to business fortunes. Attacks to steal IP are directed by individuals, your competitors, foreign governments, and those supported by foreign governments; no company is immune from these attacks. Misuse of patents, copyrights, trademarks, Web sites, logos, and products is also an epidemic that is costing hundreds of billions per year to U.S. business alone. Every business sector has recorded significant cases of IP theft, misuse of IP, gray market products, and just plain piracy or counterfeiting of products. Legal protection does not prevent the attacks. Enforcement often does not recover significant dollars, and public confidence in products is eroded.

Products are global during production, marketing, and use. The supply chain for a single product can circle the globe. Ensuring product integrity throughout a product's useful life cycle in this global marketplace requires a global, product-based strategy. Counterfeit products may be the result of high product costs, not enough legitimate supply available, products that are attractive and easy to copy, or the social pressures that exist in various markets. Your own third-party manufacturers using your specifications without your knowledge are often the source of counterfeit products. The specific reasons are multiple and varied, but they all represent criminal attacks against your revenues and the reputation of your products.

When authentic products are sold below market price in the gray market, your revenues and profits shrink. These costly attacks are most often caused by your own internal pricing, marketing, or sales executive compensation programs. Gray market activities can be stopped and the revenues recovered by understanding how it happens and then changing internal business processes.

Most companies do not have one single person responsible for the integrity of products that generate key revenue streams for the company. There may be product managers, brand managers, marketing managers, IP attorneys, and others, but most often no one person has complete responsibility for ensuring product or brand integrity throughout the supply chain and life cycle of the product. A growing number of companies are dealing head-on with these problems and have established brand protection or brand integrity functions to lower product risk, preserve consumer confidence, and increase profitability.

To manage product integrity and improve revenues while lowering product risks from internal and external attacks, a new executive-level brand integrity dashboard is required. You need to know what to ask, what to look for in your business processes, and what to measure.

This book provides the background and framework for establishing dashboards to manage products and brands for global product integrity, brand protection, and product-focused day-to-day business operations. The results will lengthen your product life cycle and increase consumer confidence.

Getting Started

Let's start with the basics of brand integrity and product protection. First of all, we are separating brand integrity from product protection, as they are different but complementary concepts. Brand integrity represents all the efforts used to ensure that the ongoing value of products or brand is maintained. Product protection is what you use to make sure that each product that constitutes your brand, or is the brand itself, (1) has a good chance of getting in the hands of your customers, in the right markets, at the right times, and (2) generates a profit for you, not someone else!

Brand: *The essence of a company: the key product name recognized in the marketplace; the name of a company; the business reputation; something of extreme value to the company and shareholders; something to be protected at all costs.*

Brand Integrity: *Those strategies, processes, features, designs, and business practices that ensure the integrity of products, intellectual property, reputation, image, and shareholder value.*

For purposes of this book we will use brand integrity (BI) as the all-inclusive term for brand protection, product protection, and product integrity.

The objectives of a brand integrity program are to retain or improve margins, maintain consumer confidence in products, ensure authenticity of products, and "keep the brand alive" in the marketplace. The strategic focus of brand integrity should follow the company's profit goals and objectives and should use the protection of key brand and product assets to enhance all other management activities. Protection of each product that the company produces is as important as the promotion used to market it. (See Figure I.1.)

Products are the individual items sold, and the sum total of all these products or even a single product may constitute the brand. Product integ-

FIGURE I.1   Brand Integrity Triangle—Produce, Position, and Protect

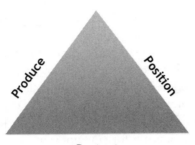

rity embraces *all those things used to ensure the integrity of a product throughout its useful life in the market.* This would include concepts, package design, markings, sales, manufacturing supply chain, distribution channel controls, market surveillance, and so on.

Developing a management philosophy that employs brand integrity as a guiding principle is not easy and usually doesn't happen often unless a crisis occurs. Over the years, we have never seen a CEO who wakes up one morning and says, "We need a brand integrity program." It just does not happen unless products have been attacked by counterfeiters, margins are eroded because of gray market goods flooding a market, or fraudulent rebates get out of control. However, dealing with an ongoing crisis is the worst possible time to establish a brand integrity or product protection program. Normally after the problem is identified and resolved, the lessons learned form the starting point for instituting a more comprehensive approach to improving and strengthening business processes.

Over the years in working on these problems, we were able to identify the following eight laws of brand integrity. They are extracted from hundreds of projects, in almost every type of manufacturing, distribution, and marketplace setting around the world. If they are implemented properly, products in the supply chain and distribution channels will have a strong probability of being safe, authentic, and available at the right price to your customers. These laws were identified at a cost of billions of dollars in brand-related losses to global businesses. Don't let the lessons learned from them go to waste!

The chapters in the book take each of these laws and provide some background on their use and operation. Memorize them—you will need them again and again!

Eight Laws of Brand Integrity

1. Brand integrity is more than legal protection.
2. If a product is valuable, somebody will try to take your profits.
3. If you do not protect your products, nobody will do it for you.
4. If you wait until your products are attacked, you will lose.
5. Protect your products, and the bad guys will attack your competition.
6. If you have different prices in different markets, someone is stealing your profits.
7. Your own products are often your largest competition.
8. Continually monitor the marketplace to lower risks and increase profits.

These eight laws form the background against which an active program of brand and product integrity management is established and managed on a daily basis. Establishing a management culture of "watching the store" for each new idea that becomes a product to be manufactured, marketed, and sold is not new. However, the responsibility for making sure that a product is protected at the right level throughout its useful life is often dispersed throughout an organization without a cohesive product integrity management plan. Legal does its job, engineering does its, brand management does its, sales does its, but overall responsibility for product integrity either becomes an ad hoc assignment or is not looked after at all. Brand integrity has also, unfortunately, been overlooked as a source of increased revenue, increased customer confidence, and increased management control and accountability.

This book provides two things:

1. Questions that the CEO should be asking his or her executives about the integrity of the company's brands and products
2. Tools to capture the attention of employees and measure their performance to increase brand integrity

Questions the CEO asks the direct-report executives about product integrity provide the necessary tools for effective executive leadership and oversight of this critical aspect of product and revenue management.

The dashboards required to set up, operate, and evaluate global brand integrity programs are provided for the CEO in each chapter of the book. They can be implemented to deal with a specific problem, handle portions of a supply chain, introduce a new product, or establish a new corporate brand integrity or brand protection function.

A brand integrity program is good business. It encourages good employee performance and customer loyalty. It is profitable because it encourages good product and intellectual property management, which translates into enhanced profits. It is good for the corporate image, as it enhances brand awareness and loyalty and extends and expands product life in the market. It also increases profitability and shareholder value.

Brand integrity is not social responsibility. Social responsibility is a function of brand integrity. While a brand integrity program may be necessary or required to comply with government regulations of the SEC, FTC, FDA, or Sarbanes-Oxley, doing the right thing with products and brands, knowing who is touching your products throughout your supply chain, and knowing who uses them is good business, whether mandated or not.

In the final analysis, having a brand integrity program is good business. In addition to demonstrating good ethical corporate stewardship and corporate citizenship, it results in tighter controls, good market intelligence, higher returns on investments, and overall good management.

All brand and product integrity programs begin and end with the stewardship of key product and brand assets. In order to collect revenues from these assets, they must be designed, manufactured, and sold in the global marketplace. This book is organized around the eight laws presented in groupings of chapters that reflect the impact of different aspects of the supply chain as products move within the company and out into the hands of an end user. Chapters 2, 3, 9, 10, and 11 discuss corporate issues as well as establishing and managing a BI program. Chapters 4, 5, and 6 deal primarily with product-related matters. Chapter 7 focuses on the market, while Chapter 8 covers "the deal."

Making brand integrity work is the responsibility of executive leadership in the company. Initiating it as an everyday way of doing business is essential to effective global competition and must be a part of the CEO's metrics used to manage the enterprise. *Best practices for brand integrity* must form the strategies for product development, manufacturing, distribution, and sales. *Dashboard questions* for follow-up must be used to track implementation and effectiveness. Compensation must in part be based on brand integrity metrics. Embedding brand integrity across all parts of the enterprise should have the ultimate goal of increasing profitability and ensuring long-term shareholder value.

The laws of brand integrity presented in the book, along with questions the CEO needs to ask the organization, provide the necessary tools to manage brands and products for long-term value.

CHAPTER 1

RETHINKING THE BUSINESS MODEL WITH BRAND INTEGRITY: AN ORGANIZING CONCEPT

Not everything that can be counted counts, and not everything that counts can be counted.

Albert Einstein

Who's stealing more from you today? The spy, the gray marketer, the counterfeiter, the computer hacker, or the white-collar criminal? Or is it just the result of bad decision making? If you don't know for sure, welcome to the club! The opportunities for profits to flow out of your business operations are greater today than ever before in history. It happens at the speed of "e-light." Only a "click" away!

The source of trouble is no longer just from employees stealing parts or supplies from the stockroom. Now trouble comes from your competition thousands of miles away in Korea, China, France, or wherever your company conducts business. Patented products are often in such demand that they are immediately counterfeited, or overseas production partners feel free to infringe upon your patent. Key products, still in the patent pending phase, are often copied abroad and sold in the United States before the original product hits the market and at prices lower than the company charges to distributors or customers. These product arbitrage attacks against the company eliminate or reduce margins and are far more serious than what happens in the stockroom.

Likewise, when the bad guys all wore black hats, or we thought that all the spies were from the Soviet Union, it was easy to focus on risks, analyze threats, assess vulnerabilities, and educate management and employees. Unfortunately, the age of black and white has changed to a world of chasing gray cats in a dark room.

Today all companies operate in the global economy whether or not their markets are considered domestic or international. Competition does not originate only in the United States or in the European Union. It comes from any location in the world if a product is in demand and an opportunity to compete profitably exists. Protecting global operations and products requires a very focused application of basic brand integrity management as well as a thorough understanding of the specific risks faced by the company and its products.

Protect what brings in the cash! While this may seem elementary and obvious, it is easy for company assets to become buried or ignored in the process of building and growing a brand or a product. During the past decade, the focus of business has been on developing a brand, expanding growth avenues, marketing aggressively, and keeping the bottom line attractive to Wall Street. Economic growth seems endless. International markets, such as China and India, provide cheap places for manufacturing and potentially huge purchasing markets. Technological advances created fast and efficient methods of communication, new products, and unfathomed profits. Protecting company assets was neglected, taking a backseat to the demands of the market and the accountants. Companies were so busy growing and expanding into the global marketplace that they didn't have time to worry about their most important possessions. With information so easily available on the Internet and new generations of products coming on the market daily, there was little interest or need to worry much about protecting information or products. Besides, many companies, especially those in the United States, honestly didn't believe they had anything to lose. Who would steal from them? Why spend money when it doesn't add to the bottom line?

Times change, sometimes faster than technology; and even before the economy started to slow down, companies started to realize that global opportunities also included global threats. Participation in the global marketplace does not mean business as usual, which many companies discovered the hard way. Owning a great product or brand requires protecting that product or brand at a level consistent with its value to the company and the competitors. Understanding the new, constantly changing competitive environment is essential for developing a successful international business strategy. Protecting key resources and information is a necessity that must be addressed and advanced by senior management and passed down to all levels of operations. A new approach is required if companies want to maintain a competitive edge, control their products and technology, and keep their profit margins attractive. A fresh look at some old issues and priorities provides a good starting point for brand integrity.

GLOBAL THREATS: WHO'S INTERESTED IN YOUR BRAND?

The simple answer is that there are virtually no secrets in the business world and few in government circles that can withstand the test of time. Companies, individuals, and several foreign governments are actively trying to learn about products and technologies that can be useful to them but financially harmful to their rightful owners. The FBI has identified France, India, China, the former Soviet Union, Korea, Japan, and Taiwan as high on the list of countries aggressively collecting business-related technology to assist their developing industries and governmental programs. Why do they do it? Because it is a very inexpensive way to get market share without doing the R&D!

Numerous companies, often staffed by former employees of companies that own the technology, do the same thing. They steal information and build competitive businesses. Smarter employees use an offshore company to manufacture the products and to avoid direct competition in the United States. The 1996 Economic Espionage Act was designed to assist U.S. companies in defending against these attacks, but to date it has had limited success because most companies did little to protect themselves from losses and in some instances contributed to the problem because of poor brand integrity efforts.

During the past decade, the trend has been to hire high-tech employees from foreign countries and to contract out sensitive R&D work to workers in foreign countries. Reliance solely on a legal contract to protect highly sensitive information in a foreign country has been a regular feature of many high-technology company operations. This is extremely risky for brand integrity. The countries that are being used for this type of development contract work are often the same ones that have active intelligence programs focused on collecting U.S. high-technology secrets. Without comprehensive safeguards, brand integrity can't be guaranteed in the future.

Case Study

We were reviewing manufacturing plant security for a client in Sri Lanka. Our client had entered into a licensing agreement with a local company to produce a private label product for the Asian market. As a part of the licensing agreement, our client was obligated to provide technical manufacturing updates and manuals to the local company. The licensing agreement had been in effect for several years when our security review was made. During the plant visit, we reviewed the materials sent from our client to the Sri Lankan company and discovered that our client had inadvertently been sending the materials not only for the licensed product but for all the technology that the company was developing.

Once we learned of this problem, we conducted an investigation to determine the scope of the potential damage and loss to our client. It quickly became apparent that the oversight was being taken advantage of by plant employees who were members of a radical political party and had been trained by the KGB when the U.S.S.R. had been active in the country. In fact, the driver for the managing director of the local company had been the driver for the KGB resident agent while he was in the country. This driver had been "tasked" to make copies of each of the manuals when they were received as well as all subsequent materials sent to the plant. These copies were delivered to the KGB.

We were instructed by our client to package up all the materials that were not directly related to the licensing agreement and return them to the United States. No further materials unrelated to the license were sent to the plant. It could not be determined at that time what economic damage our client suffered as a result of sending the "extra" materials to the company.

Two years later, a petrochemical company in Russia sent an inquiry to our client, asking for technical assistance with a production problem at a new plant being built in Siberia. Company engineers were dispatched to the plant to determine exactly what was required so that a contract could be developed. When they returned to the United States, they informed senior management that they found an exact replica of one of the company's latest manufacturing facilities for producing polycarbonate products. The problem at the Russian plant was that critical key components were lacking to get it operational.

The specifications for these key components had been developed after the discovery of the materials in Sri Lanka and thus had not been sent to the licensee. Litigation was not a possibility. So a licensing agreement was established with the Russian company that generated several million dollars per year in royalties and for the purchase of feed stocks. It could not be determined if other materials that leaked out of our client's licensing operations had been commercialized.

BRAND INTEGRITY

There is not one company that has a successful product (brand) that is not at risk to both ethical and unethical competition. The difficulty is in knowing which is which and establishing early warning procedures to identify when the company is being unethically attacked.

Globalization raised new imperatives for corporate executives:

- How do I keep my information, products, and brands safe and secure in electronic and global environments?
- Am I sure that my manufacturing partners are not taking advantage of our technology?
- How do we deal with all the clever international counterfeiters?
- Do my supply chain and distribution channels contribute to our gray market product problems?
- How can we control e-commerce transactions within the company and also with our vendors, suppliers, and clients?
- Is it possible to protect our patents and trademarks in any foreign country?

Intellectual property (as well as intellectual capital) is key to business success. Aggressive thieves are stealing anything and everything of value. Business and strategic plans must focus on product risk assessments and be adaptable to changing risk and vulnerability. Company information is often distributed to a wide group of people. This information must be protected wherever it is, for as long as it has economic value to the company. Products with significant intellectual property content must be protected as long as they have economic value to the company: the greater the value, the greater the necessity for protective efforts and measures. The market life of a product should determine what BI efforts are appropriate to use and for how long.

Why be concerned? Trade secret theft, violation of product patents, product diversion, and gray marketing activities account for the largest volume of lost profits and margins from U.S. business today and are expected to continue to increase for the foreseeable future. According to the 2005 *American Society for Industrial Security Trends in Proprietary Information Loss Survey Report*, annual losses reported from these categories by U.S. companies is nearly US$60 billion. To put a fine point on these statistics, *USA Today* reported that the FBI arrested 25 Chinese nationals or Chinese Americans in the United States in cases involving the targeting of U.S. technology in the past two years.

Many countries such as China, Japan, Korea, and India take a much longer strategic view of business development than their western competitors. In a report about a recent McKinsey & Co. study of Chinese technology companies, the *Wall Street Journal* suggests "that Chinese firms are gaining much faster in know-how and process than their western competition. How much of this rapid gain is attributable to normal business operations or from other sources could not be determined."

Losses to U.S. business products are difficult to measure accurately because no single source collects this information, and a common reporting format does not exist. Companies also do not report losses that could affect their share price or Wall Street rating. Who wants to admit to such a loss? For purposes of this book, we will divide identified losses into four areas that have particular relevance to brand integrity: research and development, manufacturing, distribution, and marketplace activities.

To some extent the exact value of the losses is not as important to this discussion as the order of magnitude present in them. Whether or not

FIGURE 1.1   Life Cycle Losses[a]

Research and development	Trade secret theft	$60 billion[b]
	Information	$53–59 billion[c]
	Internet	$300 billion[d]
Manufacturing	High tech only	$.5 million per theft[e]
Distribution		$30–60 billion[f]
Marketplace	Retail	$31 billion[g]
	Gray market	$30 billion[h]
	Counterfeit	$250 billion[i]

Notes:

[a] These losses do not include management time, lost sales revenues, lost market share, margin loss, and indirect costs associated with investigative and legal expenses and administrative costs to recover normal business activities caused by the loss.

[b] American Society for Industrial Security, 2005.

[c] U.S. Chamber of Commerce, 2001.

[d] Federal Bureau of Investigation, 1997.

[e] Federal Bureau of Investigation, 1999.

[f] Technology Asset Protection Association (TAPA), 1997, includes investigation loss, insurance paperwork, and claims.

[g] National Retail Merchants Association, 2003.

[h] Brand Protections Associates, 2000.

[i] Institute Anti-Counterfeiting Coalition, 2006, U.S. companies only.

experts can agree on the exact numbers is less important than the fact that major losses are happening across all businesses and industries. Losses are huge and growing in number and frequency.

Other issues, such as noncompliance with export controls, failure to verify end users for exported products, and ignorance about who is actually manufacturing products or effectively controlling production equipment, can cause significant losses to reputation, image, product authenticity, and patent infringements. Recent headlines have accused the apparel industry of using unfair labor conditions—of using child labor in foreign countries to produce consumer goods and of permitting poor working conditions. While the allegations may be true in some cases, they are not in others, and these accusations cause greater damage and have longer-lasting consequences than the theft of finished goods from a warehouse.

INFORMATION PROTECTION

What do you know about your competition? How much do your competitors know about you and your future plans? Can you prevent the competition from gaining access to information regarding your company? Knowing what your competitors are doing, while keeping them from learning too much about what you are doing, is an important, but often neglected, part of effectively managing a business.

In the United States, concerns about the effects of the predatory intelligence practices of foreign companies or unethical individuals must also be coupled with the current investment climate. The views of industry analysts and the impact of public reaction to changes in stock prices and returns often drive business decisions and competitive practices rather than good business sense. Consequently, companies and governments are exploiting opportunities and individuals. The results are reduced profit margins, diminished return on investment for R&D expenditures, concerns about product reliability, and eroded customer and distributor trustworthiness.

Case Study

Company A suddenly finds a new competitor in a foreign market just after sending a "sample" to a prospective Chinese joint venture partner. The Chinese company had reverse-engineered the product and sold it in developing countries at a fraction of the cost of Company A's product.

A Korean company seeks out a disgruntled employee in Company B and buys a trade secret–protected machine design. Low-cost production begins in secret, and lower-cost products compete against the company that originally developed the machinery.

Dozens of similar examples are occurring today. These are typical of the problems that international firms face in regard to the protection of their intellectual capital and the loss of markets that should be available to them.

The global business marketplace is, in many respects, a geopolitical economic warfare zone in which all companies must protect key competitive advantages and brands while expanding markets and maximizing shareholder profits. This must be done without giving away or losing the family jewels in the process. It is a lesson that most companies and executives feel does not apply to them or is not important. During the past 20 years of investigating business losses for clients, we have dealt with too many executives who continue to use a variety of rationalizations to defend decisions that violate every principle of sound corporate business management.

- "We're giving them (the Chinese) technology in this deal which is two years old."
- "We must share all our new developments with (them). It's in our transfer agreement."
- "Our R&D center is in (India) so we can cooperate more effectively with our partner."
- "We have new products that will make what we are giving (them) obsolete in three years."
- "It's cheaper, and that's where the new markets are going to be."

Taken outside the context of how information technology is collected by known predatory country-company collaborative efforts, such statements might sound like reasonable corporate decisions. When viewed through the eyes of competitors, a business might appear naive at best, and reckless in exposing secrets. Why be concerned about who's stealing your newest technology when the potential third-world customers will, for the next five years, need only the low-tech, current-generation technology you are giving them under the "great" licensing agreement your company just signed?

Failure to understand that current-level technology is valuable to global competitors is hardly a new theme in business. What is troubling is the failure to understand or remember the history of how many current global competitors came to assume positions of dominance. Japan, a defeated country that was virtually rebuilt with U.S. technology and "copy" products, has become a major competitor in large part due to close government business integration and aggressive intelligence collection on business, technology, and trade policies, which actively support and promote Japanese companies. The French and Italian governments aggressively follow a similar policy. Likewise, the Chinese, Koreans, and numerous other countries seeking to move up the global business food chain have been actively involved in "assisting" national business interests.

Why is it that many companies ignore the fact that endless predatory intelligence collection policies are employed by numerous foreign companies, countries, and individuals against the interests of a successful business? Sufficient examples exist to establish models of predatory operation, but they are seldom viewed as a real threat. Examples include:

- Countries that have national policies to collect business intelligence in support of national companies
- Business competitors that engage in predatory intelligence activities as a corporate policy or that target companies because of industry or product leadership
- Private individuals who target specific product or technology developments or seek "targets of opportunity" for personal profit
- Employees who are dissatisfied or improperly controlled and have access to high-value technology or information

Case Study

Several Chinese nationals have been identified as operating a "recruitment program" in California's Silicon Valley. The purpose of this program was to identify and recruit Chinese employees of high-tech firms who could take the technology they were working on in their U.S. companies and bring it "home" to China. Offers of higher positions, their own laboratories, ownership in new companies, better housing for relatives still in China, and so on, were all dangled as incentives. Coercion would also be used if incentives did not work. Several recruiters were reportedly active at any one time during the late 1990s and early 2000s.

It is interesting to note that numerous intelligence services of foreign governments, as well as the U.S. FBI and Central Intelligence Agency, have indicated that economic intelligence has become a major focus of the intelligence collection efforts of many countries. There are now numerous interagency programs in the United States to assist companies in reviewing their information and technology protection programs and provide heightened protection from foreign intelligence collection efforts. However, direct support to U.S. business interests, comparable to the efforts of France, Japan, China, and Korea, is not permitted.

There is ample evidence to suggest that before and during the cold war, the Soviet Union engaged in both military and business espionage to develop its space program, atomic energy program, and key industrial processes. As a deterrent, strong U.S. government measures, under the Department of Defense Industrial Security Program, focused on protecting key business production in areas where the government had an interest. While these efforts to protect government classified information in the hands of U.S. business continue, the broader issue of government protection for U.S. business from other forms of espionage or competitive intelligence collection is less than adequate. While the FBI investigates business espionage cases that are reported, its role in the prevention of losses or support to corporate executives is limited. The threat to business from, for example, Chinese economic espionage activities can include the theft of dual-use technology as well as proprietary information, technology, and trade secrets.

The Economic Espionage Act of 1996 provides criminal penalties for economic espionage or trade-secret theft that is conducted on behalf of foreign governments. It also requires that a company take reasonable precautions to protect its sensitive information. This was the first direct application by the U.S. government in establishing a standard of due care against business espionage by agents of foreign governments. Few cases have actually been tried successfully under the Espionage Act, partially because most companies have been unable to demonstrate that the trade secret was actually treated as a secret. Corporate standards concerning access to sensitive company information, R&D activities, product development laboratories, and sensitive production facilities have, in many cases, not kept pace with company growth and expansion. The priority to protect trade secrets and sensitive information is often overlooked when most companies look at expanding into foreign markets.

Of the major industrial or political powers, only the United States and U.S. corporate interests have consistently developed policies and procedures that make it difficult to compete internationally. Until recently, neither the U.S. government nor U.S. industry focused directly on global threats to competition. Instead, domestic reaction to business decisions were used to gauge the appropriateness of strategic decisions regarding non-defense-related technology transfer, protection of trade secrets, copyright enforcement, and the proper role of government to further the interests of business overseas. It is difficult to compete on a level playing field with such a narrow view of the global marketplace when company executives have failed to see the bigger picture.

A good example of both U.S. business and government focusing on only half of a serious problem is the high visibility given the piracy of intellectual property in China. The unauthorized copying of commercial products such as CD-ROMs, computer chips, cigarettes, clothing, cosmetics, and drugs is a very serious problem resulting in lost revenues and markets for U.S. products. Much attention has been placed on this issue, and the Clinton and both Bush administrations have applied pressure on the Chinese government with limited success. Success in stopping or even slowing the sale of fake or counterfeit goods has until recently been very limited and spotty at best. U.S. pressure and threats of trade sanctions have also been of limited value. The emergence of Chinese intellectual property (IP) and the globalization of Chinese business are responsible for a greater willingness to protect intellectual property rights, at least for the Chinese, and are proving to be more effective than any U.S. pressure to control IP theft.

The more serious problems of the theft, transfer, and licensing of U.S. technology developments, processes, and designs, along with the loss of development lead time, have received little attention and have not been effectively addressed by either the government or the business community. Corporations continue to give away technology for short-term financial gains while trying to control marketplace losses of commercialized products. In other words, let's enforce intellectual property rights to save today's profits but give away tomorrow's profits and market share because of minimal controls over new technology. It is an easy way to allocate future losses to increased competition rather than ineffective brand integrity. Setting up a cutting-edge technology development center in a high-risk environment where the host country has stated a goal of establishing technical superiority is a questionable practice. Lower salaries, better-trained engineers and scientists, and lower operating costs are often cited as motivating factors for locating facilities in India or China. The brand integrity risk question is often overlooked or downplayed as a concern, but the leakage of technology and process know-how and the development of local intellectual capital in the local scientific community are almost impossible to control over an extended period of time.

In today's global business environment, nothing is more important to a company than brand reputation. Whether threats come from counterfeit products, patent infringements, gray market products, or the theft of trade secrets, brand integrity is the essential ingredient for effective international competition. The strategic focus of this book is on key brand integrity issues affecting assets: company reputation, corporate or product image, product integrity, maintenance of shareholder value, and information protection.

Companies operating globally must make sure that products maintain market share, margins are retained or improved, consumer confidence in their products does not dwindle, product authenticity is ensured, and the brand is "kept alive" in the marketplace. To attain these objectives, it is essential that the most senior management executives in the company provide dedicated leadership so that brand integrity programs respond to company needs and are designed to enhance bottom-line company performance. Brand integrity measures the need to blend BI policy reviews and development with marketplace monitoring and crisis management. Key assets to be protected, corporate issues to be managed, and corresponding security issues that most often require response are illustrated in Figure 1.2.

Trying to identify where BI efforts need to be expanded or concentrated is always a difficult task. Because the list of assets, people, and intellectual property to be protected will vary from company to company, it is

FIGURE 1.2   The Brand Integrity Framework

Corporate Issues	Assets	Brand Issues
• Authenticity • Product Confidence	PRODUCTS	• IP Theft • Counterfeit • Product Extortion • Liability / Recalls
• Customer Support • "Keep Brand Alive" • "Good Corporate Citizen" • Company's "Good Name"	REPUTATION & IMAGE	• Ethics • Contamination • Compliance • Crisis Management
• Control Sensitive Data • Project Desired "Public Face"	INFORMATION	• IT Security • Trade Secret Theft
• Maintain Desired Levels of Financial Returns	SHAREHOLDER VALUE	• Due Diligence • Fraud • Value Analysis
• Protect Market Share • Protect Margins	MARGINS	• Gray Market

essential to have a clear understanding of the company supply chain (current product lines as well as products in development) and the relationship of all products to profitability. Once these relationships are understood, a focused BI program can be developed and managed to protect these assets.

Three major BI concerns are present in global operations:

1. *Protection of brand.* Company products and reputation
2. *Protection of product.* Integrity, authenticity, and reliability
3. *Protection of information.* Intellectual property, electronic transmission, and storage

These "generic" brand issues are, in theory, quite simple to manage if the following steps are taken:

- Develop BI programs for company brands and products.
- Keep company information and intellectual property safe.
- Ensure that profit margins are not eroded by fraud or gray market activities.
- Develop and maintain effective systems of control and audit.
- Provide protection for employees and against dishonest workers.

As in most decision making, the key factors in any successful operation are determining when and how to focus plans and when and how to apply the plans effectively. The single most important step in achieving profitable long-term revenue generation from products is maintaining brand integrity.

Every CEO, brand manager, and start-up entrepreneur must address three major product or brand concerns:

1. How do we bring the product or idea to market?
2. How can we sell more than our competition?
3. How do we maximize profitability throughout its useful life cycle?

This book deals with all three of these concerns from a slightly different perspective from that of the traditional business school model by adding a fourth issue: brand integrity. Unless your brand is adequately protected in the marketplace, your products will fail to return full value.

Each product or brand has risks that are specific to each stage of the life cycle. These risks need to be managed differently and effectively if maximum value is to be received. Incorporating life-cycle BI risk management into strategic business plans is a sure way to enhance competitive advantage for the company. Risk identification specific to each product, focused application of best practices to lower or manage risk, and integration of a product-based brand integrity philosophy into all decision making are the major components of a successful brand integrity program.

Protection of products, brands, and corporate activities is often thought of as "a cost of doing business" rather than "a way of thinking about doing business." The BI way of thinking and operating needs to be embedded in decision making if strategic goals for current and future business revenue are to be attained. Bottom-up product risk evaluation, top-down support, and management supervision of brand integrity efforts are required if company assets and profits are to be maximized.

Many of the principles presented in this book are well known to business executives, brand integrity professionals, and the legal community. What is different is the way in which they are applied, managed, and used to create business opportunities rather than produce barriers to effective global competition. These principles have been developed over the past 30 years of helping major corporations solve international brand integrity problems. They work; but to work effectively, they must become an integral part of corporate policy and the daily management of the business. The focus of day-to-day actions must be on managing the most important aspect of the company: its products at every stage in the supply chain and product life cycle.

Moving from whatever approach a company is currently using to a global brand integrity model will not happen without some effort. Changes in attitude, management style, and possibly even structure may be required if the concepts are to be implemented successfully. The rewards for this effort are significant in reducing operating costs, increasing responsiveness to changes in the marketplace, maximizing product life, and improving profits.

WHAT'S THE PROBLEM?

Very simply put, the problem is that in many major corporations senior management has lost focus on the most critical aspect of the business: getting the most value from the products and brands. Increased production, faster delivery to the market, aggressive marketing, creative financial engineering, supply chain management, IT prowess, and so on, are all essential, but they do not necessarily ensure getting the most from either the products or the brand. Brand managers look after products; engineers look after processes and develop new products; lawyers file patents and trademarks; HR executives hire, fire, and look after the welfare of employees; technology officers manage new products; security officers look after the security of people, facilities, and assets; IT professionals manage information flow, systems, and telecommunications. But who manages and coordinates product or brand risk issues?

Brand risk, unlike risk management, is usually diffused throughout the corporate structure. There are no specific programs to manage issues associated with specific product-related risks that arise at different stages of the product's life cycle. R&D manages the risks in R&D. Engineering or production executives manage manufacturing risks. Distribution system risks are managed by distribution, and marketplace risks are managed by sales and marketing. The corporate support functions such as legal, security, and risk management most often provide guidance, direction, and assistance to the various business units when problems arise, but product risk issues are not considered the job of any one individual. The old adage "If everyone is responsible, no one is responsible" holds true here.

While it is important to provide a safe working environment, ergonomically correct workspace, adequate parking lot lighting, and good labor relations, it is more important to protect the information, products, reputation, and image of the company in the global marketplace. Keeping the brand and products safe, preserving competitive advantage, improving market lead time, and maintaining margins are essential measures that will keep the company viable in the short term as well as the long term.

In a single-product company, if the product is being counterfeited or the patent is being infringed upon, it is a major problem that involves all senior management. If, however, the company has 10 products and only one is attacked, this is often not perceived as being significant and as requiring significant management time because "the system will deal with it." The attack on one of many products just does not have the attention-grabbing impact as an attack against a company's sole product. Realizing the sense of urgency, maintaining vigilance, and responding aggressively to attacks against any product as though corporate existence depended upon it is vital to long-term success no matter how many products or brands the company claims.

In order to manage product and brand risks, executives need to understand the vulnerabilities of their products. R&D risks are different from manufacturing risks. Distribution risks are different from marketplace risks. All require information assessments, monitoring, and best practices to obtain maximum value from the assets. Coordination of information and monitoring of changes in risk assessment or attacks may require that a position be dedicated solely to brand protection or may just require that additional responsibilities be assigned to an executive. How the process is managed will depend upon the volume of products involved, current and past risk and loss history, and strategic growth plans for the company. If new products are being developed, additional oversight is warranted.

HOW DO WE FIX IT?

Hundreds of companies go out of business each year because they have not paid adequate attention to the principles presented in this book. Hundreds of others, including Fortune 500 companies, have not returned the best value to their shareholders for the same reasons. Global competitive forces, stock analyst projections, internal compensation plans, poor internal communications, reduced employee loyalties, and lapses in ethical standards make it essential that a new way of managing for long-term profit be initiated.

We are not suggesting that a brand integrity officer (or department) is required for every company or that such a position would replace or supplement the security executive, compliance officer, or legal counsel. Rather, we believe that a new way of thinking about doing business is required. The primary strategic focus must be on protecting the products. Managing risk to products must be integrated into daily management of the company. Since risk-reduction requirements change from day to day and within each stage of a product's life cycle, management systems must be geared to collecting and disseminating timely information so adjustments can readily be made. The major outcome of using a brand integrity model is to prolong product life, maximize margins and profits, focus corporate energies on brand management, and adapt business strategies to respond to global marketplace risks.

Using BI principles, senior executives and those responsible for maximizing profitability are provided with an alternative tool for managing their business in a manner that will help lower risks, extend product marketplace life, maximize profits, and increase customer satisfaction. While it sounds like a magic bullet, it is, in fact, a return to the basics of running a successful business. The idea is to give those managers responsible for running the business a clear set of guidelines about what is expected, supply them with guidance and support, and let them do the job.

The key difference between the brand integrity approach and the way things are often done today is the attitude adopted to maximize profits. Business success comes from a balance between long-term and short-term solutions, product risk assessments, extensive use of marketplace surveillance, focused application of product-protective measures, and aggressive responses to attacks against the brand or product assets of the company. An embedded philosophy, espoused by senior executives, that brand is everything and must be protected at all costs, in all phases of its useful life, is what makes this approach successful (see Figure 1.3). Everything else is secondary. If the brand is properly cared for throughout the life cycle, maximum profits and shareholder value will result.

The shift in focus is threefold:

1. From being marketing driven and aggressive to being aggressively protective of product and brand
2. From giving managers partial responsibility for products to delegating full responsibility to them for maximizing total return on assets
3. From limiting responsibility for protecting brand integrity to making each and every company employee aware of the importance of brand integrity and responsible for protecting brand, product, and information

FIGURE 1.3   The Five Elements of Product Protection

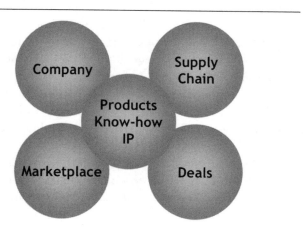

Like any other new idea, the brand integrity approach to product management must pay for itself with measurable financial value. Otherwise, why do it? We show numerous examples throughout the book that have worked and continue to work to do just that!

Shareholders, analysts, brand managers, general counsels, CEOs, and customers must all actively support and encourage the shift to a brand protection model of doing business. The major question is not "Should we consider doing it?" but "How soon can we get it up and running?"

A company that is either number one or number two in a market or brand is a clear target for any or all of the predators in the global marketplace. The U.S. government is not there to protect U.S. corporate interests, except in circumstances where national interests and corporate interests coincide or as required by law. Consequently, corporations must assess their own needs and provide required protection. Companies with the following characteristics are automatically at high risk, regardless of market position:

- Technical or market dominance in their industry
- Production of a single product
- Licensing and joint venture strategies
- Product and process protection
- Information and technology protection
- Unique marketing approaches
- Brand sensitive to compromise

A variety of analyses can be used to prioritize programs and identify activities that are essential to meet strategic plans. The most basic of these is determining whether they are "must-do," "should-do," or "nice-to-do" activities. If this basic test were applied to current efforts at ensuring brand integrity, what would we find? In many major corporations the focus is on providing an overall protection program for all corporate protective activities, with brand and product issues receiving a small portion of program time and attention unless product problems are significant management issues. Otherwise, they are only one of many competing priorities that security and loss prevention executives must balance in providing overall corporate support.

If brand issues are made the core program of corporate management, the must-do, should-do, and nice-to-do lists would look much different. Protecting products and brands would take top priority for all employees.

The must-dos would focus on aspects of product risk identification, life-cycle management, intelligence from the marketplace, customer management, supply chain protection, and IT security. The should-dos would include providing safe working environments, protecting employees, minimizing workplace violence and sexual harassment, managing physical security programs, investigating thefts, and so forth. The nice-to-dos may be such things are security surveys, investigation of minor thefts and security incidents, and parking and key control. While many of these problems can contribute to brand- and product-related problems, unless they are identified as core brand concerns, they should not be allocated budget from corporate funds. Brand managers must identify priorities and establish the must-dos and should-dos that have the highest return for protecting their assets. These priorities are based on using risk or threat analysis and applying brand integrity standards.

Brand integrity must be the overarching philosophy of company management. Think "lifetime product profits," not immediate returns, and structure operations around the product life cycle. Brand identification, promotion, and protection are essential to long-term profitability. Most information is time sensitive. The blend of sound legal underpinnings for company protection with a well-developed BI program is essential for long-term profitability. Products are the life of a company. They need to be kept healthy, protected, and managed for their entire useful life.

WHAT QUESTIONS SHOULD YOU ASK ABOUT BRAND INTEGRITY?

The CEO should have questions on his or her monthly dashboard for all direct-reporting executives that focus attention on the key aspects of brand integrity. These 10 questions address each aspect of BI oversight:

1. If you look for BI issues, what will you find?
2. Are lessons learned from BI incidents being used?
3. How much risk do products and brands have in the market?
4. Can we identify our own products?
5. Can we respond effectively to product or brand attacks?
6. Do we have reliable loss information?
7. Do we have anyone responsible for brand integrity?
8. Do we have brand integrity policies and procedures?

9. Are the brand integrity costs justified by the risks?
10. How do we compare with other companies?

The answers to these questions will provide a strategic overview of how product stewardship is being maintained within the company. Brand integrity as a core management function is rewarded, promoted, and embedded as it becomes a key ingredient of the day-to-day operations.

CHAPTER 2

BRAND INTEGRITY IS MORE THAN LEGAL PROTECTION

Management is doing things right; leadership is doing the right things.

Peter F. Drucker

The first of the eight laws of brand integrity states that, "Brand integrity is more than legal protection." This means that legal protection is only one part of a brand integrity strategy, not the strategy itself. You need more than mere legal protection, although most executives think and act as though it is enough. Certainly, it is important to have all the necessary legal protections in place, but that is hardly enough to protect products, profits, and probably jobs in today's highly competitive global business climate. It's like the United States trying to build a fence across the border with Mexico and expecting it to keep out illegal immigrants. Brand integrity is a very complex problem requiring multiple levels of solution.

ORGANIZING THE BUSINESS

It is important to get the patents, copyrights, trademarks, and trade secrets protected. But once you have them, how are you going to make sure that they are respected?

You do it by making sure that products are hard to copy, sell off-price, or steal.

You do it by aggressively marketing your product, controlling the supply chain and distribution channels, and understanding what is happening in the marketplace.

You do it by treating customers, employees, and distributors fairly and giving a good return to shareholders.

You do it by being a good corporate citizen and not having sweatshop labor.

In other words, legal protection takes you only so far in protecting your brand reputation, image, shareholder value, and profits. How you organize and manage the business is what makes the difference.

A combination of sound legal practices and documentation forms the basis of a brand integrity program, but it is only one component of the actual process of protecting brands and products. Brand integrity requires layer upon layer of cost-effective practices focused on ensuring that every product and brand has the level of protection it needs while it is producing revenue for you. Figure 2.1 describes the possible layers for a typical product.

A brand integrity program should be designed to improve profits and market share. It requires not just understanding the legal rights but also determining which brand assets are really important to the company. It is a willingness to spend management time and money to develop strategic approaches to protecting products and intellectual property. It must, lastly, develop specific programs to identify risks and threats from within the marketplace and also from within the company.

The primary goal of a brand integrity program is ensuring that corporate fiduciary responsibilities to shareholders, social responsibilities, ethical considerations, and margin improvements are met, along with using industry best practices and following case law.

FIGURE 2.1   The Layers of Brand Integrity

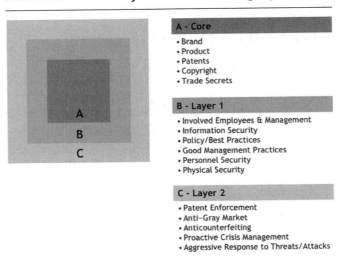

A - Core
- Brand
- Product
- Patents
- Copyright
- Trade Secrets

B - Layer 1
- Involved Employees & Management
- Information Security
- Policy/Best Practices
- Good Management Practices
- Personnel Security
- Physical Security

C - Layer 2
- Patent Enforcement
- Anti-Gray Market
- Anticounterfeiting
- Proactive Crisis Management
- Aggressive Response to Threats/Attacks

Establishing a brand integrity program involves many parts of the company, but it must focus on those products and brands that are vital to the company's financial success. Identifying the key products and brands, developing risk profiles for them, and formulating the strategic plans for product stewardship are the steps that complete building a program. Each step, though, is a *part* of building and operating a program, not the program itself. Establishing legal ownership of products and intellectual property plays an important role in the process, but by no means the only role.

In most companies the responsibility for product integrity is diffused throughout the company, but the legal department often controls product integrity and views its actions as defensive, not profit generating. Where responsibility is spread out in the corporate structure, the CFO, product management, and sometimes the security department have a role. Marketing and sales executives often take the position that if you sell more products, you don't have to worry about product integrity. If a counterfeit problem is identified, you will hear comments like, "They wouldn't buy the real stuff anyway" or "You can't stop all counterfeits; it's only a small market." Gray market products engender a similar response: "We still made our numbers. It's just a little extra margin." We have also heard executives say that "We can raise the prices a bit to make up for the revenue loss." What is not heard often is that, "It's good for business to protect our products."

An inordinate amount of reliance is often placed on the traditional legal protection provided by copyrights, trademarks, patents, and the like. Enforcement of these rights is often initiated after an attack against a product—and frequently that is too late, especially in a large company. In a small company, information about an attack might travel quickly and be handled at the most senior level, but in large corporations, there is often limited internal coordination within a single business unit. Incident and intelligence information flow is not effective or even is nonexistent. Responsibility is diffused through the corporate staff. Risk prioritization is limited or tied to the value of products or brands.

Brand integrity programs are established to focus company energy and resources to protect key business assets. Their design and structure inform all staff members of their roles and responsibilities to protect products and brands. These programs will provide the analytical tools to identify risks and attacks against brands and to develop internal responses to protect and address BI problems. The paramount purpose of the tools is to manage risks to profitability from trade secret theft or losses, patent infringements, counterfeit goods, gray markets, and dishonest customers, suppliers, and employees. If established properly, these programs will also provide benchmarks so that strategies for managing internal protection programs and improving profitability and market share can be developed and operated.

VALUE OF BRAND INTEGRITY

Brand and product are the foundation of the financial success of an enterprise. Product integrity is the foundation of a successful product. If a product or brand cannot be protected, its useful revenue-producing life will be short. If the integrity of the product cannot be maintained in the marketplace, brand loyalty will fade quickly. If integrity is maintained, it will extend and expand the product's life and value in the market. Brand integrity efforts are good for the product and its image. It is, in short, good for business to have an effective, aggressive brand integrity program because it's profitable.

There is no substitute for good products and brands to create financial success, nor is brand integrity a substitute for good product management. Likewise, tight controls, good market intelligence, and supply chain excellence will produce higher returns. Product integrity makes all these functions work together more effectively as it focuses efforts to extend product life and value over time. Not only is it good product stewardship to have a broadly applied brand integrity effort in the company, but it is good for the company. Following a set of legal requirements is not the same as producing a higher return from products because "someone is watching the store" because they want to do it, not because they are told to do it.

Legal protection forms the basis on which a brand integrity program is built. This foundation, if properly established, has a process to determine product risk and to develop plans for mitigating it. Risks and mitigation plans take many forms, not only involving merely a legal response. In public companies or in regulated environments such as pharmaceuticals, electronics, or aerospace, having aspects of a brand integrity program may be mandated for DEA, DOD, DOE, or SEC compliance.

Case Study

A shoe manufacturing company started to find counterfeit products in various markets around the world. An investigation to determine the source and to enforce patent and trademark rights identified the offending plant in Malaysia. The investigation determined that the plant was a very efficient, modern facility that was producing a shoe of high enough quality to be passed off as the real thing. Rather than take enforcement action, an offer to purchase the plant was made and accepted by the owners. The plant became a major production facility for the company and contributed to overall product and brand success.

LEGAL CONTROLS FOR BRAND INTEGRITY

While not the complete strategy, the legal aspects of brand integrity play a significant role in shaping it, managing business processes, and taking enforcement actions. Legal support for establishing product design, identification measures, supply chain contracts, sales agreements, and enforcement strategies are all major factors in maintaining BI. Figure 2.2 provides a summary of the key areas in which legal support is critical to BI.

Intellectual Property Protection

Intellectual property protection has two very clear-cut components: legal and everything else. The legal barriers provided by various forms of registration set ownership and enforcement rights, while the brand integrity program provides the means and framework for carrying out the protection program.

The legal environment for intellectual property associated with products, brands, and company operations in general is different for each product and country of sale or operation. The key questions for consideration are similar regardless of venue:

FIGURE 2.2 Critical Legal Support

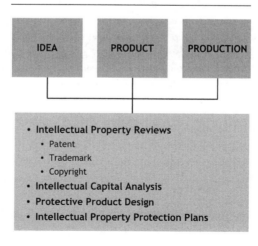

- *Patents.* Whether to register or not
- *Copyrights.* When, how, and where to register
- *Trademarks.* When, how, and where to register
- *Trade secrets.* How to handle or recover if lost or mishandled
- *Logo(s).* How and where to register and how to deal with logo squatting
- *Web site.* How to protect a Web site and deal with Web site squatting

How these questions are answered sets the legal strategy in motion to protect intellectual property. They do not, however, do anything to guide the way in which products are sold, designed, or developed or the way vendors are selected. They provide a framework to identify what is important to the company: if a product is important enough to copyright, it has some value to the company and needs further protection.

Case Study

The law department of a major corporation had budget constraints for registration of trademarks, patents, and copyrights for the corporation's global operations. Numerous products were developed and manufactured around the world by both third-party manufacturers and the corporation's own plants. The company name and logo were a highly recognized part of the industry in which the corporation operated, but because of the high cost of registration, they were not registered in all countries at the same time. A major product diversion problem developed in China for a key product. During the preparation for an enforcement action, it was learned that neither the company name nor its logo had been registered in China. They were, however, owned by another Chinese company. No enforcement action could be taken, and at considerable expense the name and logo were purchased from the Chinese company. The legal department originally believed that it was too expensive to register in all areas of the world, and China was just left off the list. The department now had to reassess its approach to determining the registration cost-benefit criteria.

Case Study

A large multinational company hired a new country manager for Malaysia. He was responsible for operating several companies, building a new plant, and overseeing new operations in a few other Asian markets. Two years after assuming these responsibilities, he was promoted to regional president in addition to his duties in Malaysia. Shortly afterward, the CEO of the parent company received an anonymous letter saying that the regional president was stealing from the company. The company investigated the allegations and determined that they were true: he had collected kickbacks from the factory construction, sold manufacturing equipment to family members, and started a company that was competitive to his employer. When confronted by senior management, he said that he did it but that the company could not take any actions against him. Upon further investigation of all his activities, it was determined that he had local legal counsel put all the company assets in his name, not that of the company. To avoid a larger scandal, a deal was made with the regional president that gave him a large settlement to quietly leave the company after rectifying all the legal filings. He continued living and working in Malaysia, competing with his former employer using the equipment that he sold to his relatives. He also established a series of fashion and advertising-related businesses that tried to get contracts from his old employer. He was turned down, not for his prior unethical behavior, but because his prices were too high.

In short, our client's company now has a process of establishing legal ownership in key markets but still lacks a process for brand integrity. Figure 2.3 provides a shorthand comparison of traditional product protection plans to a brand integrity approach, along with what is needed to close the gap identified.

FIGURE 2.3   Traditional Product Protection—Most Companies Lack a Process for Brand Integrity

Best Practices Concept	Traditional Product Protection Plans	What Is Needed?
• Product risk identification focus • Protection strategy tied to financial objectives • Coordinated process with broad participation • Best practices used to manage • Self-audits / continual improvement built into process • Measurable results • Tied to product life cycle / revenue value • Embedded in day-to-day company operations • Product / brand managers responsible for process	• Reliance on legal protection (copyright, trademark, etc.) • Enforcement action after attacks • Departmental (silo) approaches, little coordination of efforts • Incident / intelligence information flow not effective or nonexistent • Responsibility diffused throughout corporate staff • Risk prioritization not used or tied to value of products / brands	• Process to identify brand / product risks • Identification of baseline value for all IP / IC in the company • "Tools" to coordinate & operate process • Team building / training to build / use process • Reward / incentive program • Integration of BP process into company operations • Metrics for program operations

As noted above, legal protection for patents, trademarks, copyrights, and trade secrets is just a step in the protection process. There are dozens of other aspects of protecting brand and products that are equally, if not more, important. They include:

- Product design
- Packaging
- Security features
- Marketing
- Supply chain controls
- Manufacturing controls
- Distribution controls
- Marketplace surveillance
- Customer awareness

Most legal controls let you take some action if or when you are attacked. But they normally do not prevent an attack from happening any more than putting a fence around your home prevents intruders from coming into your yard. They provide some deterrent value but little practical value against a determined counterfeiter or gray marketer.

Legal documentation and enforcement provide a portion of the controls and program components, but not all the major policy and process aspects that are required to keep the products and company safe. Product protection must be around the product, around the company, around the deal, and around the marketplace. If any one of these dimensions of protection is not provided for in the brand protection plans, that oversight will be exploited. Protection must be from *information production to product production* with no gaps! All phases of the business cycle must be protected: R&D-related issues, patent pending, patented, production, distribution, and so on; all have special risks and vulnerabilities and require the right legal protection as well as controls in place to minimize risks.

Additional key points about the difference between legal protection and brand integrity include these:

1. Keep in mind that brand identification, promotion, and protection are essential to profitability.
2. Think in terms of *lifetime product profits*, not immediate returns.
3. Structure operations around the product's life cycle.
4. Reward product stewardship, not exploitation.

Clearly, not all these relate to ownership rights or enforcement. They do, however, underscore the need for a more holistic approach to the product and brand integrity. If you make a product, you need not only to market it but to protect it with good business processes, policies, and procedures for operating the company, motivating employees, and managing products.

Effective marketing and distribution of a product may be the best product integrity measures that can be used. If a product is in demand, it has an increased risk of being counterfeited or diverted. By flooding distribution channels with real products, sold at realistic pricing, the lead time required by the counterfeiter is shortened; and it also minimizes the availability of bad products being introduced into the market. Selling at good market prices also reduces the possibility of diversion. Neither product marketing nor distribution is considered a traditional brand integrity measure, but nothing works better to lower risk than to have real products readily available for sale. These measures do not rely on legal protection for anything other than sales or distribution contracts.

Intellectual Capital

What you own as intellectual property is not the only asset that requires protection. The know-how used to develop concepts, new-product ideas, designs, and manufacturing processes is not necessarily something that can be patented or even treated as a trade secret. If possible, handling "know-how" properly can provide some degree of legal protection for this valuable asset. The less tangible aspects of company operations, such as long-term employees who know how to keep your equipment operating properly or engineers who know what ideas have and have not worked, help save time and money in R&D, provide creativity in solving supply chain and other problems, and are valuable dimensions of the business. If key individuals are hired away by predatory competitors or jobs are outsourced to low-cost foreign countries, is the long-term value of the company diminished? Is intellectual capital being stolen or given away? Without a risk analysis that looks at the impact of these types of losses on brand integrity, it is difficult to provide either legal or business process solutions or options.

Protective Product Design

In order for any legal protective measure to be effective in enforcing your product rights, you must be able to positively identify your products. While this sounds simple, we can assure you that many major corporations have not been able to properly identify their products during a legal proceeding. Filing a patent in the United States might not provide comparable protection in China or India. A trademark for your company name might be valid in the United States but not in India. In fact, a competitive firm in India copied the name of our company within a few months of starting our business in the United States. We never thought to file for a trademark in India! In this situation we found out about the infringement early through good market surveillance, wrote "lawyer letters," and tried to get the Indian company to "cease and desist." The offending company management said that since we had not filed in India and we had a good name, it was going to continue using our name regardless of what we wanted it to do. It is still using it today, but only in India! Has it hurt our business? Probably not, since our clients were made aware of the infringement; but what about the potential clients that never hear about us but know about the company in India?

So can you really identify your products? Legal identification is difficult, even with serial numbers, stock-keeping units (SKUs), chemical descriptions, and patents. How would you do it? We know of several major multinational companies that could not do it. How was this possible? They had third-party manufacturers using their plans. A lack of controls over their dyes and tools, along with subcontractors unknown to them who were manufacturing their products, resulted in a lack of standardization. In one case, although its logo was on the finished product, the company could not tell whether the product was authentic using any of the methods it thought were in place because the authentic product could not be differentiated from the nonauthentic or counterfeit product. The reason? The same plants were producing the same product for the company *and* the counterfeiters!

Do you or can you trust your subcontractors? Most third-party or contract manufacturers are honest and try to provide quality products for their customers. It is, however, important to make sure that they do what they are supposed to with no overruns or unauthorized production taking place. This can be done with good contracts, inspections, unannounced audits, control of key raw materials, and other controls as necessary. Preventing unauthorized use of third-party subcontractors and verifying production volumes are steps that often help to "keep honest people honest." Some contracts can take up to 100 pages of terms and conditions to control quality and production standards! But it is worth the time, effort, and cost. This is where legal support is vital to BI.

Even with all possible controls in place, the system can be beaten. So how do you find out if your products are in the market? Well, the best way is to

FIGURE 2.4   Product Risks and Protection Options

Threats
- Copyright Infringement
- Product Extortion
- Product Diversion
- Patent Infringement
- Trademark Violations
- Trade Secret & IP Theft
- Gray Market
- Clones & Counterfeits

Protection
- Market Intel
- Protect the Process
- Physical Security
- Due Diligence
- Test Buys
- End-User Verification
- Computer Security
- Know Your Distributors
- Know Your Manufacturers
- Know Your Vendors
- Public Relations
- Training
- Enforcement
- Employee Checks

have sales and marketing staff, as well as distributors who know what is going on in their market space, report back to you. If this is not working, or as an independent supplement to it, there are commercial services that will monitor the Internet or check stores, flea markets, discount stores, and the like. Repairs, warrantee claims, or customer complaints can also provide good feedback. It is important to be listening and watching for the warning signs: products that are not performing properly, higher repairs and returns than expected, more products in the market at lower prices than should be present in that market.

Without establishing a product risk evaluation process and corresponding product and brand integrity plans, it is unlikely that effective product design criteria will be developed. Legal considerations must also be included in product design for compliance, safety, and enforcement purposes. Figure 2.4 presents the various product risks and the associated protection options that can be considered to establish a product protection plan. At the center of the risks and options is the product. What is done to the product to provide additional legal measures for protection makes the application of all the other protective measures effective.

Commercial services to monitor your products in the market can be useful, but they must be selected properly and monitored closely. A variety of services are available:

- Internet monitors for the use of trademarks and copyrights or Internet searches for specific products and pricing

- Product honesty shopping to buy products from various sources on the Internet, specialty bulletin boards, and the like
- Product purchasing for intelligence about pricing, availability in selected markets, product sourcing, and so forth
- Investigation in advance of some enforcement action against gray marketers, counterfeiters, or unauthorized distributors

Keep in mind that, as with most services, quality and reliability can vary dramatically. And, again, you must know your product and have specific goals when you are employing a commercial service. It is essential to use the correct service for the end result required. Do not, for example, hire a service to collect product intelligence and then try to use the information for legal enforcement. The methods used are often not the same as those legally required for an effective enforcement action.

There are numerous legal actions that must be taken as well as procedural steps that must be done for each type of product-related issue. Things that require legal actions are copyrights, trademarks, patents, sales contracts, compliance with import and export controls, and labeling. There are other issues that require some legal attention, but these issues are mostly business processes and controls, such as patent pending sales, trade secret protection, gray market management, counterfeit control, and deal and end-user verification.

Patent Pending

If a product needs to be released before patent protection is in place, substantial risks are present if the product is really desirable. Patent pending protection, while affording some measure of relief if the product is attacked or copied, never makes up for lost sales, reputation problems, or legal expense to enforce patent rights. It is most desirable to have the proper patent, trademark, and copyright or trade secret protections in effect before releasing a product. It is much cheaper in the long run!

If a product must be sold before a patent is finalized, it is important to have protection in place to lower the risk that nonauthentic products get into the market. An aggressive surveillance and enforcement program must be in place. It is essential that while the patent review process is in progress, this series of actions be taken:

- Specify strict contractual terms for production.
- Conduct security reviews at the manufacturing site.
- Conduct internal security reviews in the company.
- Initiate a market surveillance program.

It is important that these controls are in place, that they can be documented, and that offending products are found in the market quickly so that cease-and-desist letters can be sent. Damages are generally not awarded for products sold before they are discovered and the offending party is notified. So if you don't find them for a year, most likely all those lost sales cannot be included in any damages claimed against the offending company. Faster is always much better than slower!

Trade Secrets

One of the main criteria of the Uniform Trade Secrets Act requires that "you take reasonable measures to keep information secret." Therefore, to ensure that you will have legal recourse, you must:

- Conduct security audits of your facilities.
- Provide security awareness education and training.
- Have and maintain a security policy and procedures.
- Perform compliance reviews.
- Conduct background investigations on employees having access to secret information.
- Conduct investigations of known or suspected compromises.
- Review IT security systems and controls.

In other words, if you want something to be considered secret, you must treat it as though it were secret. It short, you must tell employees that the product is secret, handle it as a secret, protect it when it is not in use, control access to it while it is in use, control access to it by nonemployees, tell employees how to handle it, and provide them the means to protect it while it is in their possession. If you do not, most courts will not consider it secret.

Gray Market

Selling products in the gray market is generally not considered a criminal act. The source of the problem comes from violations of sales and distribution agreements. Strong contractual language that limits how and where products can be used, distributed, and resold is a good start to lowering gray market risk. But, again, legal documentation can only lower risk and assist in enforcement. Vigilance and good business controls can preclude the problems from occurring. A comprehensive anti-gray market program should have business processes that include:

- Customer verification
- End-user verification
- Vetting of outside manufacturers
- Compliance monitoring
- Due diligence on suppliers, customers, distributors, and the like
- Import and export compliance investigations
- Purchasing controls
- Internet intelligence collection

In order to collect lost margins that gray market resellers are collecting, contractual language that specifies the penalties for violations is essential.

Case Study

A company that sells an electronic component put a clause in the sales agreement that states: "The contract OEM price for 50,000 units of SKU1234 is $23.45 based on this product being used in the manufacture of computers in your factory in Malaysia. If this product is discovered outside of this channel within 60 days of shipment date, the OEM sales price is canceled and the normal Tier 2 price of $41.75 will apply for all SKUs covered on this Invoice."

It was discovered through surveillance of gray market channels that SKU1234 was being sold through Internet bulletin boards within seven days of shipment. Samples were covertly purchased and verified, and a demand letter was sent to the offending company. A revised invoice was then sent to the company, and a collection action was initiated for $915,000 ($2,087,500 – $1,172,500). The court action was successful, and the differential pricing was received.

HOW MUCH DOES BRAND INTEGRITY COST?

It depends, but usually less than doing nothing about protecting the company brand. If BI is built into the day-to-day operations, there are usually no extra costs once management restructuring takes place. There is no extra cost when starting a new operation or launching a new brand. By building on the established legal platform with supply chain controls, product design defenses, marketing strategies, distribution strategy, marketplace surveillance, and consumer education, an effective, layered BI program is low cost to operate and maintain.

BEST PRACTICES

1. Identify key products and brands.

2. Identify key intellectual property.

3. Establish a framework for legal protection.

4. Develop a brand integrity process in the company.

5. Manage products and brands using a brand integrity process.

DASHBOARD QUESTIONS

- Are ownership rights effectively protected using legal filings?
- Are prioritized product, brand, and IP legal protection in place?
- Are brand integrity plans established for all key products and brands?

IF A PRODUCT IS VALUABLE, SOMEBODY WILL TRY TO TAKE YOUR PROFITS

I have six locks on my front door, all in a row. I lock every other one. I figure no matter how long somebody stands there picking the locks, they are always locking three.

Jerry Seinfeld

Remember that threat follows value: the more value products appear to have, the more likely they are to be attacked. While you create both the value and threat by having a desirable product and promoting interest in it, you alone stand to lose if your product is not protected effectively in the marketplace. For a one-product company, the impact of a successful attack against that product can be more serious than several attacks against a company with a broad portfolio of products. Both companies can, however, suffer irreparable harm to their brand and goodwill by someone wanting to usurp their profits through gray market or counterfeit sales.

KEY CONCEPTS FOR THE IMPLEMENTATION OF LAW NO. 2

To minimize the likelihood that a product will be singled out for attack, the company's product or brand must appear to be a hard target for anyone thinking about trying to take advantage of it. "Hard" because of aggressive monitoring in the market, enforcement of your intellectual property rights, and marketing that reflects a quality image. Brand integrity enhances public perception of product value. What is important to remember is that your approach to product management and your business focus will both provide the defenses and positive management strategies to minimize the effects of an attack when it occurs.

We can remember sitting in a Jakarta law office with a client and his firm's outside legal counsel. Our client was a manufacturer of high-fashion men's clothing in Indonesia and had just told his counsel that we had evidence that a new product line was being copied using techniques that made it almost impossible to distinguish the counterfeit from the real product. After a long technical discussion, the client asked the lawyer for his opinion on stopping the piracy. The lawyer sat back in his chair, thought for a minute, and then said, "I have two answers: one as your lawyer, and the other as an Indonesian. As a lawyer, I think it will be difficult to stop the production because your production contracts are not as strong as they should be. As an Indonesian, I am proud that we have finally developed our technology to the point where we can produce such high-quality counterfeit goods." We told our client it was time for a new lawyer.

In another instance we met with a senior official in the Ministry of Foreign Affairs of Vietnam about a software piracy issue. During the discussion, we told him that it would be in the interest of the Vietnamese government to stop software piracy. He became very agitated and told us, "Those software companies are making too much money. It costs them almost nothing to produce the programs, and they sell them for hundreds of dollars. Our people cannot afford them. We need these programs to develop our country, and I [and the rest of the government] will look the other way until we no longer need them." This was and continues to be the policy in many developing countries that need high-tech goods and services but cannot afford world pricing. What will they continue to do? Steal them, copy them, gray-market them—whatever is possible until you stop them!

How then do you keep products from being stolen or put into the gray market in this brave new world of global thievery, deceit, and attacks against your supply chain? Let's first take a moment to distinguish between gray market goods and counterfeit goods. *Counterfeit goods are not genuine products.* Most often they are copies made by persons who have nothing to do with your supply chain. They usually are inferior in quality, materials, and functionality and sometimes can present safety concerns. In all cases, counterfeiting is illegal. The people involved are criminals and are frequently associated with organized crime.

Gray market goods are most often genuine products being sold outside the normal authorized distribution channels at below standard pricing. In most cases, gray market products are legally sold but usually violate distribution agreements, customs import and export regulations, and sometimes company internal sales policies. Those involved in gray market activities are most likely aggressive businesspeople that understand markets and pricing and are very good at arbitraging your products against your own sales and marketing programs. Gray marketers are most often not criminals but exploiters of opportunities created by your company. Gray market products can frequently be the single largest source of competition your own products have in the market. One additional concern about the existence of gray market distribution channels is that they can often be used to introduce counterfeit products. Mixing gray market products with counterfeit ones can bring additional revenues to the gray marketer and additional risks to consumers.

Six BI rules exist that can help focus management in thinking about how to protect products from these attacks. They are:

1. Losses are often due to management problems, not security issues.
2. Losses are best controlled by those responsible for operations.
3. There is a cost to providing time delays and barriers against attacks.
4. Losses will be lower when there is more employee involvement and more personal interest and when company goals and viewpoints closely parallel personal goals and viewpoints.
5. Those with the most access can cause the most serious problems.
6. A balance is required between BI and business objectives.

So let's spend a little time talking about these rules as they apply to BI Law No. 2: *If a product is valuable, somebody will try to take your profits.*

A NEW WAY OF THINKING IS REQUIRED

We begin first, though, by asking this question: How do you protect your products from being attacked, make sure that your customers can purchase only genuine products in the market, and keep your profits safe? In truth, it is almost impossible to protect against a determined attack. What is possible, however, is to minimize the impact of an attack when it happens by having the systems in place that manage the products. This necessitates a slightly different way of thinking about what is important to the long-term success of the company and then requires the structuring of operations and management practices accordingly. The following concepts are useful for structuring a brand integrity approach in the company:

- The primary focus of management should be the product or brand.
- Brand integrity should be integrated into day-to-day operations at every step of the product cycle.
- Product needs (requirements) change at each stage of the life cycle.
- There should be a focused application or approach to management time and resources by using best practices.
- Financial results should be measured to determine cost-effectiveness.
- Application should be flexible.
- The product life should be prolonged.
- IT and supply chain issues should be integrated into a brand integrity approach.
- Corporate management and governance concerns should be related to brand integrity concepts.

Executive management must ensure that product managers are, in effect, brand integrity managers. They must provide "self-directed self-protection" that (1) takes responsibility for products and brands from cradle to grave, (2) takes control of the supply chain and market monitoring, and (3) applies aggressive enforcement of all legal rights over products. In short, brand integrity requires a rethinking of brand stewardship that expands the traditional four Ps—*produce, promote, price, and package*—to five Ps, by adding *protection*.

Protecting brand is a top-down activity. Product protection is done from the bottom up. These two complementary forces operate together against both gray and counterfeit activities to set the tone, identify key product requirements, establish best practices for operating, and give life to day-to-day program operations.

The Six Rules as They Apply to BI Law No. 2

1. *Losses are often due to management problems, not security issues.* In almost all investigations that we have handled, the root cause of a product-related attack was a management failure that caused the problem to occur. Is the product's moving into the gray market caused by a clever arbitrage expert or by a sales incentive plan that

rewards only top-line sales rather than margins? Is the fact that a product is easy to copy the result of a counterfeiter targeting your product or the lack of simple safeguards to discourage copying? If you ask various security consultants why there is so much business crime, they will all tell you the same thing: "Management is just not watching the store!" It's easy to take production or distribution shortcuts, disregard warning signs of potential risks, and react only when there is a serious attack. Because financial costs are associated with avoiding a potential risk, the thinking is, "Let's see what happens and deal with it if it becomes a problem."

The identification of product risks should be a key responsibility of management since a risk identified and handled is one less opportunity for attack. Managers need to be more like owners than semi-interested stewards. They need to care about the business and products and be able to react to executive management questions concerning what is important and how to deal with a situation. It requires a different philosophy to take ownership and responsibility for a product, live with the product, and get the most from the product.

2. *Losses are best controlled by those responsible for operations.* Products must be valuable to those managing them. If managers do not have a close, vested interest in stewardship of the product, it will be difficult to expect them to assume the day-to-day responsibility for protecting the product and managing it for profitability. A product manager who has overall responsibility for getting long-term profits will have a different attitude toward management than one who is being pushed for and expecting maximum quarterly returns. Decisions about improved product design, the reliability of new customers, or supply chain security will not be viewed as being as important as the need for higher sales this month to whoever wants to buy. Product managers should want *good* business, not just any business.

3. *There is a cost to providing time delays and barriers against attacks.* Everything costs money. Management time to think about problems, solutions, changes to production processes, security features such as RFID, and so on, has a cost. Each additional level of protection for a product costs something but also should deliver a commensurate benefit. The more layers of protection used, the more benefits there should be. Knowing how much to use therefore becomes important to balance risk, cost, and benefit. Each

security feature provides a time delay against an attack. More sophisticated measures, such as holograms, were at one time thought to make product identification and authenticity more difficult for counterfeiters to duplicate. This advantage lasted only for several weeks as holograms were themselves duplicated. Did the use of holograms justify the expense? For some companies it did, as not all counterfeiters were able to obtain the counterfeit holograms and could not make copies that would sell. Each product risk has a different set of criteria to measure value for money spent on brand integrity that must be tailored to lifetime revenue expectations.

4. *Losses will be lower when there is more employee involvement and more personal interest and when company goals and viewpoints closely parallel personal goals and viewpoints.* Getting employees to take a personal interest in the welfare of the business or a specific product is key to lowering risk and attacks. Employees who work with the product day to day should have the best information on how to ensure its safety and profitability. Marketing managers should have good product intelligence to understand where and how products are vulnerable to gray market or counterfeit attacks, competitive products, pricing issues, and opportunities. Sales executives should know the competition. They must know where the competition and gray market are a threat to profits, manufacturing, and product design and find ways to lower the risk of copy, contamination, or unauthorized production.

A team of employees with an interest in making the product or brand successful will ensure that real-time marketplace information on risk and opportunities is incorporated into business and brand integrity planning.

5. *Those with the most access can cause the most serious problems.* The basic problem in brand integrity efforts is the involvement of dishonest or unmotivated staff who are not interested in preventing losses. In several industries, the most successful gray marketers are former employees of the companies being attacked. These former employees know how the systems work and can take advantage of special pricing plans to get the product for off-price sales, can manipulate rebate programs, and can obtain preferential pricing and terms. The milking of your system by former employees is a serious problem. All your vulnerabilities are well known to key staff and, if these staff members are not managed properly, you will provide opportunities for severe losses during and after the period that they are employed by you.

Likewise, current employees who know the system well can work with others outside the company to siphon profits. Harmful practices such as approving new customers that are discounters, wrongfully manipulating returns or rebates, getting better pricing, engaging in channel stuffing, and the like, can all be managed by key staff without arousing suspicion.

6. *A balance is required between BI and business objectives.* This is the part where we talk about the *zen* of brand integrity. Getting the right balance so that neither the business objectives nor the protection of products is subordinate or superior to the other is the goal. The two need to be blended to work "just right" for the environment in the company. Products should not be overprotected, but they should be reviewed for risk on a regular basis. Protection plans should then be adjusted to reflect risks, threats, and attacks. The yin and yang are equally important to increasing sales while protecting all . . . Promoting all but losing none . . . Developing new while nurturing old. It's not impossible—it just requires the right attitude and good information.

KNOW YOUR ENEMY

Gray market goods are products intended for sale in a certain region or channel, often at discount pricing, which are then diverted to unauthorized distribution channels to be resold in other regions or channels at lower than standard prices. These channels often provide an entry point for counterfeit and substandard goods to also flow through them.

Gray market goods are usually organized on a tiered distribution model: distributors–resellers–end users. Gray market operations are highly profitable businesses with little or no overhead. The price differential between geographical regions creates opportunities for gray marketing. The following contribute to gray products in channels:

- Promotional pricing
- "Meeting-the-competition" pricing
- OEM product diversion
- Rebate programs not adequately managed
- Stock rotation scams
- Price protection scams

How Are They Organized?

Your competition is most likely a global organization that can have your product available worldwide within a day. Such organizations offer better prices to resellers and end users than do authorized distributors. They have access to the inventories of other gray marketers and can ship from multiple locations to multiple locations overnight by drop-shipping from strategically located warehouses around the world. They may have access to your production schedules and have new-product information and pricing before your dealers get that information. They also can manipulate sophisticated rebate, discount, and returns programs.

How Do They Do It?

There are three categories of gray market attack:

- Resellers that claim competitive situations with nonexistent end users to obtain steep discounts or that overorder quantities on approved "meet-competition" deals
- Brokers that pose as OEM customers and OEMs that broker products intended for system integration
- Distributors that sell to resellers for "meet-competition" prices and then buy products back at a lower price and claim additional discounts on special incentive discount programs

What Is the Impact on the Company?

One main impact is lost profits from lower margins. There are also excessive payments on programs that involve volume discounts, stock rotations, and price protection. In addition, back-office administrative costs are increased, and channel relationships are often damaged. The last major impact is the inability to manage channel inventories and sales forecasts.

Products Move Globally

The time value of money and price arbitrage are the key concepts that drive the gray market. In the movement of products, time is everything. Technology and transportation allow easy purchasing and rapid delivery globally. The gray market requires little warehousing space, as just-in-time delivery is the norm. Orders are filled by drop shipments from multiple sources and locations.

We investigated a case in which a low-cost product was sold to a gray marketer that allegedly was selling the product in Asia. According to the customs certificates, the product was shipped from California to Singapore to Hong Kong and back to California in three days. Normal delivery time using company channels for this routing was ten days. Another shipment went from Canada to London to Hong Kong and then to California in three days! Orders were being shipped to bonded warehouses at airports, then were consolidated, and were drop-shipped to distributors or end users without the need for the gray marketer's own warehouse facilities.

Who Is the Opposition?

The gray market is typically managed by young, entrepreneurial, aggressive businesspeople. The market consists of growing and global businesses whose employees are knowledgeable about products, have considerable marketing ability, and are usually technologically savvy. These businesses most often cooperate with multiple other gray marketing companies operating in syndicates, cartels, or multinational corporate-style structures. They are characterized by interlocking ownership or relationships between companies and distributors. They tend to be differentiated by product lines or geography. It is very unlikely that a gray marketer that handles computer equipment will sell consumer goods. But those who deal in both will do so on a massive scale, especially in household and higher-end consumer goods.

There are four general categories of gray marketers:

- *Traditional—those using the telephone and the Internet.* This category includes large distributors with international operations, OEMs, medium-sized distributors, and the mom-and-pop distributor.
- *E-commerce only.* These are brokers, bulletin boards, and multi-level marketers.
- *Situational.* The two main subsets of this category are employees who use legitimate operations to increase personal sales or margin goals and opportunists who take advantage of a deal.
- *Criminal.* These dealers use fraud to acquire products and to exploit operational loopholes in a system. They also seek to avoid tariffs, duties, and fees when shipping, selling, and distributing.

No matter which of these approaches gray marketers use, they operate at a lower overhead than that of your operations, they cut costs, and they exploit your systems. They work at it full time with a great incentive package: they can keep whatever they divert from your channels. If you are not aware of this threat and if no one is looking for the attack while it is ongoing, your profits are out the door.

Case Study

We investigated a very aggressive gray marketer who focused his business on a specific high-volume computer peripheral. He was able to develop special order relationships with salespeople in Asia who sold to him at 45 percent below then current U.S. and E.U. wholesale pricing. In a 90-day period he acquired and sold $23 million in product via bulletin boards and distributors. He operated from a 10 × 10 room in his home in the Seattle area. His net profit was over $1 million per month working about four hours per day. He never touched the product, never took delivery of it, and after 10 months of operations, closed down his business.

How Do You Stop It?

Knowing that the problem exists is the first step. Knowing your customers gets you half the way there. Applying sound business processes using the principles in this book will lower your risk and help you earn better margins without raising prices.

HOW ARE YOU ORGANIZED?

The primary goal of business is to provide the best return on assets, investments, and operations to company shareholders. Brand integrity provides the focus and organizing principles for managing brands and products for maximum long-term financial returns—and for reaping short-term gains as well.

There are immediate internal and external benefits from the use of a brand integrity philosophy within a company:

Internal Benefits
- A link between the company's financial strategy and brand integrity activities

- Additional focus on high-risk–high-value products
- Improved market intelligence
- Employee involvement in brand integrity
- Increased coordination between departments
- Additional support for key executives

External Benefits

- Increased confidence in company products
- Assurance of product authenticity
- More effective maintenance of margins
- Increased shareholder value

Establishing a direct link between company strategic goals and the use of brand integrity principles to organize company operations provides direct benefits to the company. These benefits are centered on increases in coordination and communications related to the handling of key brand and product assets. Since a continuous risk evaluation program is in use, intelligence about marketplace activities is constantly being gathered and is available to all executives for decision making. It is necessary to direct all information about prices, product availability, competitor activities and plans, the emergence of questionable products, and so on to a brand manager to assist in adjusting protective marketing and production plans.

Monitoring the marketplace also ensures that any questions of authenticity caused by counterfeits, gray market products, and the like are immediately detected and addressed without delay. Pricing, customer concerns, and discount and rebate issues that affect margins can be closely monitored. When regional sales vary significantly, or new customers are making large purchases, or low-price products are being detected in the market, internal fact-finding is conducted to identify the source of the problem, which can then be fixed quickly. Margin loss due to sales and marketing management problems can be monitored to ensure that profit margins do not erode. Rebates, discounts, and special offers and pricing all generate either profits or losses, depending on how well they are managed. Brand integrity programs establish monitoring processes over these activities to ensure that maximum value is returned to the company, not to gray marketers, sales executives, or clever distributors.

BENEFITS TO YOUR COMPANY

Benefits from instituting a brand integrity program cut across all levels of the company. They include:

- Improving overall company financial performance
- Increasing operational responsiveness
- Providing specific managers with additional information and resources

Linking product protection to corporate strategy might seem like a prudent and natural thing for senior management to do. Unfortunately it does not often happen. Security and BI executives will often be the ones responsible for telling senior management staff what they should be doing, set up the metrics for evaluating BI, and measure their own performances. Brand managers also often make product decisions based on strategies that do not consider product risks from counterfeiting, the gray market, or the impact of losing market lead time caused by theft of intellectual property. Yet there are numerous cases where product strategies have estimated 12 to 18 months of product revenues without significant competition, only to actually have 1 to 2 months without significant price and margin erosion caused by copy products.

The loss of new-product lead time is a significant issue in revenues, reputation, authenticity, and customer loyalty. But it is something that can be minimized if appropriate risk identification and protective priorities are established early in the product planning process through the application of a brand integrity planning program.

Equally damaging is the loss of margin through either the predatory product arbitrage practices of gray market traders, resellers, and dealers or the unethical or illegal activities of employees trying to make sales quotas, rebate, or promotional program goals. Few if any sales programs factor in margin retention rather than sales volume as a basis for compensation programs. Likewise, few companies perform due diligence investigations on clients or end users to verify that the products being sold will not enter the gray market and damage both long- and short-term margins of the company. These problems can be minimized by instituting a brand integrity program.

A brand integrity program can be applied to an individual product, a group of products within a brand, specific corporate activities with a broad impact on the company, or all corporate activities. It must be tied to the overall strategic plans for whichever plan or product it is going to be used to protect. Figure 3.1 describes the various segments of corporate operations and where they can be applied.

FIGURE 3.1   IP Product Risk Continuum

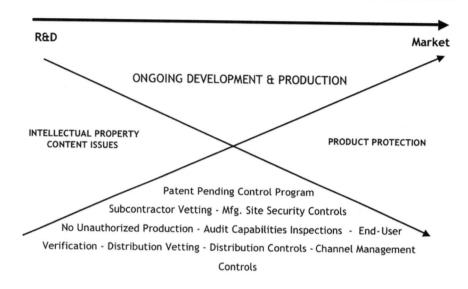

LINK BETWEEN STRATEGY AND BRAND INTEGRITY

The link between corporate business strategy, brand strategy, and brand integrity must be very direct. The application of best protective practices in each phase of the product life cycle ensures that risks particular to that

FIGURE 3.2   Typical Life-Cycle Risks for Products and Brands

R&D	IP losses, trade secret losses, product development plans and strategies
Manufacturing	Contract manufacturers exploiting products for their gain (and your loss) Premature product release, unauthorized production, quality control issues cause by the sale of scrap product Counterfeit, clone, reconditioned products sold as genuine
Distribution	Theft from supply chain of finished, semifinished, or raw materials and products
Market	Fraud in rebate, discounts, returns, damaged goods Gray market, parallel imports, and end-user problems Sales quota, consignments

portion of the product chain are managed cost-effectively. The risks associated with R&D or for any product with high intellectual property content are different than they are for consumer consumables. (See Figure 3.2.) Products that have all their costs associated with development and very limited marginal costs are particularly susceptible to significant losses if the IP is compromised before the useful marketplace product life is reached. Where every sale after cost recovery is almost pure profit, each lost sale caused by compromise of IP (theft of trade secrets) is a dollar-for-dollar drain on profitability.

Typical life-cycle risks are currently managed using a combination of legal, investigative, and product-line management resources. IP issues are normally considered from the perspective of enforcing IP ownership, with corporate security or outside investigators determining the facts and supporting various types of legal action: injunctive relief, infringement enforcement actions, counterfeit product raids, gray market purchasing, and the like. Product managers who receive information from customers, sales representatives, or product returns most often bring problems to the attention of legal counsel. The assumption is made that if legal protection is present through patenting, licensing, or contract manufacturing, then little can go wrong that is not manageable by legal action.

In the global marketplace, if the only protection that a company relies upon is enforcement of legal property ownership rights, that company will soon experience severe losses. For example, in countries such as China or India, such enforcement efforts are likely to result in expense and significant management time, but little actual relief. Brand integrity requires vigilance in the market, aggressive and prompt response to identified instances of attack against a product or brand, meticulous legal filings to protect IP (within each country), and nonstop public relations programs.

COORDINATE WITH BUSINESS STRATEGY ACROSS FUNCTIONAL LINES

The requirements for protecting products or brands cut across corporate functions but must be the responsibility of the brand or product manager, who can apply, coordinate, and revise as situations dictate.

Products with a high IP content require higher levels of legal attention, greater protective measures, and tighter controls during R&D and manufacturing than after they have been in distribution channels and the marketplace. Trade secret (rather than patented) products, which have a high IP content, may require additional vigilance even while in the marketplace. New products that have a high IP content and that have short product cycles, such as high-tech electronics that have a 12-month cycle, may require continuous surveillance until the new-generation product is released. It may then be downgraded from a high IP security risk, and the next-generation product takes its place on the high-surveillance list.

Case Study

We were asked to investigate the theft of a prototype product taken when a computer hard drive was ripped out of a server in the company's R&D center. The hard drive contained all the plans, technical data, and software of the next generation of company products and also held the plans for the follow-on products. The investigation determined that the theft was perpetrated by a security guard at the plant working there on behalf of another company with ties to the Indian government. The company responsible for the theft attempted to commercialize the product, but for a variety of reasons it was unable to do so. This theft was valued by the company at over $1 billion in potential loss had commercialization taken place.

It is imperative for products with high IP content to constantly shift protective priorities based upon strategic decisions related to changing technology values, anticipated revenues from the products, and global markets. The requirement to manage risk and apply best protective practices must be a part of the brand manager's portfolio. This assumes that intelligence related to attacks against products flows from the field, protective strategies have been developed, implementation plans are ready for execution, staff support is available to assist with technical problems, and a product-risk tracking system is in use.

The link to corporate strategy must be used to proactively update plans for product protection to reflect key financial goals. If a new product is to be introduced and is expected to contribute significant revenues over a two-year period, a brand integrity plan should accompany the market entry strategy for the product for that period. For example, if a new product is to be introduced while the patent is pending, special provisions to manage the manufacturing process should be implemented to prevent clones from entering the market while the new product is still in its initial penetration of the market. Patent pending issues can be exacerbated when foreign contract manufacturers are involved unless tight controls, inspections, and market intelligence are used to minimize the opportunities for the goods to "leak" from manufacturing channels.

The challenge to the brand manager is to ensure that engineers, production managers, legal counsel, and sales and marketing managers all understand the risks to the new product and will handle their respective responsibilities to monitor the marketplace and report attacks and questionable occurrences in a timely manner. If they are to be effective with this BI responsibility, their roles must be adequately delineated in a product protection plan, training must be provided, best practices and policies need to be implemented, and effective coordination must be put in place.

The glue that binds all these coordination and operational activities together is the plan, which provides a common understanding of the value of protecting the product or brand wherever it might be in the marketplace. Embedding the brand integrity philosophy throughout company management is the key factor in operating a successful, self-directed, and ongoing program. Good, well-motivated people are required to make a program work. Tying compensation and rewards to plans for protecting products and brands based on company-specific standards sets the stage for success. A well-designed best-practices program to identify, measure, and respond to product life-cycle risks provides the tools to operate the program. Senior management who are sensitive to brand integrity will stress the relationship between profitability and product protection and thereby set the tone for ongoing employee participation in the program.

BENEFITS TO SPECIFIC MANAGEMENT

Having worked with numerous executives to solve their unique problems, we have determined that each executive has different issues to resolve when a brand integrity problem develops.

For the CEO, key issues include:

- Fact-finding for prospective partnering, production, or alliance relationships to ensure that representations are accurate
- Confidential analysis of the information protection program within the company, facility, or country or in a specific product line under development
- Verification that executive applicants are representing their background, reputation, and skills truthfully

- Sensitive internal investigations into allegations of questionable executive behavior and misuse of company assets, funds, or information
- Independent review of product distribution and supply chain channel protection
- Crisis management support for product extortion, contamination problems, or counterfeit products that harm reputation and credibility

Key issues for the CFO are:

- Independent testing of distribution channels for compliance with company sales policies, rebates, and discounts
- Investigation of fraud, theft, and product diversion problems
- Support of internal audit staff in reviewing instances of questionable ethical conduct

Certain other executives—the CIO, the operating unit executive, the general counsel, the brand manager, and the security professional—are tasked with specific responsibilities.

The CIO

- Reviews IT systems for compliance with established security standards
- Provides computer forensic support to investigate attacks against, or losses caused by, compromise of the IT system
- Supports the development of internal security policies, procedures, and standards to protect sensitive company information

The Operating Unit Executive

- Ensures that the monitoring of licensing, manufacturing, and subcontractor relationships is appropriate for the degree of risk to the key products being produced

The General Counsel

- Investigates questionable business practices, FCPA, Sox 404 concerns, and ethics policy compliance questions
- Investigates violations of patents, patent pending matters, and copyright infringements

- Investigates theft or suspected theft of trade secrets, or compromise of proprietary information, at foreign and domestic facilities
- Provides investigative support for general litigation for theft, infringements, fraud, or loss of intellectual property, work in progress, or finished products within corporate operations

The Brand Manager

- Ensures that products are being sold at proper margins and that fraudulent transactions are not affecting sales, rebates, or discounts
- Monitors markets around the world for specific products in regard to pricing, unauthorized sales, and availability
- Purchases products from the Internet to verify supplier and pricing
- Checks the reputation and reliability of new customers, distributors, resellers, and end users
- Investigates counterfeit products, product contamination, and extortion
- Investigates suspected kickbacks, unauthorized rebates, discounts or returns, theft of returned products, and sale of rejected products to consumers
- Provides investigative support for legal actions against contract manufacturers who are producing unauthorized products and selling into the market
- Provides investigative support, including sourcing information, if substandard products are being sold as regular quality rather than seconds

The Security Professional

- Provides investigative support for counterfeit products, due diligence, fraud, theft of trade secrets, and related types of loss or risk situations around the world
- Performs security reviews of facilities or operations, provides employee security training and awareness, and develops information security programs

CONFIDENCE IN PRODUCTS

The loss of customer confidence in a product or brand can be fatal to a company unless the cause for this loss is quickly identified and dealt with candidly. Loss of confidence can result from poor quality control, improper testing, defective components, counterfeit goods, product extortion, distribution delays, malicious rumors, and the like. Some of these, such as poor quality control and distribution delays, are internal problems. Others, such as counterfeit goods and product extortion, are external problems.

Case Study

A product that was patented, but not marketed in Taiwan, was targeted by an infringing pharmaceutical company—which sold hundreds of thousands of dollars of product before the client learned (through a local dealer) about the infringement.

The investigation revealed that the product was being illegally imported and sold to a major client of the patent holder. That client was unaware that it was buying unauthorized production. The investigation also determined that the importer could be prosecuted without endangering the relationship between the product's rightful owner and the client. The importer's company was raided, and the illegal products were confiscated.

Internal Problems

Internal problems include such issues as poor quality control, distribution delays, defective design, and questionable advertising. These problems are often the easiest to fix, as well as the easiest to minimize or control in the future; but what often proves most difficult is to demonstrate that they have been cleared up.

Different problems are handled in different ways. For example, changing offending advertising in concert with using effective public relations programs can make any adverse public reaction to the offending advertising go away quietly. If accidents or deaths resulted from product defects, the litigation strategy will have a direct impact on customer confidence and must be handled accordingly. If the cost of the litigation, including damage awards, is potentially high, the case may well be handled differently from one that is likely to be less costly; less costly cases are more apt to result in a quick settlement that would restore immediate confidence and allow for continued sales of the offending product. Internally caused brand problems are usually handled within the company and do not require that extensive fact-finding be conducted outside of company operations.

External Problems

Externally caused brand problems range from counterfeit goods, gray market products, clones, and diversion of licensed technology to product extortion, patent infringements, and malicious rumors. These problems all require extensive fact-finding conducted outside of normal company channels. These brand problems often go to litigation; and where criminal statutes have been violated, law enforcement will sometimes be involved.

Regardless of cause, anything that erodes confidence in a product or brand must be addressed using an established protocol to avoid inadvertently making the problem worse. This assumes that crisis management plans have been developed, executives have been trained in how to respond, and internal procedures have been established to identify the cause of the problem and resolve it quickly.

Johnson & Johnson, in the famous Tylenol case, handled its contamination problem so well that the publicity surrounding the situation enhanced the brand image and customer confidence, rather than lowering it. Johnson & Johnson's response provides a model for how to organize for and respond to these types of problems. It is also necessary to identify other areas in which companies could begin to be preventative rather than reactive and to lower risk from cloning, counterfeiting, diversion, manufacturing problems, and product reliability problems.

Case Study

The Tylenol murders occurred in the autumn of 1982, when seven people in the Chicago area in the United States died after ingesting Extra Strength Tylenol medicine capsules which had been laced with cyanide poison. This incident was the first known case of death caused by deliberate product tampering. The perpetrator has never been caught, but the incident led to reforms in the packaging of over-the-counter substance and federal anti-tampering laws.

Johnson & Johnson was praised by the media at the time for its handling of the incident. While at the time of the scare the market share of Tylenol collapsed from 35% to 8%, it rebounded in less than a year, a move credited to J&J's prompt and aggressive reaction. In November it reintroduced capsules, but in a new, triple-sealed package, coupled with heavy price promotions, and within several years Tylenol had become the most popular over-the-counter analgesic in the United States.

A number of copycat attacks involving Tylenol and other products ensued during the following years. However, the incident did inspire the pharmaceutical, food, and consumer product industries to develop tamper-resistant packaging, such as induction seals, and improved quality control methods. Moreover, product tampering was made a federal crime.

Additionally, the tragedy prompted the pharmaceutical industry to move away from capsules, which were easy to contaminate as a foreign substance could be placed inside without obvious signs of tampering. Within the year, the FDA introduced more stringent regulations to avoid product tampering. This led to the eventual replacement of the capsule with the solid "caplet" as a drug delivery form and to the addition of tamper-evident safety-seals to bottles of many sorts.

FROM WIKIPEDIA, THE FREE ENCYCLOPEDIA

Anything that brand managers can do to help employees better understand the key components of the supply chain and the risks associated with them to products and brand is a beneficial first step. While brand managers might not be able to comment on who might be the best manufacturers for a product, they can certainly require that a due diligence review be conducted on all key current or potential manufacturers in the company supply chain. They can also maintain surveillance over their continued operations to ensure that any significant changes in their ability to provide the type and quality of service in the supply chain are noted and reported to company management.

Clearly the ability to have a strong contract with key supply chain partners is essential to protecting company interests in the marketplace. Unless contracts contain, at a minimum, the following provisions to protect product brand integrity, it will be difficult to protect products in production or to investigate abnormalities that develop during the product cycle:

- Due diligence investigation for all key manufacturing partners and ongoing monitoring of them throughout the life of their company relationship
- Identification of where actual production is taking place—including company, location(s), and subcontractor(s)
- Knowledge of those who have copies of plans, molds, material lists, and so on
- Compliance with company production security standards by contractor and subcontractor facilities
- Security audits before starting production

- Agreements to have periodic and unannounced security compliance inspections
- Marketplace monitoring to ensure that unauthorized production is not entering the channel

Brand managers must monitor for any gray market goods around the world and use the various watch lists for Internet, field reporting, or both. They should also monitor distribution channels daily for price, availability, and related issues to assist marketing executives in understanding the flow of products in the marketplace on a real-time basis.

PREVENTING DIVERSION OF LICENSED TECHNOLOGY

The problem of having clones of company products in the marketplace is significant since the loss of sales, market share, and confidence are all related directly to new technology.

Case Study

Company Z licensed a company in Korea to produce private label computer technology to be used in an OEM environment. Company Z is providing both the manufacturing technology and the chips for production purposes. Finished OEM products look and behave exactly like Z's product except that they have a private label on them.

Another license was arranged with a Chinese company with production to begin in China within three months.

An audit of the current manufacturing and distribution process at the Korean facility was conducted. All aspects of the complete set of brand controls were instituted for the China licensee immediately.

These products are likely candidates for either excess production or diversion into the gray market as clones or counterfeit products. In order to reduce these risks, security measures are required, beginning at the time the licensing process is being negotiated and continuing through the start-up of the licensing arrangement, and extending throughout manufacturing and distribution.

The recommended brand integrity plans for the proposed production-distribution cycle should include:

- *Supplier credibility*
- *Production contract terms*

- *Security of the manufacturing site(s)*
- *Security of Company Z's intellectual property*
- *Security of the finished products*
- *Accountability of production*
- *Verification of the location of all production sites*
- *Protection of the distribution for finished products*
- *Quantity management*
- *Market surveillance*

Each of the above security features is required to ensure that there are controls over every aspect of the cycle and that production quantities can be verified. Additionally, each of the following steps should be implemented for the contract manufacturer.

Contract Negotiations

- *Licensee due diligence before the contract is signed*
- *Site security standards agreed to in the contract*
- *Periodic unannounced audits agreed to in the contract*
- *Inspection and audit of chip inventory and finished production specified in the contract*
- *Controls over scrap and overruns specified in the contract*

Start-Up

- *Preproduction security survey conducted*
- *Required security upgrades implemented before production begins*
- *Possible placement of undercover investigators (UCs) into the workforce*
- *Production security audit after 60 days*

Manufacturing

- *Use of undercover operatives in plants*
- *Monitoring plant(s) via audits*
- *Surveillance of marketplace via Internet, marketplace analysis*

Distribution

- *Security over finished products in distribution channels and in the warehouse*

AUTHENTICITY

The authenticity of products is an increasingly vexing problem for global business. Counterfeiting, copyright violations, and piracy plague virtually every business and type of product. Aircraft parts, automobile parts, watches, drugs, cosmetics, food, drinks, liquor, clothing, computer equipment, software, and anything else that can be produced at less cost than the original are being copied and sold. Putting aside the safety issues in using substandard counterfeit equipment, counterfeiters produce at less cost and sell at less cost than originals.

Case Study

An American chemical company established a joint venture (JV) with a Chinese company to produce industrial materials for the China markets. Patent and trade secret–protected technology was transferred to the JV, which was staffed by PRC employees, with U.S. technical management. After several years in operation, a competitive product, which was of exactly the same composition as that produced by the JV, was discovered in the marketplace. The U.S. parent company that supplied the technology to the JV decided to take enforcement actions against the company copying its product. The parent company directed the JV to begin legal proceedings. The Chinese partner in the JV declined to take any action. Subsequent investigation determined that a relative of the JV company president was producing the copy product. Since the technology was provided to the JV for use in China, only the JV, not the U.S. company, could take enforcement action. And so the copy product continued to be sold in the market.

Various rationales explain why copies are produced and sometimes ignored by foreign governments. Here are some typical examples:

- "The software is too expensive for the average person, and the counterfeiter is performing a good service."
- "There is no such thing as intellectual property. Ideas belong to everyone."
- "It's easy to copy the product, and everyone wants to buy it. I'm really not hurting the company by copying its product."
- "The people we sell to know that we are selling copies but don't care since they can't afford to buy the real one."
- "Versions come out too often, so people buy copies to keep the costs down."

Whatever the reason, copies cause lost sales, cheapen the brand, and raise questions about prices on the street and the reliability of the products that are sold by legitimate dealers. We have seen cases in which dishonest employees have taken real products out of stock, put counterfeit goods on the shelf, and sold them as authentic so they could sell the real goods to friends at a discount.

This situation caused brand credibility and customer relations problems because the counterfeit goods did not hold up as an original would in daily use.

How do you manage a counterfeit problem in the marketplace? Some companies we have worked with are very aggressive and want to find out who are the ones doing it and stop them immediately. Others, while wanting to stop the problem, do not want to alert the public that there are counterfeits in the market. They feel that if they tell the public about a counterfeit, consumers might switch brand loyalties rather than try to stay away from the one offending product line. Still others, such as Procter & Gamble in China, have taken aggressive and very public steps to inform the public about counterfeit products, police the market, and initiate legal action against those found knocking off their products. No single approach fits all circumstances or management philosophies.

The brand integrity philosophy is simple on this topic. Where a counterfeit is suspected or identified, the offending party should be hunted down and a stake put through the heart of the operation. No quarter, no prisoners, no compromises. Your brand is sacred and must not be compromised for any reason. Use sales staff, dealers, customers, investigators, and the like—whoever is appropriate for the particular problem to police the marketplace—to find counterfeits. Once found, "Take it down, close it down, lock them up" is the only program that should be followed. Your customers should know this approach; the bad guys should know this approach; and most of all, your brand managers should know this approach. Nothing less than a full-bore, take-no-prisoners approach to protecting your products will provide additional protection in the market. People will know not only that your products are real wherever they are found, but that you will not tolerate anyone taking advantage of either your customers or your brand without suffering severe consequences. You want to be viewed as a hard target by the bad guys.

Case Study (Typical Investigative Plan)

There were indications that unauthorized Company B products were possibly being produced and distributed by various companies and individuals in China. There was also strong evidence that gray market products were freely available in South China. This investigation was to determine how these products were being manufactured, distributed, warehoused, and sold to end users; to identify those responsible for these activities; and to develop an action plan for follow-up investigation to interdict these products before they entered the China market.

The precise nature of the existing problem was not fully known by Company B. Developing intelligence information, determining the extent of the problem, and discovering the sources of the unauthorized products in the South China region constituted a primary focus of the initial activities during the project.

Operational Plan

The preliminary investigation of the situation was conducted to review the market for selected Company B products in China. This review was to determine which major sources of the products were significant contributors to the current loss in revenue within the region. This project was conducted in South China during February and March 2005. The purpose of the review was to:

1. *Collect information about the availability of products below predetermined price points.*
2. *Determine the availability of selected products in distribution channels in selected South China locations, from distributors, and from merchandisers.*
3. *Analyze Internet availability of selected products coming from sources within China.*
4. *Develop a source analysis of products in selected channels.*
5. *Determine the relative magnitude of questionable products resulting from gray market, OEM, clone, recycled, and counterfeit sources.*

The investigation consisted of interviews, field investigations, and identification of the sources of product availability in South China, and all activities were conducted in a discreet manner using interviews, covert surveillance, and information collection techniques. Knowledge of the existence of the investigation was limited to only very senior management within Company B and the legal department. It was recognized that the investigative environment in South China was difficult, and accidental disclosure of the investigation could prove detrimental to successful completion.

Information to Be Provided by Company B

The following information had been requested from Company B. The information was essential for cost-effective conduct of the inquiry. The information was provided at the start of the inquiry along with a briefing for the field manager assigned to the project.

1. *All details regarding the suspect companies and all available information already collected*
2. *Major suppliers and dealers currently purchasing the legitimate Company B products*
3. *Leads developed to date by regional Company B sales and marketing staff*
4. *Background information related to the key products*
5. *Information on the recent licensing of the products for manufacture in Korea and China*

Phase 1—Interviews and Fact Gathering

An investigation was launched to determine the source, the people involved, the methods used, and the distribution channels of the questionable Company B products. In order to do this, interviews were conducted and other investigative techniques were used to collect the following information:

1. *Identify the source(s) involved in the sales and distribution process.*
2. *Identify the outlets and buyers of the product and the volume being sold.*
3. *Monitor Internet outlets, trade publications, and related media in China for products fitting established price profiles.*
4. *Identify the ultimate source of the questionable products, and determine the methods by which they were brought into South China.*
5. *Discover the methods used to distribute the products.*
6. *Determine the warehousing and shipping system.*
7. *Identify potential sources to provide additional information about the questionable operations.*

In order to obtain the above information, the following investigative techniques were used:

1. *Interviews with Company B sales staff*
2. *Interviews with dealers and resellers*
3. *Field interviews to develop alternative sources of products*
4. *Internet scanning*
5. *Product purchasing*
6. *Forensic examinations and reverse engineering (provided by Company B)*
7. *Background investigations on prime suspects developed during field data collection*

It was estimated that this phase of the investigation would take no more than 30 working days. A report was, however, submitted as soon as enough information was available to make it practical to meet with legal and company management to determine the follow-up investigative requirements.

After Phase 1

Phase 1 of the investigation obtained sufficient information about the distribution, marketing methods, and volume being sold, and phase 2 involved a broader look at unauthorized activities outside of South China. It was important to identify unauthorized dealers who were engaged in marketing activities in other parts of the country where there was suspected distribution of Company B's products. These activities were identified and interdicted as well. Coordination with Company B's management was necessary on a continuing basis.

UNCONTROLLED COUNTERFEITING

Uncontrolled counterfeiting of products that are important to a developing economy is a special category of concern.

Case Study

The managing director of a large European manufacturer of agricultural products was summoned to the Ministry of Agriculture in a developing country and was accused of sabotaging the economy of the country. The major cash crops of five provinces had failed because the products of his company were not working. His company would be held responsible if riots broke out, people would starve, and crops would be devastated for the entire year. The minister produced samples of the offending product, statements from farmers claiming to have purchased the products from cooperatives, and receipts from the cooperatives showing that they had purchased the products from the company.

The managing director asked for some time to look into the matter and was granted two weeks. An investigation was immediately started to analyze the product, check the distribution chain, and interview the farmers.

Through chemical analysis, it was discovered that some of the samples were genuine product, some were diluted genuine product (less than 5 percent active ingredients), and the balance of the samples contained colored sand (no active ingredients). Under the growing conditions in the country, there was no way that the diluted or inactive products could perform properly.

The investigation determined that a distributor who was selling to the cooperatives had mixed counterfeit and diluted products into the deliveries to them and sold the real products outside the country at a higher price than the subsidized local prices. Once it was proved that the company was not responsible for the problem, the Ministry asked for assistance from the company to rectify the problem.

The distributor left the country, but even so, the company faced several years of trying to rebuild the brand since the farm cooperatives had started using a competing brand to avoid further problems.

Consequently, when the company uncovered another counterfeiting problem involving a different agricultural product in that same country, the company resisted telling the public (or the Ministry) since the samples found were only diluted, not counterfeit—they would work, but just not as effectively. The company was reluctant to give up any more market share to its competitors because of the second attack. In the end, the customers became unhappy with the results obtained from the product and changed brand anyway.

PATENT AND TRADE SECRET PROTECTION

The brand manager often is not involved in making the decision on how sensitive company information is to be protected (e.g., patent versus trade secret), and the decision to register a patent or use it as a trade secret is often made without input from security or BI managers. However, once that decision is made, how the information is handled and used becomes a major factor in how business operations are conducted and managed from a BI perspective.

If a decision is made to produce and market a product that is still in the patent approval (patent pending) process, brand, BI, and security managers should be involved in planning how sensitive information or the product is to be handled until the time that full protection is in place. This period in which a new product is in the marketplace without registered protection requires special precautions to ensure that clone products are not sold using your protected designs or information.

The *Nike Inc. vs. Wal-Mart*, 138 F.3d1337 (1998), decision suggests that it is essential that once a patent-protected product is put into the marketplace, it must be closely monitored for clones, counterfeits, or nongenuine copies appearing for sale. Patent infringers must be identified and notified promptly; otherwise damages or legal remedies may be limited to the period after which they had been notified, rather than for any and all damages caused by the infringement. Consequently, protecting patent pending products requires that the production process and manufacturer be well known and additional security precautions be taken during the production process. Marketplace surveillance is necessary for the timely identification and notification of anyone copying the product. This additional security has extra costs but can save the product and its introduction into the market.

In most countries, three major organizations—police, customs departments, and various ministries such as the Department of Commerce or MITI (Japan)—provide support in the efforts to prevent damage to company brands. These organizations can be very helpful but must be used in a selective manner to attain the required corporate goal. In the final analysis, each company must determine what it wants to do about a counterfeit, gray market, or patent infringement problem and use the appropriate tools to meet its requirements.

The police in many foreign countries are often not very helpful with these problems unless the situation has become a political issue or they are working to assist with a legal enforcement action directed by legal counsel. Likewise, customs departments can be helpful, but their degree of involvement, enthusiasm for assisting, and competence varies considerably around the world, and they should be used with great care. Some national trade and customs ministries can assist with broad tariff and trade matters and bring pressure for various types of political reform and regulatory changes that can have an effect on when and how attacks against products can happen. Their efforts are usually strategic, are not often tactical, and frequently will have limited effect on a specific case of product attack. The company is usually on its own in dealing with these problems and must act accordingly.

To Whom Are You Sending Information?

All U.S. companies are required to comply with U.S. government trade regulations and enforcement programs. Trade regulations prohibit the sale of restricted products to designated individual customers, businesses, or countries. In addition, some U.S. government programs are designed to detect and prevent money laundering by drug dealers. However, these are not the only reasons that it is essential that you know who will be receiving the patent pending technology. It is necessary to conduct due diligence investigations on all contract manufacturers involved in the production of your product. It is also essential that you check the credibility of all your contract manufacturers and suppliers.

Limiting Access to Information

In order to be sure that the patent pending technology is not misappropriated, it is essential that proper physical security and procedural policies be enacted to protect the technology. Physical and information security audits should be conducted at all manufacturing sites, transportation and logistics sites, and the facilities that store the finished product. The audits will establish a benchmark for both the physical and the information security, from which improvements can be made. Audits should be conducted far enough in advance of the transfer of technology to allow time for the recommended improvements to be implemented. Periodic audits should be made to ensure that the required standards are being maintained.

Monitoring Production

In addition to normal verification methods such as audits and inspections, undercover operatives can be very successful in determining if technology is being inappropriately used by contract manufacturers. An investigative agency can recruit and place undercover operatives within each manufacturing facility. These operatives will monitor production and provide timely reports on the activities within the factory. While extremely valuable, these techniques must be used with great care. If discovered, trust relationships with suppliers can be severely damaged.

Monitoring the Marketplace for Infringing Products

Using an established network that surveys a given market for patent-infringing, counterfeit, and gray products is essential. These systems should monitor the traditional marketplace for these items as well as check for their availability through e-commerce.

The basic points of the program consist of the following key steps. (Chapter 7 will provide a more detailed discussion of these points.)

1. Review the corporate philosophy of security through interviews with key management.
2. Identify key corporate protective requirements.
3. Conduct a baseline study of the physical security equipment currently installed.
4. Review the current levels of the security staff's training and experience.
5. Review the existing employee awareness training program.
6. Review current company licensing contracts.
7. Establish controlled manufacturing facilities with audit, inspection, and QC features.
8. Provide field surveillance for product problems in high-risk countries.
9. Establish an ethics program.
10. Develop a product marking and identification system.
11. Establish a program for the coordination of enforcement activities.
12. Assess the current threat level and existing security program activities to reduce exposure.

The results of the strategic business analysis will create the framework for analyzing all the risk management and security issues that must be addressed during the project. The management of those issues will eventually be integrated into the analysis and the resulting report.

Case Study

Substandard automobile replacement parts were found in an Asian market. The products were causing both liability and distributor problems, as they were being sold through unauthorized resellers.

An undercover investigation determined that an organized ring of employees in the OEM facility were stealing not only original parts, but scrap and defective parts as well, and selling them to resellers. It was also learned that the expatriate plant manager knew about the situation, but did nothing because he was being blackmailed by the ringleader for taking bribes.

The details of the alleged theft were verified. After confronting the plant manager, he confessed his involvement, he was fired, and the theft ring was closed down. An undercover operative was kept in place for several months to ensure that the ring did not begin operating again.

GRAY MARKET PRODUCTS AND PRODUCT DIVERSION

Gray market products are essentially original products that either are not authorized to be sold in a particular market location or are obtained by deception at lower than normal prices and sold in a predatory manner in the same market locations as authorized products. In either of these situations, the product price is lower than that of the product normally obtained through legitimate distribution channels.

Another way of looking at gray market goods is that the concept of "buy low, sell high" has been hijacked. While there are countless variations on how diverters and gray marketers obtain goods from legitimate sources, the goal is simple: get the lowest prices possible regardless of the method, and make the highest margins possible. The products make no difference; the margins do.

Diversion and gray market sales can attack any product. The characteristics that a diverter selling gray market products looks for include:

- Products in high demand
- Sales and rebate plans that can be manipulated
- Company sales strategies that provide for differential pricing around the world
- Incentive plans for sales staff that recognize sales volume, not margin
- Products with high internal margins and high value-added content

- Strong internal pressures on sales staff to meet pricing from the competition
- Financial pressures on the company to meet quarterly sales or earning forecasts
- Poor internal procedures for the verification of product end users before the sale is made
- Dumping of products to reduce inventories
- Lack of audit and controls at the point of manufacturing or distribution

It is almost impossible for diversion to take place unless one or more of these factors are present in a company with a desirable product.

Since selling products below suggested retail pricing is not illegal—and is often considered desirable by the general public—how can it be prevented? In reviewing numerous legal actions that have been brought against diverters, most courts have ruled that once a product is sold for the first time, it no longer belongs to the company that produced it. The *law of first sale* applies. This simply means that once a product is sold, the buyers can do anything they want with it: keep it, resell it, or destroy it at their pleasure. The producer loses control of the product and can do nothing about it. Consequently, making sure that it is properly sold in the first instance is paramount to reducing gray market exposure. Unless fraud or deception can be demonstrated, the gray marketer is guilty of nothing more than making a good deal for himself and his customers.

The effects of the gray market and diversion can appear very quickly via the Internet and, if not managed immediately, can destroy sales, margins, employee morale, and customer confidence.

Case Study

A distributor approaches Company X, requesting specific computer components at a reduced rate for resale to a new OEM. Company X has a sales policy that provides differential price points for various manufacturing purposes. Since the sale proposed by the distributor is for an OEM end user, the unit price is significantly lower than the regular distributor pricing. This means that the normal $50 wholesale price of the component could be as low as $30 for a large OEM order. Company X buys 10,000 units for its OEM customer.

Instead of selling all the components to the OEM company, Company X sells half of the units to a reseller at a substantially reduced price. The reseller in turn moves the product through established retail and Internet channels, and the general public purchases the product at bargain prices.

Company X distributors now face unfair competition for the product and will lose sales. Company X loses $200,000 in margin on the sale since the normal price for distributors would have been $50, and sales and distribution channels are now disrupted for this product. Company X may also be responsible for guarantees or warranties that covered different sales options.

While the distributor may have engaged in fraud to purchase the products, Company X never verified the existence of the OEM or the end-user purchase order before the products were sold and shipped.

Gray market products easily find ready buyers since the price is always below that of identical products being sold by legitimate outlets. Buying gray market products at the retail consumer level is not illegal; arranging for product purchase using fraudulent means is. The line between ethical and unethical can be very gray.

The major issues to be concerned about with the gray market are the following:

- Loss in margin
- Loss in sales as distributors and resellers are unhappy and move to other brands
- Loss in confidence from the general public
- Increased warranty and returns issues
- Limited control over sales and lack of accurate sales forecasting by regions
- Impact on manufacturing based on incorrect sales forecasts
- Lower employee morale and an increase in questionable employee transactions
- Energy lost on positive company activities due to gray market problems

Additional questions, like the ones below, need to be addressed by brand and company management. These questions deal with the core business issues affecting the day-to-day management of the sales and marketing functions in the company.

- What level of gray market activity will the company tolerate?

Contracts

- What is in use for each vendor, distributor, and manufacturer?
- Who approves? Develops?

Warranty

- What are the terms?
- Who manages enforcement?
- What is the procedure?
- What has been the history of returns during the past six quarters by product? Is this an issue?

Channel Sales

- Where are the big changes in global sales?
- What is happening in the sales channels?
- Are there any trends?
- What is strange?

Special Pricing

- Who approves of the special pricing agreements?
- Who checks?
- What are the procedures?
- What were the large accounts during the past year?
- How are rebates and promotions handled? Audited? Enforced?
- Who signs up the distributors? Resellers?
- Who establishes and enforces the sales policy?
- What sales shifts have been evident during the past year?
- What incentives have been given to distributors during the past six quarters?
- Do the same terms apply globally? If not, what are the differences?

OEM

- Where are the big increases? What has been the pattern for the past six quarters?
- Who approves the special sales pricing?
- Who handles the OEM account, and what controls are in place?
- What contractual agreements are made with OEMs?
- Are the sales verified for volume actually used, as opposed to volume sold?
- What actions are taken if end-user verification sales are not as reported in the original OEM contract?
- Do the same terms apply globally? If not, what are the differences?
- How are rebates and promotions handled? Audited? Enforced?

Returns

- What is the return policy?
- What happens with returns by region?
- What happens with returns by product?
- What has been the history by product during the past six quarters?
- What happens with the scrap?
- Who determines that a product is scrap?
- Who selects the scrap vendor, and what controls are in place to manage the scrapping program? What contracts or agreements have been made? How will enforcement be handled?

Refurbished Product

- Is there a refurbishment program?
- If so, who decides what is to be refurbished and what is scrap?
- How is the refurbished product distinguished from the original product?
- Who manages the refurbishment program?
- What procedures are in place to oversee the program?
- Is this a local, area, or global program?

Security and Brand Integrity

- What enforcement action is taken, and who requests the action?
- What is the policy on vetting all new distributors, resellers, OEMs?
- Is due diligence completed on all new vendors, manufacturers, distributors, and resellers?
- Who verifies the large deals? How will end-user verification and compliance be handled?
- Who decides when an investigation is necessary?
- Are employee background checks a requirement?
- What is the company policy on enforcement?

Audit

- Channel management
- Special deals
- Returns
- Rebates

Miscellaneous

- Who selects freight forwarders?
- What shipping controls are in place?
- Counterfeit products—have they been an issue?
- Clones—what agreements are currently in place and for what products?
- Is there a way to identify any pending manufacturing agreements so that vetting and verification of the product volume are monitored?
- Is there an employee awareness program in effect?
- Are OEMs, distributors, and resellers informed about their obligations and the nature of the problem?
- Team effort—are all key functions involved in the process? These include
  o Sales
  o Finance
  o Legal
  o Security
  o Audit
  o Communications and PR
  o HR
  o Manufacturing
  o Shipping
  o Returns
  o Refurbish and scrap

SHAREHOLDER VALUE

Case Study

The medical processes of a European company were stolen by an employee of an Asian subsidiary and sold to a local manufacturer. That manufacturer produced clone products for sale "as real" in the country. Because the local manufacturer cut some production corners, the product did not perform as the original and caused widespread health problems. The local government blamed the European company for selling substandard products and causing great economic loss to the country. At the request of the European company, we launched an investigation and determined how the theft had taken place. The offending manufacturing plant was identified; and blame was placed where it belonged. The government was convinced that the local manufacturer had caused the problem and absolved our client.

Reduced shareholder value can also come from sources that try to damage the reputation of a brand or product by starting rumors, planting false newspaper stories, issuing unfavorable analyst reports, writing nasty Internet chat room messages, attacking IT systems and Web sites by hacking, etc. Each of these attacks can have a serious impact on the company operations in general or on a targeted product or brand. For example, Procter & Gamble's crescent-shaped moon was linked to witchcraft! High-value clothing manufacturers are frequently linked to sweatshops in Asia and Latin America.

Product extortions are, however, very focused attacks against a product, with the intention of coercing the company to pay money to prevent the extortionist from carrying out a threat to harm the public using the product. The best-known examples are Tylenol, grapes from Chile, Glycol (candy in Japan), and Yeo's (a soft drink in Singapore). These are often high-visibility situations—the public is aware of them and watching what actions the company takes to solve the problem and protect the product from the attack.

Even with the best program, a company can still be a target for gray market, counterfeiting, or improper subcontractor manufacturing practices. Dealing with the cause of these problems can be time consuming, but if done properly, it can be a profit-enhancing, risk-reducing experience in which management shows that it exerts effective stewardship over the assets of the company. The measures often used to determine if management is doing a good job are share price, earnings, and the enhancement of brand value through advertising, promotions, public relations programs, good corporate citizenship programs, community involvement, and the like.

The value of brand integrity can't be overestimated. A strong program ensures increased market share, maximizes margins, manages authenticity issues, and builds consumer confidence. Thus, shareholders are satisfied because investment expectations are realized.

BEST PRACTICES

You can build a strong program if you:

- Focus on the most important aspect of the business—keeping the product safe in the market.

- Don't lose sight of what's important—total results, not just quarterly performance.

- Maximize profits by using daily opportunities to improve results.

- Restructure product life-cycle thinking.

- Analyze the various risks in the product life cycle.

- Develop systems to manage product risks and opportunities.

- Motivate and provide incentives for employee participation in the process.

DASHBOARD QUESTIONS

1. Are programs in place to prevent counterfeiting and diversion?
2. Are product risk profiles monitored and updated?

CHAPTER 4

IF YOU DO
NOT PROTECT YOUR
PRODUCTS, NOBODY
WILL DO IT FOR YOU

We're from the government; we're here to help you.

Urban legend

The "You can do it, we can help™" (Home Depot) approach is the right idea! At the end of the day, protecting your property is up to you. Whether your property is inside a well-guarded warehouse, on a truck going to a customer, or on a store shelf, it's up to you to find the right kind and level of protection. Likewise, if your products are counterfeited or gray-marketed, it is up to you to decide how to handle the problem. How much or how little you choose to do is almost exclusively your decision. The Department of Homeland Security may have something to say about how your overseas cargo is imported, or your insurance carrier may have some standards for physical security; but beyond these things, it is up to you.

Making the decision about how much product protection should be a part of the day-to-day operations of the business involves adapting to the global business environment and focusing employee efforts on every product's value to company revenues.

TYPES OF PRODUCT PROBLEMS

Product problems come in all shapes and sizes:

- Overruns
- Unauthorized production

- Knockoffs
- Irregulars
- Seconds
- Gray market items
- Nonauthentic production
- Counterfeits
- Parallel imports and diversion

Whatever they are called, they spell trouble for the real products in the market. If you have ever been to Stanley Market in Hong Kong, the Silk Market in Beijing, or street stalls in Bangkok, Kuala Lumpur, New York, or Moscow, you have probably seen all these types of products competing side by side. How do you separate the real from the counterfeit, the seconds from the gray market items? How do the average consumers do it? Do they even care as long as the price is right and the quality is OK for that price? How do you get the nonauthentic products off the market without looking like you are trying to keep the price higher than it should be?

Responding to attacks, like most things in brand integrity, requires proactive measures to lower the risk of a product being attacked in the first place. The legal steps of patent, copyright, trademark, etc., are all necessary but are not effective unless and until:

- The violating products are found in the market.
- You know where they are coming from.
- You know who is making them.

Unless you know the ones who are doing it and where they are doing it, you are like the police trying to stop drug trafficking by arresting street peddlers. It just does not work unless you understand the entire network and shut all of it down.

Product-protective measures, production security, and aggressive marketing are far and away the best solutions to prevent these attacks. Flooding a market quickly with your products does not give the counterfeiter and gray marketer a chance to "pick cherries." You need to let them eat your dust. Having both a growth strategy and an "old-age" strategy for protecting products as well as for marketing them is key to long-term survival. The Hula-Hoop, Beanie Baby, and Cabbage Patch Kids have all had various degrees of success in making sure that they stayed ahead of the knockoffs. It is no coincidence that the companies that produced these products are all very aggressive in protecting their products in the market against counterfeit and gray market attacks.

When you have a problem, it is essential to respond quickly with crisis management plans, including legal and enforcement actions such as the following:

- Injunctions
- Restraining orders
- Anton Piller orders
- Raids and seizures
- Product destruction
- Public relations programs

WHY A PRODUCT PROTECTION PROGRAM?

"The best offense is a good defense" is preached in almost every sport and proclaimed by the military as a way of thinking about winning or appearing to be a hard target to attack. This same philosophy has been validated by study after study of criminals and their targeting of victims, the conclusion being that if you look vulnerable or weak, you stand a much greater chance of becoming a victim. Most studies of crime against business have shown the same results: weakness will be exploited.

Translating these simple and commonsensical observations into day-to-day business practice or process is, however, a difficult task. How do you determine what "looks vulnerable"? What does weakness look like in every-day business practices? How can you have a profitable business and still protect yourself? The chances are that someone, somewhere, has looked at what you do, how you do it, and what you produce and has decided to find out just how well you are watching the store. If we limit our discussion of risks to just the two major ones—counterfeiting and gray market—you can be assured that someone has looked at your products and decided that either you are a good candidate for making knockoffs or for gray marketing or you are not worth the trouble.

Any product that is in production, particularly one that has high market visibility and penetration, is the best target, as the market has already been established and nonauthentic products can easily be sold at discount prices to people who already have been convinced of their value. It is true that most counterfeit and gray market goods are concentrated in high-value, small items such as pharmaceuticals, cosmetics, watches, clothing, luxury goods, liquor, CDs, DVDs, and cigarettes. Still, anything up to and including aircraft parts, machine tools, petroleum products, and automobiles are regularly attacked.

Since products normally have specific profit goals at each stage of life, it is critical that those values be weighed against the risk of loss at each stage when attacked. This risk needs to be addressed with appropriate brand integrity (protective and defensive) measures, processes, and techniques to lower the risk, thus making the product appear to be a hard target for the bad guys. Products start with an idea and end, it is hoped, with profits. At each step along this value chain, there are risks that can spell either disaster or opportunity for your operations. Two of the key areas for products are research and development and manufacturing.

What are some of the bad things that can happen in R&D?

- Other companies or countries steal ideas, processes, and new products.
- Your employees take your ideas and start their own company.
- Your employees go to a competitor and sell your ideas.
- Your patent is infringed upon, or another company produces your product while your patent is still pending.
- Competitors "file around" your patent or file your patent in a country where you did not choose to file.
- Your engineers quit before they file a patent for you, start up their own company, and then file the patent as their property.
- Your trademark or copyright is infringed upon or filed while or before you are in the process of filing ownership rights.
- Your strategic product development plans are taken, giving the competition a road map to your future product development.
- Engineering test data are taken.
- Prototypes are taken and reverse-engineered, so that next-generation products can be produced more quickly than you can produce them.
- Product pricing or production processes are taken to give competitive advantage to contract manufacturers or competitors.

What are some of the bad things that can happen in manufacturing?

- A contract manufacturer clones your products before you get yours into production.
- Competitors hire away key production staff to produce similar products.
- Critical raw materials are stolen, forcing production to stop.
- Labor problems caused by social activists curtail production or impede the shipment of finished goods.
- Subcontractors, without your knowledge, are discovered by the press to be using child labor.
- Molds and dies are misplaced, halting production.
- The finished product is deliberately contaminated before shipping.
- Nongenuine components are substituted in products, causing safety concerns.
- Quality standards are not maintained, causing high rejection rates by customers.
- Your production know-how and plans reside with a third-party manufacturer that will not return them at the end of the contract with you.

Each aspect of the product life cycle in R&D and manufacturing must be mastered from information, risk, and opportunity perspectives.

RESEARCH AND DEVELOPMENT OPERATIONS

It is very important to maintain product protection in an R&D environment. The integrity of the ideas and the longest possible lead time before competitors learn about the product must be ensured. Secrecy of plans, programs, and products must be maintained so that risks or threats are identified at the earliest possible time and appropriate investigative, legal, and administrative steps are taken to solve the problems.

Not all companies have an R&D function, but most have trade secrets, patents, copyrights, trademarks, licenses, or some other process that is the primary way funds are generated for the company. To the extent that this is some type of proprietary information, process, or design that needs to be protected, it is essential that brand integrity management be established and used.

PRODUCT PROTECTION ENVIRONMENT

Various corporate and market forces drive the product protection process in a company, including:

- Reaction to problems affecting brand and products
- Security breaches, theft of trade secrets, and so forth
- Competitive advantage issues
- Cost control and reduction initiatives
- Management attitudes about protecting the brand and products

Within the company, various levels of operations and management have differing goals and objectives that need to be addressed if a BI program is going to be successfully implemented. These levels include all employees involved in R&D, manufacturing, supply chain management, distribution, and sales and marketing, as well as executives and administrative and support staffs. The individual groups must understand the company brand integrity philosophy and concepts, the responsibilities involved, the degree of involvement, and the personal value to them. How the program is initiated will vary depending on the current management tools in use. If a Six Sigma or ISO balanced score card is utilized, or any of the other strategic and performance-enhancing systems are used, implementation will be slightly different in process, timing, and effect on different levels in the company. All these systems, however, can be used to develop a BI strategy, coordinate with existing product plans, devise program goals, and implement product plans.

BUILDING A PRODUCT PROTECTION PROGRAM

You need to keep these three rules in mind when you build a product protection program:

Rule 1. Threat follows value.
Rule 2. Products must appear to be and really be a hard target.
Rule 3. Product protection enhances the public perception of product value.

Understanding what products have real value to the company is always the starting point for establishing a product protection program. Whether it is for a single product or the entire range of products, the process starts with an internal and external risk-threat evaluation of which products have significant revenue value to the company. Reputation, image, IP, etc., all have value, but all have different values depending on various factors: importance to current and future revenue, company reputation, consumer safety, etc. This analysis includes:

- Reviewing intellectual capital and intellectual property to identify key contributors to key current and future revenue streams
- Selecting those products that currently provide the major contributions and ranking them by long- and short-term revenue contributions
- Identifying anticipated contributions from future products and ranking them by expected contributions until expected normal competition appears
- Preparing an analysis of the risks and threats to each product along its expected revenue contribution
- Developing risk-mitigation and risk-reduction plans and budgets corresponding to useful life expectations
- Preparing a cost-benefit analysis for each product to determine the level of brand integrity to be applied

This type of analysis will permit a product-focused application of BI that reflects the impact for alternative intervention strategies to maintain revenue generated by key products.

In working with individual products, the focus should be on providing support for the corporate requirement to protect profitability and margins in all phases in the product cycle. *The goal should be to provide comprehensive information about product and brand management in order to develop tailor-made options that assist in the mitigation of risks to corporate profitability from theft or loss of trade secrets, gray market products, patent infringements, counterfeit goods, and untrustworthy customers and suppliers.* (Such related corporate support functions as IT, HR, security, and legal often have direct roles in managing product protection issues. How their input is used in making decisions about strategy, best practices, and implementation needs to be coordinated during the planning process, and is discussed in Chapter 10.)

Different Approaches for Each Product and Brand?

Product protection differs for individual products based on their relative financial contributions to the company. They will, however, have a common strategic approach within the same company: enhance brand value by lowering risk to these key brand and product assets. How this philosophy is translated into programs for specific products or brands may vary considerably depending on the strategic value to the company.

BI for an after-market automobile part will differ from that for a new type of PDA, just as a generic drug has lower BI requirements than a newly introduced asthma product. While these might sound like commonsense distinctions, they reflect the relative revenue values associated with those products by the companies that produce them. The asthma drug may not be as highly valued as a new AIDS treatment, but possibly higher than a hormone replacement therapy. The decision to protect or not is a company- and product-specific one.

Each phase of the product cycle has different risks associated with either the value of the intellectual property in the product or its marketplace value. In most products the intrinsic value of the IP is built into the market price of the product and does not require the same level of protection as when it was in the development stage. Figure 4.1 identifies the continuum along which protection is provided as it moves from pure IP within R&D to product protection in the marketplace. Clearly there may be significant IP in the product that needs to be protected in the market, but the methods used

FIGURE 4.1   The Protection Continuum for IP, from Research and Development to the Marketplace

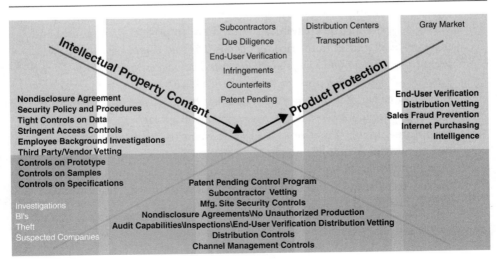

are significantly different from those used when it was in an R&D facility. It is this type of difference that characterizes the application of brand integrity. The security for products is handled differently than that for intrinsic IP, but the IP in products may require special monitoring for the useful life of the product.

Case Study

A new pharmaceutical was introduced three years ago. Before the drug was released, the IP was highly protected. However, now that the patent has been issued, everyone knows exactly what the chemical composition is and how to produce it. The product now requires marketplace monitoring to ensure that counterfeits or clones do not appear and dilute product earnings before the useful life is reached. This is a significant dimension of brand integrity.

How was product protection provided before? It usually depended upon the company and the product, but mostly, surveillance would take place using salespeople, agents, distributors, doctors, and the like, who might report problems or unusual products. The sales manager would then notify a product manager, who might investigate, involve legal (and possibly security) to investigate the matter further, and take some type of enforcement action.

To determine when to apply brand integrity, an evaluation of the circumstance surrounding the introduction of a product or the underlying IP needs to be conducted. BI concerns are similarly present when decisions are made about the location of new ventures, selection of joint venture partners, and sharing of key technology with foreign partners.

Case Study

There were a number of product protection issues related to using key IP in an R&D strategy. First-generation technology was being considered for deployment to India for use in establishing a manufacturing JV in Bangalore. The following factors were present in the proposed operation:

Business Environment
- *High-risk environment for theft, misuse of IP*
- *Government targeting for specific types of technology*
- *Low levels of acceptance of IP protection concepts in the business community*

- *Poor record for enforcement of IP rights of foreign companies operating in India*
- *Difficult work and living environment for expatriate engineers*

Key Issues

- *High risk of compromise of the technology that was to be transferred to the JV and the facility*
- *High risk of compromise of the technology that was to be developed by the JV and the facility*
- *Retention and loyalty of R&D staff hired in India*
- *Operating environment for expatriate engineers*

Mitigation

- *Comprehensive brand integrity program for the JV company*
- *Total IP control program*
- *IP insurance for IP transferred to the JV and the facility*
- *Background investigations for the JV and facility employees, contractors, vendors, suppliers, and customers*
- *Effective physical security program for all the JV facilities and those that will house the company IP*
- *Marketplace surveillance program*
- *Ongoing brand integrity awareness training for all levels of the JV and facility employees*

Should the company allow its key IP assets to be used in this project? It depends on how much risk tolerance the company has. In this situation, the company declined to transfer the technology and continued development in the United States.

Case Study

A U.S.-based chemical company opened a joint venture in China to produce a specialty product that contained a component that was protected by a trade secret. Raw materials were purchased locally except for the "secret sauce" ingredient, which was produced in the United States and sent in liquid form, with several inert chemicals added to the sauce to disguise the basic material compounds that the trade secret protected. After two years of operations, a local competitor appeared in the market with a similar product. Although it seemed as though it were an exact copy of the JV product, analysis of the local product determined that the secret sauce was not copied correctly, causing the copy product to significantly underperform the original. In addition, several attempts to gain access to the U.S. data system were attempted from a Chinese source but were unsuccessful. The JV continues to operate successfully with this product protection technique—producing the secret sauce in the United States. Local marketing executives use the identified deficiencies in the copy products to enhance marketing of the original formula product in China and Asia. Some market share was lost but was regained. Enforcement actions are still pending in local Chinese courts.

Product Protection Planning

Having someone responsible for understanding product risk, conducting root cause assessments, and devising design and operational plans is essential. There are many ways to establish product risk; Figure 4.2 outlines one method. In establishing product risk, the intrinsic features of the product must be evaluated, and so must the market, legal, and organizational considerations. Figure 4.3 provides an overview of the basic features of a product that can be the subject of product protection redesign and planning. Figure 4.4 shows how the product protection plans can be integrated into the overall brand integrity plan.

Product Protection Management

Some organizations may identify sufficient product protection (PP) planning activities to justify hiring an executive for this responsibility. This

FIGURE 4.2   Market Risk Profiling Tool

Drivers	Elements		Risk Evaluation Questions & Scores	
			Risk Evaluation Questions	**Score**
Product	Financial	Volume		
		Price	How many units are shipped annually?	
Market		Position in revenue cycle	Is volume increasing or decreasing?	
			What is the distributor list price of the product?	
	Physical	Characteristics	What is the gross margin of the product?	
Legal		Manufacturing process	What is the range of special pricing used across geographic areas?	
		Level of product protective technologies employed	What is the price differential across regions?	
Business Processes			• Create additional risk evaluation questions to determine the level of risk associated with each product.	
	• Develop additional details on specific topics		• Score each question:	
			• 1 - Low Risk	
			• 5 - Medium Risk	
			• 9 - High Risk	
			• Weight and aggregate scores by element	

FIGURE 4.3   Protective Layers

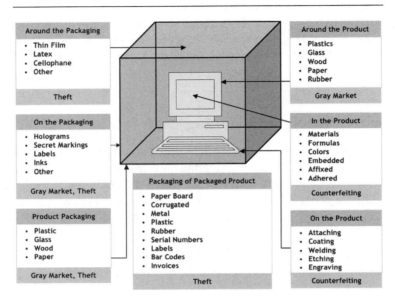

Around the Packaging
- Thin Film
- Latex
- Cellophane
- Other

Theft

On the Packaging
- Holograms
- Secret Markings
- Labels
- Inks
- Other

Gray Market, Theft

Product Packaging
- Plastic
- Glass
- Wood
- Paper

Gray Market, Theft

Packaging of Packaged Product
- Paper Board
- Corrugated
- Metal
- Plastic
- Rubber
- Serial Numbers
- Labels
- Bar Codes
- Invoices

Theft

Around the Product
- Plastics
- Glass
- Wood
- Paper
- Rubber

Gray Market

In the Product
- Materials
- Formulas
- Colors
- Embedded
- Affixed
- Adhered

Counterfeiting

On the Product
- Attaching
- Coating
- Welding
- Etching
- Engraving

Counterfeiting

position would normally be responsible for managing counterfeit risks and threats against company products and lead the development, implementation, management, and measurement of product protection plans. It is

FIGURE 4.4   Corporate Brand Integrity Model

Strategic (Corporate-Level) Plan

- IT Security Guidelines
- Telecommunications Security Guidelines
- Products
- Personal Security Guidelines
- Physical Security Guidelines
- Intellectual Property Security Guidelines

Operational (Site-Level) Plan for Site 1
Operational (Site-Level) Plan for China
Operational (Site-Level) Plan for Asia
Operational (Site/Program/Country) Plan for Site N
Tactical Plan for Product Security

Product Integrity
IT Security Backup/Recovery Plans
Market Surveillance
Distribution Controls
Product Protection Plan

primarily a prevention program management position that develops standards for the following:

- Intellectual property
- Package design
- Labeling
- Manufacturing
- Delivery system design
- Customs compliance

The actual development of the design for intrinsic product features would be the responsibility of R&D and product management using these standards with support from the product protection position. Additional tasks might include:

- Lead new technology development efforts for track-and-trace systems.
- Develop product authentication efforts.
- Lead the effort to identify high-risk products in development or the market.
- Review and approve product protection plans.

Policy Guide: Risk Analysis Lessons Learned

After reviewing its operations, a major pharmaceutical company identified these areas to reduce brand vulnerability:

- Incorporation of anticounterfeiting technology, for example, new product labels
- FDA advocacy
  - o Increased secondary wholesaler oversight; distributor and repackager surveillance and enforcement
  - o Tougher penalty for noncompliance
  - o Responsiveness to counterfeit attacks—tracking, sourcing, lab analysis, turnaround time
  - o Packaging guidelines
- Business process improvements
  - o Diversified product integrity team
  - o Practices to protect patient health
  - o Increased cooperation with law enforcement agencies
  - o Promotion of public policy to eliminate counterfeiting

- Governance
  - Policies
  - Communications
- Pricing
  - Structures
  - Reimbursement
- Employee programs
  - Incentives
  - Compensation
- Business agreement standards
  - Sourcing agreements
  - Distribution agreements
  - Employee agreements
- Business relationship due diligence
  - Business partners
  - End customers
  - Employees
- Business practices
  - Business design
  - Awareness training—employee through customer
  - Compliance programs
  - Enforcement programs
  - Incident management and reporting
- Product management
  - Legitimacy standards
  - Traceability standards
  - Intellectual property strategy
  - Regulatory strategy
- Performance measurement
  - Reporting
  - Controls
  - Market awareness
  - Competitive intelligence
  - Business intelligence

GLOBAL BRAND INTEGRITY PROGRAMS

Global product protection programs must be designed to help the company protect its products and information wherever they are found. The programs should offer a variety of approaches based on the products' needs and individual market requirements. Depending on the situation, these programs encompass:

- Theft of trade secrets, patent pending, and IP investigations
- The establishment of product security characteristics to minimize risk from copying
- Gray market tracking to identify channel distribution and management irregularities
- End-user verification
- Global intranet and direct product purchasing and intelligence gathering
- Due diligence investigations
- Background investigations—both internal and external

Protection of a Specific Product Line

This is the core of brand integrity: developing and managing the protective efforts for a single key asset. It is a microcosm of all the analytical, managerial, program, and communication skills required for a comprehensive program involving all aspects of the company's products. It is often the best place to start with a program as well, since it provides a limited scope within the company (unless there is only one product) to develop the correct balance of policies, procedures, and programs.

Product security features may be required to ensure brand integrity for high-risk items. A wide variety of technological features are available to clearly identify the real product and distinguish it from copies. These features may include:

- Unique packaging
  - o Sealing of shipping cartons
  - o Inner boxes
  - o Individual product packaging including film wrappers, product containers, seals for product containers, and holographic labels
- Product-marking technology
  - o Organic
  - o Inorganic
  - o Molecular modifiers
- Advertising and public relations programs

RESEARCH AND DEVELOPMENT

Rule 1. There are no secrets; there is only lead time.
Rule 2. Most information is time sensitive: valuable today, worth less tomorrow.

With enough time, desire, and money, any secret can be uncovered. R&D takes place to commercialize new ideas, and eventually the product will be released for sale. The critical time is while the product is in development—that is when theft or loss of it could harm the commercial viability of the product and the initial market entry sales.

It is critical to the growth, survival, and financial success of a company that its intellectual capital and intellectual property, such as trade secrets, patents, copyrights, and licenses, be kept secure. In addition to protecting company information, it is essential to ensure the loyalty and personal integrity of employees; provide a secure working environment, effective control procedures, and appropriate levels of legal documentation; and maintain a good flow of industry intelligence. The major risks associated with protecting R&D information are:

- Predatory intelligence
- Shared R&D operations
- Protection of third-party intellectual property

Predatory Intelligence

As previously discussed, there are individuals, companies, and governments that actively try to obtain sensitive company information without paying for it or getting permission to use it. All information, particularly when it is related to future revenues of the company, needs to be safeguarded against possible attacks. Protection of proprietary information is a key element of a BI program.

The United States is still the number one economic and military power in the world. It is also number one on the hit parade for people who want what it has in both sectors. Make no mistake about it. There are very real risks from those seeking to build up their military capabilities at the expense of any company or country that has valuable technology. There are many people who want to take your research and product leadership and convert it to their use without paying for it. There is a hidden but very real war going on around the world in both sectors today.

There are three categories of these predators:

- Intelligence agents
- Government-sponsored attacks against trade secrets and proprietary information
- Privately sponsored theft of R&D, strategic plans, and financial results

Industrial spying is very common and is actively engaged in by governments, companies, and individuals against both defense- and nondefense-related information. Defense-related U.S. technology, for example, was the suspected target in the following categories of activities (National Counterintelligence Center Report, 2001):

- Commercial and individual collectors accounted for 58 percent of attacks (32 percent individual, 26 percent commercial).
- Government-sponsored spying (e.g., military attachés) accounted for 22 percent.
- Government-affiliated spying (by institutes, laboratories, universities, etc.) made up 20 percent.

What are secrets? They can be marketing strategies, manufacturing processes, new inventions that are patent pending, recipes, or methods of doing something new. Basically they are anything that provides its owner with a competitive advantage and that is treated like a secret or has value.

- *Does it matter who takes your trade secret if it is the single most valuable asset in your company?* Not really. You are still going to be out of business. The only thing you will have is someone to blame!
- *Does it matter if China is actively recruiting engineers from high-tech companies to return to the motherland and bring their company secrets with them?* Yes it does if they work for you and take your technology back with them!
- *Does it matter if the latest generation of technology is being produced by a JV in India and that all of that technology and all of those production processes associated with it are now in the hands of a future competitor?* Yes it does.

How Do Attacks Happen?

Open-Source Collection   Open-source collection means the collection of information that is readily available. Some of it takes more effort to find than other information. It can be obtained by reading:

- What a company says about itself
- Newspaper and magazine articles
- Papers written by employees

It can also be found by:

- Requesting information via e-mail or letters
- Exploiting Internet discussion groups
- Exploiting multinational conferences, business information exchanges, or joint ventures
- Misleading open-source collection

Approximately 70 percent of the information about what a company is doing can be obtained from these sources. So make sure that you know what your employees are publishing or talking about at meetings.

Illegal Collection   This is the covert collection of sensitive information that a company does not want to share outside its organization and employees. This might involve:

- Acquisition of export-controlled technologies
- Theft of trade secrets, critical technologies, and critical information in host countries
- Agent recruitment, co-opted employees, and U.S. volunteers

Who Are the Ones Who Are Doing It?

Anyone who wants what you have will try to steal it. Most often the thieves do not want to let you know that they have taken it, and they certainly don't want to pay you for it! What kinds of people have we seen steal information from companies?

- The Indian security guard who has an advanced degree in electronics and who wants to work weekends and the night shift
- The engineer from Korea who has worked for seven high-tech companies over the past five years
- Your new JV partner in China who is being funded by the People's Liberation Army
- The IT service company that supports your software development in India
- The employees of your R&D center in Singapore who have gone to work for a start-up company
- The employee who was downsized during the last round of reductions and now has a job offer from a competitor

How Are They Doing It?

They do it anyway you can think of. It may be surprising, but most thefts of IP are fairly simple. If you were a thief, you could:

- Mirror-image a hard drive that contains the data.
- Download a copy of the required files and e-mail them to an accomplice (or an e-mail account set up just for this purpose).
- Steal a laptop with the data from a traveling executive or engineer.
- Pay someone to give you a copy of what you want.
- Hack into the IT system.
- Steal a password from someone who has access to what you want.

There are more sophisticated methods, but most of the thefts of trade secrets or proprietary information do not require anything fancy. More information on IT systems is condensed in smaller and smaller files, making it easy to take, conceal, send, and store.

If someone is motivated to steal from you, that person will find a way to circumvent your controls and take what he or she wants. The controls should, however, allow you to monitor unauthorized transactions or sensitive files for access, preferably on a real-time basis. This will give you early warning that something has happened. While after the fact, at least you know that you have a problem and can take remedial action quickly. Many cases of theft are initially discovered because of this simple control.

What Can You Do to Lower Risk?

Knowing what is important is the first step in the process. Once you know what is of value, you can set procedures in place to lower the risk of attacks happening:

- Know what is important to protect.
- Have a good security program.
- Investigate employees before you hire them.
- Take good care of your employees.
- Have sound legal agreements with staff and third-party manufacturers.

- Create strong IP protection for products.
- Take aggressive action when an infringement is discovered.

Case Study

A supervisor noticed that an R&D employee, developing software for a new electronic product, was copying files that he was not authorized to use. After checking the computer transaction logs and determining that copies had been made of the R&D files, the employee was confronted. The supervisor reported the compromise to company security officials, who investigated the problem and notified federal authorities. While the supervisor was contacting authorities, the employee purchased two new computers for his home, made multiple copies of the information, and sent several copies to different ISP addresses. He also called for a FedEx pickup at his home to send additional copies to Korea. He then returned the computers to the store, saying that he did not like the way the computers performed.

The incident was investigated for violation of the 1996 Economic Espionage Act, and the suspect was arrested at the airport while en route to Korea; he was charged with grand theft.

In this case, the company had an effective security program, excellent system documentation, and observant supervisory personnel. Consequently, potentially serious damage to the company's new product was minimized.

Trade Secrets

A strong BI program promotes the protection of intellectual property during product development, usually with comprehensive security and legal support. In companies where in-house security support is not available, commercial services are most effectively provided on a bundled basis, especially for companies without an internal security professional who provides guidance and support. Available services include:

- Security audits
- Awareness education and training
- Policies and procedures
- Compliance reviews
- Background investigations

- Investigation of known or suspected compromises of information
- Investigations of theft
- Audits of the IT security system and the imposition of controls

Investigations into Theft of Trade Secrets, Patent Pending Products, and IP

Suspected theft of trade secrets requires timely investigations and damage control. Immediate and aggressive actions are vital to protect R&D investment, product development, and product-introduction lead times. Retrieval of the stolen information is difficult and time consuming and must be initiated as soon as the loss is discovered.

Getting the information returned is sometimes not possible, but pursuing legal action, as a result of the investigation, can prevent the stolen information from being used against the economic interests of a company.

When the loss is related to a product that has patent pending protection, the need for a timely investigation and enforcement action is extremely critical. Identifying where a product is being sold and taking immediate and decisive legal action are essential steps to maximize financial recoveries and damages from those infringing on the patent pending product.

Shared R&D Operations

The decision to share product development is often made in order to comply with product strategy, to minimize development cost, to fulfill market entry requirements, or to shorten development time. How the IP is developed using this process, what IP is shared with partners, and how developments are capitalized upon are significant BI issues.

IP and subsequent products are clearly intended to add revenues to company operations. The relative value of the investment of intellectual capital, financial investment, and management support must be weighed against the risks associated with sharing next-generation and beyond IP outside the company. If that decision has been made using an appropriate risk-threat-value analysis, how that IP is to be protected becomes the major BI concern. Application of the appropriate BI processes can be implemented.

Protection of Third-Party Intellectual Property

The technology needed to develop products often cannot be completely generated within the company. Licensing agreements are a common means for getting the technology that will be incorporated into a new product. When this third-party information is acquired, it must be protected at the same level as that of comparable technology in the company. There are often contractual agreements that specify the security to be provided for that information. Severe penalties are often imposed if that information is lost, stolen, or compromised. Consequently, whenever third-party technology is to be used, either a specific BI program must be initiated, or the entire level of the involved company product needs to be raised to the level required by the third-party provider of that technology.

MANUFACTURING

Protecting the manufacturing process is in many ways more complicated than protecting R&D activities. More people, locations, suppliers, and activities are involved. It requires constant attention to get the right balance between achieving cost-effectiveness throughout the supply chain and ensuring that BI principles are applied. Calibrating BI to make sure that supply chain partners are following established processes means that you must attend to the following:

- Supply chain management issues
- Product security
- Process protection
- Raw materials controls
- Finished-product protection
- Contract manufacturing
- Offshore manufacturing
- Unauthorized production
- Patent pending production
- Social responsibility issues

Many corporations, even small ones, operate their own manufacturing facilities and also contract for additional capacity or specialized manufacturing support. There are, likewise, multiple suppliers of raw, semifinished, and finished products that go into the end products. Often this additional manufacturing is conducted away from the main facility of the company and very likely in a foreign country. Consequently, even a small manufacturer can have the same range of BI problems as a major multinational corporation.

Case Study

A manufacturer of children's clothing used a contract manufacturing facility of a large Asian company to produce several lines of clothing in Saipan, another few lines in Guatemala, and a few more in Sri Lanka. The products are inspected by company employees and shipped directly from the manufacturers to the customer warehouses with printed and bar-coded inventory labels. The salaries paid are considered fair in each of these countries.

One day the company is notified that it was being sued for violations of child labor laws, substandard working conditions, and abusive practices. These actions were brought on behalf of the workers in all three countries by a labor rights coalition. International press coverage was very prominent and named the company, accusing it of making huge profits at the expense of abused adults and children forced to work for substandard wages. The group asked for boycotts of the company's products and the stores that carried the clothing.

An investigation into the allegations determined that while wages were not up to U.S. standards, working and living conditions provided to the workers as well as wages were much better than those paid to other workers in the region. It was also determined that the allegations were concocted by a group seeking to organize labor in these factories and were themselves involved with running sweatshop activities in the Philippines.

Problems such as the one described in the case study are all too common. Manufacturing does not take place in isolation from all the competitive, political, and social factors present in the global marketplace. Attacks that are launched by an activist group to promote a social responsibility agenda, a labor union to further the workers' rights movement, or an anti-globalization group to impede manufacturing operations are increasingly common. These attacks have little if anything to do with the effective management of the company's manufacturing process. They have everything to do with being in the wrong place at the wrong time and being targeted by a group promoting its own social agenda.

This is not to suggest that companies are blameless in closing their eyes to contract manufacturers that cut corners in their hiring practices, do not provide safe working conditions, squeeze their employees for extra unpaid work, or pay low piecework rates. However, even where ISO manufacturing certification is present, continual vigilance is necessary to ensure that manufacturing standards required in production contracts are maintained. It is not enough to make sure that product quality is present in the products. It is also critical to make certain that the conditions under which they are produced could stand up to the acid test. Protecting brand image from allegations of abuses in the manufacturing process is one of the more serious BI issues that can arise. For example, the *Wall Street Journal* reported in November 2006 that Nike stopped using a contract soccer ball manufacturer in Pakistan when an allegation of child labor was substantiated.

Cost, quality, capacity, and delivery are likewise critical features of the manufacturing process. They drive the process of selecting which factory will produce the product, where it will be done, and how it will relate to the company manufacturing strategy. The relationships established with contract manufacturers, joint ventures, and strategic partners directly affect how products are priced, shipped, and marketed. While many of these manufacturing decisions are finance and marketing driven, they have significant BI issues:

- Do you know the background of the potential JV partner? Where does its financing come from?
- What is its strategic goal in seeking your business?
- Does the partner have a history of abusing manufacturing relationships? Does it exploit technology for its own financial gain?
- Does it engage in unauthorized production?
- Does it have a history of patent infringement, product cloning, or copyright violations?
- Have there been any criminal charges because of worker abuse, safety hazards, and so on?
- Does it have associations with known narcotics traffickers or other organized criminal activities?
- Has anyone from your company actually visited the facility unannounced?

All of the above types of problems have surfaced during due diligence reviews of potential manufacturing partners in Asia, Europe, and Latin America in the past three years. No manufacturer would like to have a visit from the DEA informing it that shipments of its products from Asia or Latin America are being used to smuggle drugs into the United States, but more than a few have had this experience. Several companies, unfortunately, have had these visits in the past few years with the attendant international press coverage. Likewise, no company wants to have its products sold in money laundering schemes that are later exposed to the international media. The brand image problems are again difficult to address after the problem is exposed.

Clearly, there are significant financial advantages to using overseas manufacturing facilities. The vast majority of these operations are effectively managed, but it is the exceptions that prove the rule.

Case Study

A Hong Kong businessman, seeking to sell a manufacturing facility just across the border in China, approached our client. Since the client was interested in expanding its manufacturing base in Asia, a representative and the businessman traveled to China to view the property. The plant seemed to fit the requirements exactly. The specifications were what was needed for the product line, and the sale terms were reasonable. The client had a routine review process that required a due diligence investigation on both the businessman and the property.

The investigation determined that the businessman did not own the plant and had no authority to negotiate its sale. He had paid a plant employee to "take a westerner" for a plant tour while it was closed for lunch. And he had a history of fraudulent real estate schemes in both Hong Kong and China.

The client declined the purchase offer.

Supply Chain Management Issues

Establishing strict contractual terms with all supply chain partners is the most critical aspect of ensuring effective BI for the manufacturing process. The standards must be applied to each aspect of the relationship for quality, accountability, security, audits, IT security controls, information protection, production controls, unauthorized production, and control over molds, raw materials, dies, and IP. The terms must be agreed to in advance and be a part of the overall contract. If the vendors lack the ability or technical expertise in implementing any of the key aspects of BI, the company should provide it. Any breach in the security provisions of the BI agreement must be handled by the company immediately whether it is related to the product, IP, Internet, or marketplace.

Product Security

Products will not provide full financial value to the company if they leak out of supply channels before they are sold through normal means. BI at this stage starts at the point when the product is at the end of the production cycle and is placed into inventory at either the company manufacturing facility or the contract site. Theft, damage, hidden defects, and substitutions of counterfeit products into inventory can all have a serious impact on brand image, reliability, authenticity, or margin. It is the BI program that will analyze the risks present, establish programs, monitor activities, conduct fact-finding if problems arise, and direct enforcement actions as required.

Process Protection

Both proprietary and nonproprietary manufacturing processes can be used during the production of company products.

Case Study

A tire manufacturer operated a series of tire retread centers around the country. These centers specialized in truck, bus, and large-vehicle tires. Two types of retreads were sold: full caps (covering the whole tire) and top caps (covering the tread and partway down the sidewall). The company allocated 25 pounds of rubber for full caps and 20 pounds for top caps. The rubber was applied using specialized equipment to old tires that had been rigorously inspected and approved for use.

A truck using a set of recapped tires experienced a blowout that resulted in the deaths of several people when the truck struck a bus on a major highway. An investigation ensued that determined that the tire, while produced by the company, did not have a DOT approval code on it. An internal investigation was conducted to determine how an unapproved tire was sold by the recap center.

It was discovered that employees were manipulating raw rubber inventories and exploiting a weakness in the system. Since most recaps in this part of the country were top caps, five pounds of rubber was considered excess for each tire produced. This meant that for every four tires produced, there was enough extra rubber to cover another tire without showing an inventory shortage. With the volume of tires in production, the facility was able to produce an additional twenty tires per day without having them show up on the inventory records. The problem was finding the old tires to recap. This was solved by employees taking discarded, unsafe tires from scrap piles and recapping them. Other employees then sold them as authentic recaps in the sales department. The sales were not recorded in the company accounts. It was estimated that several thousand tires were produced and sold in this way before the accident.

Upon determining what had transpired, the company fired all the employees, closed the plant, and moved all the equipment out of that state immediately. It took responsibility for the accident caused by the defective tire on the one truck but made no acknowledgment of the other tires on the road.

The brand implications of both the rogue employees and the way in which the incident was handled were staggering for the company. Fortunately for the brand, no other deaths occurred and no other claims were made against tires from that center. If it had been otherwise, the actions taken would have had serious brand repercussions.

Raw Materials Controls

If raw materials are not available at the right time and place, manufacturing schedules cannot be met, customer deliveries are affected, and brand damage can occur. If raw materials are substandard, damaged, improperly handled, delivered to the wrong location, or not delivered on time, production will also be adversely affected.

It is important to see that all partners and suppliers providing raw materials are adequately vetted to ensure reliability. When just-in-time delivery schedules are a normal part of the manufacturing process, how and when products are delivered is critical to the process. Inventories are normally kept as low as possible, consistent with expected usage, to decrease manufacturing costs. Consequently, anything that disrupts the supply can quickly affect the manufacturing process. Ensuring that key raw materials are closely monitored and protected is an important BI function.

Case Study

A high-tech manufacturer used large amounts of gold in its production process. This highly refined gold was delivered weekly to ensure availability for large-volume production that continued on a 24/7 schedule. The gold was secured in a high-value storage facility in the plant.

Immediately after a large delivery, armed robbers attacked the security guards at the plant, forced them to open the high-security area, and took the entire shipment of gold. Production at the plant ceased six hours later and could not resume until an emergency shipment of replacement gold was obtained three days later. The gold, valued at $278,000, caused a production loss of over $45 million from one product line. It also caused the company to lose several customers, who in turn had been forced to shut down production because the components being supplied were not delivered on time.

While there was little more that the company could have done to prevent the loss from occurring, the loss of the key raw materials caused serious brand damage. Additional security measures were added to the plant to try minimizing the damage should another robbery be attempted. Not all BI efforts are successful against a determined attack. They can, however, reduce the impact or make the company look like a more difficult target and thus have the bad guys go elsewhere.

Finished-Product Protection

Most attacks against brand assets take place when the product is finished and ready for entry into the marketplace, as this is when the product has its most direct value. Attacks can include theft, contamination, damage, counterfeiting, patent infringement, copyright violations, and gray market. Determining the likelihood of each of these categories is an aspect of brand asset risk analysis, and developing the appropriate countermeasures is a vital aspect of operating the BI program.

Several key risks require special attention, as they increase the risks to a product because they occur early in the production process and can have a major impact on financial results.

Patent Pending Production

Specific methods need to be implemented to protect products for a limited time until there is full patent protection. A comprehensive program must be in place that ensures that production security, site inspections, internal monitoring, and marketplace surveillance are in force until the product has full international patent protection. This program is essential for a six-month period from the time the manufacturing site is determined to the final patent approval in order to prevent unknown manufacturing and introduction of products.

Unauthorized Production

Similar to the unauthorized production of patent pending products, unauthorized production can be a problem for any product. It generally will take place within a contract manufacturer's facility or another plant that is given access to your processes. The product is usually touted as genuine and is sold outside of your normal distribution channels. It can disrupt your customer channels, likely cause warranty or guarantee problems, and account for lost profits. Since quality can be an issue, the reputation and brand image problems will also be significant. Market surveillance and aggressive enforcement of contract manufacturing terms are a must to minimize exposure to this type of problem.

Case Study

Our client manufactured its products using a contract facility in Thailand. The company's distribution channels began to notice that identical but unauthorized products—products that were not coming through regular distribution sources—were being found in various Asian markets.

The investigation determined that the contract manufacturer had added an extra shift to the two authorized by the client. The extra production was being sold through a company owned by the manufacturer's brother. The brother's company was ordering additional raw materials from the same sources as our client used and was storing them off-site to avoid client QC and manufacturing audits.

When confronted, the contract facility settled with our client, and our client introduced tighter controls over raw material availability and audits. When the contract period was concluded, our client hired another manufacturer. It was learned that similar schemes were a regular practice of the previous manufacturer. This would have been uncovered had a due diligence review been done before the manufacturer was hired.

CONTROLLING PRODUCT PROBLEMS

Let's take a quick look at the various types of techniques used to reduce product problems in key BI areas of concern.

Gray Market

Systems to monitor channel distribution should include:

- Customer verification
- Purchasing controls
- Internet intelligence
- End-user verification
- Screening of the third-party manufacturing site
- Compliance monitoring

- Investigations
- Due diligence
- Import and export compliance investigations

Channel Distribution and Management Irregularities

Product arbitrage occurs from internal processes such as the following:

- Differential pricing of products
- Deep discounting for special customers or situations
- Poorly supervised rebate or incentive programs
- Compensation programs tied to sales quotas

The continued flow of products through unauthorized distribution channels causes problems with authorized distributors or resellers and will absolutely erode margins.

Patent Pending

In order to protect patent pending products that are introduced into the market, the follow steps are required:

- Conduct internal security reviews.
- Conduct manufacturing site reviews.
- Perform brand integrity audits.
- Start a market surveillance program.

These steps should be continued until the final patent is issued.

Trade Secrets

Trade secrets were previously discussed, but remember: "To trust is good; not to trust is better." Keep the number of people who have access to any secret information to a minimum. Very few companies are successful at keeping a secret a secret. Coke is one of the few that has done so over a long period of time. Secrets are regularly stolen, taken to another country, and used to manufacture competing products. Secrets are difficult to maintain, and the Asian adage that "there are no secrets" rings true. As noted before, usually lead time over the competition is all you have.

End-User Verification

Verifying who is buying your product is critical, as the law of first sale makes it very difficult to tell others what they can or cannot do with your products after title passes to them at the time of the sale. Therefore, to minimize the exposure to gray marketers, due diligence investigations on clients, potential clients, end users, and distributors are critical. The purpose of these investigations is to foster good business and prevent bad business. Legitimate customers will not complain.

Internet Product Purchasing

An effective product purchasing program needs established buyers, people who are considered a part of the system. This kind of program provides an opportunity to monitor different markets where your products might be sold without your knowledge.

Due Diligence

An effective due diligence program includes:

- Access to databases of known diverters, gray marketers, and criminals
- Research
- Field investigations
- Interviews with customers and suppliers

Checking the Deal

Every deal is important for earning profits and for preventing access to products by those wanting to take your profits. A system should be in place to verify each purchase order to ensure compliance with the company's brand integrity policies.

How to Do It?

Several "tools" are needed to put together a brand integrity program. They include:

- An internal process for identifying brand assets that are important to the company

- A brand audit program
- A marketplace and gray market tracking and monitoring program
- Reviews of the current BI policy
- The development of a new BI policy

Internal Process

The process of identifying brand and product risk includes a look at products, reputation, image, and intellectual property. The value of each of these assets to the company must be quantified. Then strategies for monitoring risk can be developed. These strategies will lower product and brand risk, minimize the risk of margin loss, and increase the credibility of products in the marketplace.

Brand Audit Program

Identification of specific brand assets is critical. It is essential to know what products are to produce key revenue for the company now and in the future. Issues and risks will vary by individual products but include value, impact, marketplace protection, and, finally, strategic program design and operations.

Marketplace and Gray Market Tracking and Monitoring

To monitor and track the marketplace and gray market activity, it is necessary to complete an analysis of the marketplace for each key asset. A system to monitor channel distribution must be developed, and an analysis of product arbitrage opportunities needs to be prepared. Senior management must quantify the process for determining value and assign it to all products.

BEST PRACTICES TO LOWER RISKS

- Use strong nondisclosure agreements with employees.
- Apply strictly enforced security procedures and policies for access to R&D facilities.

- Conduct comprehensive background investigations on all R&D-related employees.

- Establish IT controls and system features to closely supervise access to sensitive data, and tighten controls over Internet and intranet communications from R&D personnel.

- Closely monitor all IT systems.

- Control and monitor the dissemination of sensitive and proprietary information during technical meetings, at seminars, in papers, and with contacts with foreign university or institute personnel.

- Audit control systems.

- Establish protocols to quickly respond to breaches in security or control systems.

- Aggressively investigate and enforce your rights when a suspected theft, loss, misappropriation, or infringement takes place.

- Monitor competitors to ensure that you know what they are doing, planning to do, or would need to do to gain advantage.

BEST PRACTICES TO PREVENT MANUFACTURING-RELATED PROBLEMS

- Conduct thorough due diligence on all contract manufacturing partners and subcontractors.

- Establish cost-effective physical controls for access, surveillance, and movement control inside the facility.

- Maintain tight raw material controls and accountability.

- Establish spotchecks for all parts and component inventories.

- Maintain effective labor relations programs in the facility.

- Establish a quality program such as six sigma, ISO, or TQM.

- Audit production processes on a regular basis.

- Conduct periodic safety and security reviews of the facility.

- Focus corporate energy and resources to protect key business assets.

- Provide analytical tools to identify risks to and attacks against your brand(s).

- Develop internal responses to product protection issues and problems.

- Provide benchmarked strategies for managing internal protection programs.

- Maintain and improve profitability and market share.

DASHBOARD QUESTIONS

1. Have product-specific protection plans been developed for all key products?
2. Have product protection and IP control procedures been developed and audited for R&D and manufacturing?

IF YOU WAIT UNTIL
YOUR PRODUCTS
ARE ATTACKED,
YOU WILL LOSE

An ounce of prevention is worth a pound of cure.

Old proverb

Think positive . . . It will happen. Assume that your products will be attacked. If they are not, that probably means no one thinks they are valuable enough to steal. If that's the case, it's time to rethink your product line!

Once a product is released, it's fair game for anyone interested in taking away profits. Even products in your manufacturing supply chain that are in preparation for delivery to your distribution centers are at risk.

When you launch a product, always think about how you can defeat an attack against it. How can you defend it in your main markets? How can you prevent an attack from happening? More importantly, can you afford to defend yourself if you are attacked? Can you even afford to find out if you are being attacked? These are key questions that need to be addressed in the day-to-day management of your products. If you plan on doing other than product exploitation, how you handle the product throughout its life will impact profitability and longevity.

The key is prevention. Attacks against each product and brand, as well as the supply chain that delivers them to your customers, need to be minimized. To do this effectively, you need to know what weaknesses there are in the products and the delivery systems. It is also important to make sure that your product managers are reviewing risks for each product and that individualized protective plans are developed.

Brand integrity is effective in dealing with these problems because it is embedded in the management processes of the company; it is not merely an overlay. It works because managers are "risk-opportunity" aware and know their control processes and their people. They also understand the risks specific to their products at each stage of the life cycle—all the bad things that can befall them and ways to keep those products safe throughout their life. They understand that it is better and less expensive to *keep* the products out of trouble than to *get* them out of trouble. They use BI concepts to improve sales opportunities, grow business, and introduce new products because they are aware of the total environment surrounding their products and brands in the supply chain, including manufacturing and distribution.

HOW TO KNOW IF YOU ARE BEING ATTACKED

Your brand or product management team should be the first to know if there are problems in the market. If counterfeit products are turning up, the team should know about it, manage any fact-finding, and recommend improvements to the products and the supply chain. As we have already noted in our case studies, counterfeiters either work parallel to existing distribution channels or try to penetrate them to sell nonauthentic products. If they are trying to sell into your channels, the easiest way to do it is through distributors who buy off-price and gray market products. Counterfeits are often made to look like the real product that is being gray-marketed, or the real gray product is mixed with counterfeit. In any of these situations, the counterfeit is being sold to unsuspecting customers.

The single point of contact from inside the company and from customers and distributors should be the brand team. If quality issues are what trigger customer concerns about authenticity, then company quality assurance must bring product management into the review process immediately after a problem surfaces. If customer safety or regulatory issues are involved, then the company should follow notification procedures as well as take remedial actions with the product itself.

BI at the Supply Chain Level

Is there sufficient product at risk from gray market or counterfeit products to warrant establishing the position of supply chain executive? If so, that position should be made responsible for managing all the risks to and threats against the supply chain. This should serve to minimize the risk from diversion and lessen the chance of introducing counterfeit products into the chain. The development, implementation, and management of effective supply chain integrity across all global operations should be a key goal for this position. The primary BI objective would be the development of prevention programs.

The person in the product protection position would also be responsible for the following key activities:

- Develop procedures to ensure a secure supply chain so that customers buy only genuine products.
- Monitor the supply chain from cradle to grave.
- Manage due diligence investigations for all supply chain relationships.
- Develop supply chain compliance standards.
- Develop standardized agreements and performance standards.
- Make sure there is information flow between supply and distribution channels.

Comprehensive support for product security also can be provided along each step of the production process. That means that beginning with R&D, security controls need to be established and security awareness programs provided for employees. Products should incorporate unique design characteristics and security features to lower risk. While products are in the various stages of production, specific security, product surveillance, and monitoring programs are required. When products are released into the marketplace, anti–gray market programs, anticounterfeiting programs, and IP enforcement are used to ensure the integrity of products. When a new product is being introduced, security planning should be included, along with marketing and distribution plans.

The supply chain risks inherent in manufacturing and distribution are different and vary with the type of product; value of the product; point in the product life; area of the world in which it's produced, distributed, and sold; and desirability. Methods for keeping brands out of trouble, successfully marketing them, and obtaining maximum return vary by industry, type of product, geography, and company management systems. The old adage that "the best defense is a good offense" applies here. An aggressive marketing and sales program may be the best defense against counterfeiters, a sales commission program that stresses margin and volume lowers the risk of gray market problems, timely competitive intelligence can help determine new product entry strategies, and pricing information can improve product margins. Basically, the quicker you bring a product to market and sell it, the less time counterfeiters have to copy it and "eat your lunch."

Supply Chain Issues

There are problems specific to each aspect of the supply chain as well as the chain itself. In 2005 the Government Accountability Office (GAO) reported that only about 11 percent of importers, 564 out of 4,357, with C-TPAT certification have been verified by customs. This is an extremely small number of companies that have taken all available steps to secure their global supply chain and increase efficiency for the movement of their goods. When companies have supply chains that extend over multiple countries, instituting a program that ensures global supply chain integrity is essential. Programs that assist in providing secure channels and increasing delivery times for products are just good business.

SUPPLY CHAIN COMPONENTS

Each aspect of the product life cycle must be mastered from an information, risk, and opportunity perspective. The areas of concern for key products in the supply chain are:

Distribution
- Product storage and warehousing
- Shipping controls
- In-transit protection
- Government compliance and controls

Marketplace
- Counterfeits, clones, and unauthorized production
- Patent and copyright infringement
- Patent pending infringement
- Gray market and parallel imports
- Black market
- End-user verifications
- Fraud; abuse of discounts, rebates, and commissions

Supply Chain
- Procedures for secure channels from production to customers
- Verification procedures for cargo security (C-TPAT membership, etc.)

- Global supply chain and distribution agreements
- Implementation of the BI supply chain protection program, which involves making organizational and operational changes including:
  o Developing appropriate policies to foster the brand integrity philosophy for all company operations
  o Establishing best practices to operate all aspects of the program
  o Providing implementation guidelines
  o Agreeing upon metrics for evaluation of major aspects of the program
  o Publishing protocols to manage unusual situations
  o Knowing when to call in expert support
  o Knowing when to call for legal advice
  o Having the confidence to handle incidents and crises

What are some of the bad things that can happen in the supply chain? Here are some typical examples:

- Customs inspections slow down transportation to distribution centers.
- Contraband is found in container cargo.
- Counterfeit goods are shipped as legitimate orders.

Moving your products from manufacturing sites to either customers or company-controlled warehousing is a significant challenge to brand integrity.

Distribution

What can go wrong in distribution? Examples of some of the bad things that can happen include these:

- Products are hijacked before getting into normal distribution channels.
- Goods are damaged in storage.
- Employees pilfer products.
- Returned goods are not managed effectively.
- Orders are filled and shipped incorrectly, causing high returns and reduced profit margins.

- Goods are not shipped in a timely manner, causing JIT systems to break down.
- High labor costs, lack of mechanization, and overstaffing reduce profit margins.

Marketplace

And now for examples of some of the bad things that can happen in the marketplace:

- Counterfeit products in the market cause authenticity problems.
- Gray market products damage pricing, distribution systems, and dealer confidence.
- Substandard and scrapped goods are sold at discount prices.
- Collusion between sales staff and dealers increases discounts, rebates, or product returns.
- Tainted products used by customers cause illness or death.
- Defective products injure customers.

Case Study

A high-tech company operated an important production facility in Malaysia. The facility shipped a major product to a client in Tokyo on a weekly basis. The product was shipped by air cargo, but shipments were experiencing regular and significant losses before they arrived at the Tokyo facility.

An analysis of the delivery process was conducted. Products were placed under surveillance, which included transport from the manufacturing facilities to the bonded warehouse at the Kuala Lumpur International Airport, to the bonded air cargo warehouse, onto the air cargo aircraft, from the Subic Bay air cargo facility to Narita International Airport, through the air cargo facility at Narita, through the transport company facilities, and finally to the receiving dock at the client company in Tokyo.

It was finally revealed that some of the product never left the company manufacturing site in Malaysia. Employees working with the trucking company falsified shipping documents and shipped pallets of the product with short counts of boxes. Since the products were palletized and heavily wrapped with plastic, it was not possible to verify actual counts until the boxes arrived. The stolen products were sold to dealers who resold them in the gray market outside of Asia.

The employees confessed their complicity and, along with the truck drivers, were arrested and jailed. It took some time for the client's brand reputation to be restored with the customer. Lost profits from the stolen products were never recovered, nor were the lost sales resulting from the gray market products recouped.

Product Storage and Warehousing

Rule 1. Products in the warehouse are the same as foreign currency. Someone knows how to convert those products into dollars if you don't watch them closely.

Rule 2. An ounce of prevention is worth a pound of cure.

Reliance on warehousing for managing inventories is not as significant a problem for many companies at it once was. Warehouse inventories are a major concern because of their cash value, the cost of holding the inventory, and vulnerability to loss. They also represent an additional step in the product cycle that many companies are trying to minimize by shipping directly to customer locations. Anything that can be done to quickly move the product into customer hands will lower costs, reduce product loss exposure, and improve profits.

Where warehousing is required, controls need to be monitored closely to minimize product leakage. Numerous systems exist for product control, including C-TPAT guidelines that mandate specific procedures for handling cargo at all stages of movement, storage, documentation, and receiving. A complete discussion of these guidelines can be found at www. cBI.gov/xp/cgov/import/commercial_enforcement/ctpat/security_guide line/guideline_port.xml.

RESTRICTED SHIPMENTS

The U.S. government and the European Union have restrictions on selling various types of technology to governments that are placed on restricted lists. It is the responsibility of the selling company to know its customers and ensure that nothing is sold to them that would violate regulations and have sanctions imposed by the various governments involved. Depending on the product or technology, the responsibility for compliance may rest with the sales, marketing, or shipping department. Whichever one is responsible, it is essential that all compliance matters be a part of the BI program to minimize damage to image and reputation and to mitigate the legal consequences of selling or shipping restricted goods.

The list-restricted categories include:

1. *Debarred Parties List.* Parties denied export privileges under the International Traffic in Arms Regulations (ITAR) as administered by the Office of Defense Trade Control (DTC).
2. *Denied Persons List.* Parties denied export privileges as administered by the Bureau of Industry and Security (BIS). The list may be found in the Export Administration Regulations, 15 CFR Part 764 Supplement No. 2.
3. *Entity List.* Entities subject to license requirements because of their proliferation of weapons of mass destruction. The list may be found in the Export Administration Regulations, 15 CFR Part 774 Supplement No. 4.
4. *Specially Designated Nationals, Terrorists, Narcotics Traffickers, Blocked Persons and Vessels.* Parties subject to various economic sanctioned programs administered by the Office of Foreign Assets Control (OFAC).
5. *Unverified List, Unverified Parties List.* Parties to past export transactions where pre-license checks or post-shipment verifications could not be conducted, and persons in foreign countries in transactions where BIS is not able to verify the existence or authenticity of all parties to the transaction, requiring heightened scrutiny by the exporter as set out in 15 CFR Part 732 Supplement No. 3.
6. *U.S. Treasury Department, Office of Foreign Asset Control* (www.us treas.gov/offices/enforcement/ofac/sdn/index.shtml).

Source: U.S. Export Administration (http://chaos.fedworld.gov/bxa/prohib.html)

Currently, numerous companies purchase products in these categories. Sales staffs are often either unable or unwilling to conduct rigorous vetting or feel that an overly restrictive customer-screening program will adversely affect their sales capabilities.

CHECKING THE DEAL

It is therefore essential that a company establish a compliance due diligence process that is independent of the sales department. This due diligence process applies to all new customers worldwide and should build in the following capabilities:

- Screen all new customers for restricted products before delivery.
- Conduct investigations quickly and efficiently.
- Maintain a database of all data collected related to potential customers.
- Ensure that all information that has been collected and maintained is subject to attorney-client privilege.
- Be cost effective.

Product orders can often be processed within days or weeks, depending on availability or customer requirements. The screening process must include the ability to provide at least a preliminary investigation and a final report on each company. Preliminary reports should be available rapidly and a final report shortly thereafter. Customers and potential customers should not know (where local laws permit it) that an investigation is being conducted during or after the investigation.

The ability to conduct a thorough due diligence investigation of potential customers without their knowledge varies from country to country. In most western countries with the availability of databases and online public records, such investigations can be conducted quickly and at relatively low expense. In developing countries or those without reliable database records, much of the investigation involves identifying primary records and conducting extensive interviews and field investigation. In the countries of the former Soviet Union, in China, and in other countries that tightly control access to what would normally be public records, time and expense can be even higher. If for various reasons the governments of those countries are involved with the company being investigated, the expense may be even higher, especially if they are trying to conceal their involvement.

Many industries have only a few companies or individuals that are actively involved in deal making, manufacturing, or distribution. Most of these companies or individuals are known to each other and to those working in supporting roles. To collect information about any one of them often requires that covert investigations be conducted to identify data about the true ownership of a company, the reasons why a product is being ordered, or the ultimate end user of the product.

Since various individuals often develop numerous corporate structures to conduct illegal transactions, it is essential that a database be established and maintained. This database should include all directors, owners, shareholders, officers and management staff, corporate entities, governmental organizations, relationships to other companies, and corporations with links to either military or scientific organizations. This database should be updated with each new customer order.

The investigative questions, at a minimum, should be focused on identifying the following:

- All directors, officers, key management, and owners
- Locations of all subsidiary companies
- Relationship(s) to restricted organizations, individuals, and entities
- Commercial reputation
- Financial stability and history
- Business reputation

The sales-production-delivery cycle governs how much time is available to conduct a complete investigation and prepare a final report on the findings. If the investigation takes too long, it will interfere with the timely delivery of the client products. Consequently, a two-phase approval process is recommended.

In the first phase, the investigation should provide a preliminary report on the company and a provisional recommendation to sell or not sell to it. The preliminary report should be issued within three to five days and should be based on a review of the following information:

- Corporate records
- Review of all electronic database information available in the country of registration
- Litigation history and credit reports (as available)
- Any derogatory information discovered from open-source or public information (the hope is that there will be none)

If the company is properly registered and if it does not have any known derogatory information or any open-source information identifying it with a category or owner or director that would constitute a violation of export controls, provisional permission to sell to it can be granted.

In the second phase, the investigation must follow up all leads developed during the first phase, conduct all required field interviews and site visits (as required), and verify all information provided by the customer. This part of the investigation phase would seek answers to the following questions:

- Is the customer able to use the product for the purposes permitted by export control regulations; for example, does the customer have the requisite facilities, personnel, technical support, and so forth?
- Does the client have direct or indirect links to organizations that would disqualify it to purchase the products?
- Is there any indication that these products would not be used for the purpose specified by the customer?

All of the above information should be provided to the company to help it determine the suitability of the customer. A final determination would then be made on whether to ship the product to the customer, suspend the order and request clarifications from the customer, or terminate the customer.

MARKETPLACE

The marketplace is a very difficult place for both buyers and sellers today. Buyers can unknowingly purchase counterfeit or gray market products, contaminated or defective goods, or out-of-warranty merchandise. Sellers can have their goods counterfeited, stolen, cloned, or gray-marketed and their reputations damaged without their knowledge. Any of these situations creates a BI problem that must be quickly and effectively addressed by the company.

Case Study

A high-tech electronic products manufacturer experienced a significant drop in sales within the United States, while the Asia-Pacific region was having record sales. It was discovered that fraudulent purchases were being made at discounted prices in the "high-sales" region and then were being sold to distributors and resellers in the "low-sales" region. Margin losses amounted to over $100 million during a six-month period.

The investigation revealed that several companies were working together to fraudulently buy and then resell products outside normal distribution methods, as well as through Internet multilevel sales organizations and bulletin boards.

An investigation of the transactions and distribution channels identified who was involved, documented the distribution methods by purchasing suspected gray market products, and collected sufficient evidence to bring both criminal and civil actions against the ringleaders. The margin saving for one product line amounted to over $25 million per quarter.

The objective of a BI program is to enhance the company's ability to get and increase good business and avoid bad business and asset-risk situations. All kinds of bad things can happen to products and brands if managers do not pay attention to the marketplace. Monitoring the market to see what is happening with key products, gathering channel distribution intelligence, finding out what customers are saying, and checking on purchasing volumes all give indications about stability, problems, and opportunities. BI risks that result in significant and direct losses should be a major focus of the marketplace program efforts.

Counterfeits, Clones, and Unauthorized Production

Worldwide, the problem of product counterfeiting is one of the most significant threats to product and brand integrity. Numerous associations and organizations exist to support individual corporate efforts to address this global problem. The problem is, for the most part, caused by criminal enterprises for which internal controls are not particularly effective. In May 2006 the U.S. Congress passed the Stop Counterfeiting in Manufactured Goods Act. The Act provides for the confiscation of an entire factory if even a single counterfeit label is found in it; this is so even if the factory may otherwise be used for entirely legitimate purposes. (Whether this Act will be successful in lowering the incidence of counterfeiting still remains to be seen.)

Clones and unauthorized products are another matter. Most of these problems can be minimized with effective business processes once the root causes are understood. These causes may vary by business, but most have similar characteristics:

- The legal environment does not favor your company, or laws do not even exist.
- Written agreements with anticounterfeit or diversion terms are not in place.
- Audit and enforcement terms are not defined, nor are they available.
- There is a lack of communication with customers and distributors about the risk of buying through unauthorized sources.
- Packaging cannot be tracked back to specific customers.
- Customs controls are not in place.
- Packaging is difficult to authenticate.

When your own factories or third-party manufacturers decide to make extra revenue by producing extra products and selling them "out the back door" at low prices, this unauthorized production is damaging to your company and distribution network. Customers, on the other hand, are getting a bargain. Fortunately, in this case, the activity does not pose product-reliability problems since these off-price products are real, not counterfeit ones. It does, however, disrupt the market and cost sales revenues.

Patent and Copyright Infringement

Patent infringement can take place from two distinct sources: (1) counterfeiters and (2) companies that once were authorized to manufacture the product and that continue manufacturing after the permission has been withdrawn. Both categories can present revenue loss problems, but the manufacturer that once was an authorized producer is more dangerous as it has your formulas and often knows your customers. It can then undercut prices, confuse customers, and ruin distribution channels. It is therefore important that contracts be carefully written and after-contract surveillance occur to ensure that the manufacturer abides by the terms of the severance agreement.

Counterfeiters should be handled aggressively to determine the ultimate source of the illegal production, and enforcement should be taken to shut down the operations quickly. As far as we are concerned, there should never be any tolerance for product counterfeiting, although we have spoken with company and legal representatives who disagree with this approach. They feel that people know that they cannot buy a $1,000 watch for $25 and therefore are not too concerned about that level of copy product. They believe that the cost of chasing these street-level dealers is not worth the expense. They may be correct, but unless they have carefully analyzed the impact on brand image and reputation rather than just the cost of litigation versus the value of product price, this may not be the best approach. Perhaps if the target of the investigation were the organized ring producing the watches and distributing them to street-level sellers, this approach might have more impact on the overall problem and increase the value of a company's brand rather than assuming that customers know that they are not getting a genuine product for that street price.

Patent Pending Infringement

This issue has been discussed at some length already. It is a serious problem for certain classes of products, but there are specific programs that can mitigate risk if applied before production commences.

Gray Market Tracking

Product arbitrage is most often caused by problems internal to a company such as differential pricing of products, deep discounting of standard pricing for special customers or situations, poorly supervised rebate or incentive programs, or unrealistic compensation programs tied to sales quotas. They can also be caused by deliberate fraud on the part of employees, unethical distributors or customers, or a combination of all these factors.

Regardless of the cause, the unchecked flow of products with prices below those normally charged to customers or distributors will result in critical problems with established distributor systems and dealer contracts and especially will cause a severe loss of internal company profit margins.

Gray market tracking programs often begin with due diligence investigations to identify those who are buying your products and their real intentions for doing business with your company. Marketplace surveillance is initiated using both the Internet and traditional methods to track products around the globe. Investigations related to specific questionable transactions are conducted to understand how internal control systems were compromised. Improvement programs are recommended to minimize the reoccurrence of losses caused by either internal or external sources.

Access to an extensive database in the industry of known diverters, gray marketers, and counterfeiters is essential and should be used in support of due diligence, end-user verification, and contract manufacturing verification.

End-User Verification

The ultimate user of a product is oftentimes more important than the entity it is sold to in the first instance. If the *law of first sale* limits control over what is done with a product after it passes to the first purchaser, understanding who will handle the product and what the person really plans to do with it is extremely important. Selling to a company that says it is a manufacturing company and plans to use the product for OEM purposes will often result in special pricing. If the company, in turn, doesn't manufacture but instead sells the product in the market, in reality it becomes a discount broker. This often causes significant margin loss and channel disruption. Thousands of situations like this occur every day. They could be avoided if proper screening of potential customers had taken place.

Due diligence investigations on the background of clients, potential clients, end users, distributors, and the like are an essential part of keeping profits up and good business coming in the front door. This strategy should be used to ensure that people with intent to do harm to your business are weeded out before they can do any damage to you.

Global Electronic Monitoring

Through an international network of Internet locations, investigators can monitor the electronic trafficking of products for a company. Products are purchased to determine pricing, availability, source(s), and the way in which unauthorized distribution systems function. Intelligence gathered is used for litigation, channel management, and the monitoring of suspected gray market activities or in stings against fraudulent operators.

Individual product lines can be monitored, specific types of products at specified price points purchased, or entire distribution systems monitored around the world through a single, discreet, controlled, and knowledgeable group of product specialists. This type of service has saved millions of dollars per quarter in profit margin for companies that have experienced leakage from established distribution channels. Similar services monitor Internet sites to ensure that copyright and trademark infringements do not occur or are identified for enforcement actions in a timely way.

UNDERSTAND YOUR SUPPLY CHAIN

A few additional BI program features should be present regardless of the type of products, potential global location, organizational style, or budget involved. They are basic to the effective operation of any BI program, but especially to those of the supply chain.

Background Investigations—Both Internal and External

The people who companies hire or contract with present potential security risks and problems. Thus, to hire a senior executive, product manager, credit manager, manufacturing partner, or distribution system manager without conducting a thorough background investigation is not good business practice. These types of positions and relationships require a complete executive background investigation regardless of where the person is going to be assigned.

Knowing whom you are doing business with as a potential joint venture partner, contract manufacturing facility, outsourced distribution service, trucking or freight forwarder, or any related service is essential to minimize the risk to products and margins. This type of investigation should be a part of developing every business relationship.

Due Diligence Investigations

Knowing whom you are doing business with, before signing a contract, is the best protection against fraud, gray marketing, and compliance problems. Numerous companies conduct thousands of due diligence investigations each year. They estimate that significant misrepresentations are present in about 20 percent of the cases. In fact, many of the fraud and gray market cases investigated have shown that if an investigation had been conducted before accepting the company as a client, derogatory information would have been available, thus eliminating the company as a possible customer.

By using a comprehensive database of known diverters, gray market-ers, and criminals; by conducting field investigations; and by interviewing other customers of and suppliers to the subject company, a true picture of the proposed customer emerges. This picture enables the responsible executive to make an informed decision concerning the types of customers the company will do business with.

Customer due diligence investigations can be brief or involved, depending on the nature of the relationship being considered. The main point is that the investigation should be undertaken, and it should be appropriate to the risk involved in taking on the potential customer as a business partner. It is critical to know who will assume responsibility for your products after they leave your control. If the company you are investigating has a good track record of doing what it says it does with other people's products, chances are it will do the same with yours. If it has a history of deceit, fraud, or product arbitrage, it is unlikely that the company will change its spots for you.

Stay Ahead of the Problem

Problems related to product integrity and discounted or off-price products are visible to customers, competitors, and your staff. We have worked with clients that had serious problems with counterfeit products but that have decided not to tell customers about the problem even though there was a product safety hazard. The concern was that if they told the customers about counterfeits, it would confuse them. In one case, the company changed the labeling, added some holograms, and just kept selling the product until the counterfeits were removed from the field by the sales staff. An intensive investigation found the source of the counterfeit product and got it off the market.

The tables can easily be turned on the company with gray market products. Customers are often the first to know about your products showing up at off prices. The company learns about it when sales drop, margins go down, dealers complain, or there are more warranty claims than sales.

Take a walk down the streets in midtown Manhattan or central London; amble through Wan Chai in Hong Kong or Chatterchuk Market in Bangkok. As you stroll through any of these places, you will find Rolex, Piaget, Burberry, Levi, Chanel, and others that are either counterfeit or gray depending on how much you are willing to spend. Both consumers and manufacturers know about these products, and both make different decisions on how to react. Some high-value-product companies try to eliminate as many fakes as possible. Others make a decision that informed consumers *will know* that you can't buy a Rolex for $59 and thus it's not important to try to stop every knockoff being sold on a street corner. But what about counterfeit Viagra, Lipitor, or countless other pharmaceuticals or alcoholic beverages such as Johnnie Walker, where a life safety issue may be present? Even when brand owners have aggressive BI programs, getting the public to believe that it is not getting a bargain is difficult to sell.

BI includes aggressive anticounterfeiting and anti–gray market programs that are used to identify problems and take enforcement actions to get products off the market. In cases of regulated industries, there is often a requirement to inform the regulators, such as the FDA, that a problem exists and to cooperate with the agency until the problem is resolved. In nonregulated industries, the decision on informing the public about counterfeits is totally up to the company with the problem. Should shareholders be informed about these problems? Should shareholders be informed about lost, compromised, or stolen intellectual property or trade secrets? What about product tampering or recalls? Should they be publicly announced or quietly handled? Do you wait until a problem is solved before making an announcement? Never tell the public about it? Industry practices run the gamut.

A decision about when, how, and if to announce product-attack problems is a company management responsibility with significant BI implications. The best practice in these matters is to disclose the problem at the earliest opportunity consistent with the facts of the situation. In life safety situations, as soon as the nature of the problem is known, regulatory and consumer notifications are essential even while the investigation and recalls progress. In non–life safety situations, prompt disclosure to key customers while an investigation is under way is important but should not be made until an investigation determines the source of the products and enforcement actions have been taken.

Applying the principles of Law No. 4 ("If you wait until you are attacked, you will lose") here means that you tell people about the problem as a defense against future attacks. Counterfeiters and gray marketers assume that you will keep quiet about these attacks or look the other way, giving up a portion of your market to their low-cost alternatives to your authentic products.

Can you investigate each incident of gray market or counterfeit products? Probably not. Can you try to identify when and how attacks are occurring? You bet! Can you identify who is doing it and develop a systematic program to interdict or eliminate the threat? Absolutely! In fact, you must do it to maintain brand integrity.

Another way that you stay ahead of problems is by knowing who has access to your product information. Basic due diligence investigations of those involved in your supply chain are often enough to significantly lower the risks of being attacked by suppliers, vendors, and customers.

APPLICATION OF THE DUE DILIGENCE PROCESS

The depth, timing, and sensitivity of the due diligence process will vary depending on the stage of the product's life cycle, the product's contribution to profitability expectations, and existing vendor relationships. The three basic categories derived from these factors are:

- The risk to ongoing operations and product lines
- The risk to new production or products
- The selection of new contract manufacturing vendors

Based on these three categories, it is essential that a company respond in the following ways:

- Develop specific criteria for establishing product risk profiles so that investigative levels can be established.
- Identify critical production requirements and levels of control needed for key products.
- Specify vendor expectations for production capabilities, continuity of operations, financial stability, and integrity of ownership.
- Set realistic timelines for the completion of the investigation before selection decisions are made.

- Allocate sufficient budget for the level of due diligence required.
- Develop guidelines for including investigations in new project and strategic product planning.

The following four policy guide case studies present different types of due diligence inquiries to determine how inquiries should be conducted and to verify the suitability of suppliers, vendors, and key employees.

Policy Guide: Due Diligence

In building a prudent and responsible business plan and relationship, it is appropriate to know the background of a future business partner(s) and its principals, subsidiaries, suppliers, contractors, and vendors. Thus, due diligence investigations need to be conducted prior to entering into business relationships between the company and other entities throughout the world. The independently obtained and unbiased information will form a foundation on which to begin the evaluation of a potential relationship between qualified parties that is mutually productive and profitable.

Policy Guide Case Study: Geopolitical Risk Assessment—Scope and Approach

Numerous issues associated with international operations can cause problems related to the BI supply chain. The key issues in regard to company operations and the continued ability of the supply chain to operate properly are:

- Crime and risk to personnel in the region
- Corruption issues affecting business operations
- Governmental stability and intervention in operations
- Information protection and product or brand integrity
- Operational integrity (protection of business operations)

While important, employee health and safety issues not directly related to geographical location, such as medical facilities and environmental concerns, are usually not significant enough to severely impact company operations. The risk review for these types of issues is different in scope and complexity from those cited in the above list.

In order to determine the risk for operations in any country in which a considerable portion of the supply chain is located, risk reports related to the specific activities need to be conducted. These reviews are best performed on-site.

During the site visits, arrangements should also be made to obtain local security assistance if needed for country management or travelers in the event of an emergency situation that requires immediate local support.

Each country report should provide an overview of the current risk situation specific to company operations, anticipated problems during the next 12 months, and recommendations to manage these risks.

If significant changes take place in the business or risk environment or if criminal or terrorist events occur that change the risk for company operations, an immediate country update should be provided.

The time required for these reports varies depending on the discretion needed when conducting the on-site work. If the review is overt and known to the target company, one or two days are normally sufficient to complete the fieldwork.

Policy Guide Case Study: Background Investigations—Scope and Approach

Since various degrees of information are required when a worldwide company must select a supply chain service, a multitasking approach is necessary to meet the company's needs. A contract investigations firm should be retained to conduct this project.

In order to provide the company's preselection team with the background information needed to make prudent business decisions, a due diligence investigation would be initiated. It would have to meet the following criteria:

- The investigations are conducted quickly and efficiently.
- A database should be maintained of all the data collected related to entities and key participants.
- All information should be collected in a sensitive and confidential manner.
- The investigation should be cost effective.

Since business decisions need to be made within either days or weeks, depending on the company requirements, the screening process must include the ability to provide at least a preliminary investigation and a final report on each identified company and participant. Preliminary reports must be available within four working days and a final report within ten days. The businesses and individuals who are the subjects of the due diligence investigation must not know (where this is legal) that the investigation is being conducted. This would include the time during and after the fact, unless so stated otherwise (notification could occur via a prescreening process exchange between the company contact and the future entity or by some other means). Issues regarding criminal records and credit checks requiring individual consent would be exceptions and handled on a case-by-case basis.

Issues and Concerns

The ability to conduct a thorough due diligence investigation of potential new ventures without the subjects' knowledge of the investigation varies from country to country. In most western countries, the availability of online databases and public records allows such investigations to be conducted quickly and with relatively low expense. In countries where there are stronger government controls over information, gathering information can be difficult and the investigation requires a different approach.

Recommended Approach

A thorough examination would be conducted to find information about the entities and individuals involved and to validate their representations. The selection process governs how much time is available to conduct a complete investigation and prepare a final report on the findings. If the investigation takes too long, it will interfere with the timely ability to make an informed decision. Consequently, a two-phase reporting process is recommended. In the first phase, the investigation would provide a preliminary report that includes general findings. The preliminary report would be issued within three days from the time the investigation began and would be based on a review of the following information:

Corporate Records Check

- A review of all the electronic database information available in the country of registration
- Litigation history, criminal record checks,* and credit reports (as available)*
- Open-source and public information, especially to rule out the presence of derogatory information
- Screening and comparison with existing databases

If the entity (or individual) is properly registered and if there is no readily identifiable derogatory information or any information identifying it with improper or questionable activities, this would be so stated in the preliminary report.

*In the United States, the European Union, Singapore, and Hong Kong, individuals must provide a signed release.

The second phase is the completed investigation. In this phase, investigators follow up all the leads developed during the preliminary investigation, conduct all required field interviews and site visits (as required), and verify all the information developed. The investigators would conduct activities to answer, at a minimum, the following questions:

- Are the entities or individuals who they represent themselves to be?
- Do they have the requisite facilities, personnel, technical support, etc., so represented?
- Do the entities or individuals have direct or indirect links to other entities or individuals that could constitute or be a conflict of interest or raise other compromising types of concerns?
- Is there any indication that the entities or individuals would or could be involved in detrimental activities or have ulterior motives?

When a company has a worldwide presence, conducting due diligence investigations of possible supply chain contractors, as well as the individuals and entities who work with them, may often require a global response. This process, especially outside the United States, must be handled in special and unique ways. In other countries, political and governmental systems, record keeping, and openness to public scrutiny of business and other financial records are varied and complex. Consequently, investigations usually take more time to conduct and are more expensive than they are in the United States.

Within any industry, few companies or individuals are actually involved in deal making, manufacturing, or distribution. Most of these individuals are known to each other and to those working in supporting roles. To discover information about any one of them often requires that covert investigations be conducted to collect data about the true ownership of a company, the reasons why a product is being ordered, or the ultimate end user of the product.

Policy Guide Case Study: Risk Assessment—Scope and Approach

On-site security inspection for supply chain contractors should be a standard part of every contractual agreement written by the company. Security standards at any vendor site should be comparable to those at any other company-owned and company-operated facility. Certifications should be obtained from all vendors, specifying that they are maintaining controls at the required levels after survey findings are implemented. Audit provisions should be included and periodic audits performed by the company.

If these services are to be provided by a contract vendor, they should be performed using the company's standards, preferably utilizing a standardized audit program managed with a software program. The use of this type of program will significantly reduce costs and improve reporting, follow-up, and accountability. The average audit using the software for a manufacturing plant will take less than one day.

Where special security requirements may be essential, such as in patent pending production, plans and strategies for ensuring additional protection need to be employed. In a patent pending case, for example, extra measures would be needed until patents are issued.

Policy Guide Case Study: Business Continuity Planning— Scope and Approach

Reviews of high-risk BI management and operating systems within supply chain contractors can be accomplished using the software system described above. Such systems as IT, crisis management, emergency response, and business resumption can be audited using the program.

Equally important is the identification of alternative supply sources or the vetting of those alternative sources identified by business unit management using criteria identical to those for the primary source.

Contingency plans for the facility or for the business unit to operate the business when the contract supplier is shut down must be developed based on the field review findings. The cost for developing these plans can vary widely depending on the shortcomings of the facility, the country in which the facility is located, and the significance of the facility to the entire manufacturing supply chain.

The aspects of due diligence outlined above have to be a part of the selection process for every contractor in the company supply chain. The depth and breadth of the inquiries must be tailored to match the relative BI risk, the value of the product, and the value to anticipated revenue. Investigations must be a part of the strategic requirements for the manufacturing and distribution supply chain. Many of the due diligence issues identified through investigations are key data for effective supply chain planning and thus should be available early in the planning process.

The due diligence investigation of all the aspects is best completed as one overall assessment of any business partner. If it is not done as a whole, it will be more costly, and often it will not result in a balanced assessment. Investigations will keep you ahead of problems. If you know the risks you are taking in running your business, you can focus on them and reduce the need for crisis management.

BEST PRACTICES TO PREVENT DISTRIBUTION-RELATED PROBLEMS

Distribution

- Introduce a quality process such as Six Sigma, ISO, or TQM.
- Install a mechanized inventory control system.
- Screen trucking companies for criminal and quality concerns.
- Require a background investigation for all new employees.
- Minimize exposure of goods through palletizing, shrink-wrapping, and unitized packaging.
- Utilize enterprise software to manage supply chain shipping.
- Initiate best practices to prevent marketplace-related problems.

Marketplace

- Join an industry group attacking industrywide problems such as anticounterfeiting, antipiracy, and anti–gray markets.
- Establish internal control practices that reduce collusive behavior by employees and outsiders.
- Monitor deals for reasonableness, margin maintenance, and compliance with approved internal controls.
- Perform due diligence on every new customer, partner, distributor, and dealer.
- Monitor your market space for pricing, competitor actions, and new-product intelligence.

Supply Chain

- Obtain customs certification for supply chain practices (where required).

- Develop standardized supply chain agreements and performance guidelines.

- Monitor and enforce compliance with established standards.

DASHBOARD QUESTIONS

1. How many product attacks have taken place this year?
2. What is the financial impact of these attacks?
3. What process is being used to identify risk?
4. Who is responsible for managing product risk in the company?

CHAPTER 6

PROTECT YOUR PRODUCTS, AND THE BAD GUYS WILL ATTACK YOUR COMPETITION

When you feel the winds of change, build a windmill, not a wind-break.

Mao Tse-tung

Market leaders, single-product companies, and high-tech developers all have different risks. Your products, your place in the "food chain," marketplace perceptions, and existing product protection are all factors associated with your risk. When an existing product protection system signals an early warning of an aggressive attack, the type of countermeasures you take to defeat such an attack often makes the difference between being a victim or a victor.

Not all companies will have a gray market or counterfeit problem, but the likelihood is that if a product is successful, it will be attacked. The success of the attack will be determined by how well you have protected yourself and how quickly you respond. The current business model used by many companies today to deal with counterfeit attacks against their products includes the following:

- Secured ownership rights
- Incorporated design features
- Packaging controls
- Aggressive enforcement

- Surveillance if required
- Public awareness and education

A number of elements will be present when a counterfeit attack takes place against your products. These include the following:

- Criminal acts (99.9 percent of the time!)
- Packaging design problems
- Product identification issues
- Loss of customer confidence
- Inadequate market surveillance
- Life safety concerns (in some cases)

The gaps between what you should have in place and the avenues that contribute to counterfeiting your product are the starting blocks when looking for product risks. These gaps are often pointed out after a product is in the market and customers, gray marketers, and counterfeiters exploit them. Hackers and software analysts regularly take delight in pointing out gaps in Microsoft operating systems, and motion picture pirates penetrate prescreenings to duplicate films before their official release. Chinese companies have been known to release high-tech devices simultaneously with the release of the same products by Silicon Valley companies. Sometimes these gaps are found before a product release and can be remedied, while at other times a crisis management situation produces the lessons learned that ultimately fix the problem.

The most critical time for an attack is in the new-product introduction process. The time between development of the concept and product release is when a product is most vulnerable to significant long-term revenue loss. Do all companies and products have an equal risk for being attacked at this or any other time in their revenue life cycle? The answer is both yes and no. As previously discussed, if your company is targeted for any reason by a determined person, the chances are that an attack will occur unless you have taken extraordinary means to prevent the loss. Even then, nothing is fail-safe.

The concept of crime prevention through environmental design (CPTED) has become an accepted part of crime and loss reduction efforts around the world. The basic premise of CPTED is that by incorporating appropriate design features into a physical environment, the susceptibility to criminal attack can be reduced. The concepts behind CPTED have been developed and refined by psychologists, architects, police officers, and criminologists and are based upon studies of crime incidents, evaluations of demonstration projects, and trial and error.

CPTED hasn't eliminated crime, but it does, in fact, work well. It is increasingly a part of municipal building codes and design standards, and CPTED features in homes and buildings are used to attract customers. The design of a particular environment discourages the type of behavior that is unwanted by the users of a particular building. It produces a safe living, commuting, entertainment, or public facility. If done properly, it is extremely cost effective, aesthetically pleasing, and user friendly.

The principles of a brand integrity program are very much like those of CPTED, as they apply proven management, loss prevention, marketing, psychological, and legal techniques to make corporate brand and product assets less susceptible to criminal and marketplace attacks. A BI program ensures early warning of problems or attacks and provides for timely responses and crisis management. Most importantly, it relies on general management and employee participation in the process rather than on a large specialized security or BI function to manage the effort. Its principles apply equally well to building and to operating brand integrity programs.

A criminal attack takes place only when ability, opportunity, and desire are all aligned in favor of the criminal. If the desire to steal your design is present but you are able to establish robust barriers to a level that criminal ability cannot match, the attack will not be successful. Similarly, if your controls do not provide an opportunity for the attack, it likewise will not be successful. Desire to attack your products can also be lowered if BI barriers appear, and actually are, more difficult to attack than those of another company. Continually raising the bar for a would-be attacker is essential to stay ahead of the competition, move potential risk away from your products—and keep the criminals moving to another company.

HOW TO STOP ATTACKS

If for some reason your company or products look like either an easy target or an attractive financial opportunity, counterfeit or gray market products will surface. Something being done in the market or the company is sending up a smoke signal saying, "Here I am. Take my profits." So how can you stop attacks? In other words, how can you implement Law No. 5, "Protect your products, and the bad guys will attack your competition"? There are six principles you can apply:

1. Don't let it happen in the first place.
2. Be a hard target.
3. Make someone else a target.
4. Avoid the "deny everything–admit nothing–make counterallegations" approach.
5. Admit the problem, fix it, and move on.
6. Aggressively promote and protect brands and products.

You don't blame customers, gray marketers, or counterfeiters for brand attacks. You blame yourself. Most brand or product attacks are self-inflicted—the result of inappropriate sales or incentive plans, inappropriate pricing policies, poor product design, faulty supply chain, and so on. These problems result from poor market intelligence, poor enforcement, bad management decisions, and premium pricing.

Many executives around the globe are looking for a free lunch and are willing to eat yours if you are not careful. Today's marketplace is more competitive, less ethical, not bound by "niceties," global, more aggressive in exploiting vulnerabilities, and focused more on the short term. You are, in reality, fighting a secret war against pirates and lost profits to retain full value from intellectual property. Not viewing this issue as a high priority is done at your peril. If viewed as defensive policy and not profit-generating activities, there are problems ahead. Losses can't be covered by "selling more and not worrying about it," as some executives would have you believe. The philosophy that says, "Don't worry about a little counterfeit product. Those people would not buy the real stuff anyway" or "A little gray market won't hurt us. We still made our numbers; it's just a little extra margin" is shortsighted and not good business. Extra costs cannot always be passed on to legitimate customers; you can't always charge higher prices to make up for lost revenue.

Success in the age of e-commerce, global enterprise, and instant communications requires the ability to continually innovate. It also means getting inside the reaction cycle of the competition and never losing that initiative in the marketplace. It further requires that the promise your brand makes to consumers truly will give them the experience your image, advertising, and product integrity tells them will be present. Given that the various products that make up the cash flow of the company are subject to both positive and negative internal and external pressures, it is essential that management systems be able to respond to slight deviations from established norms. The ability to sense these changes, respond quickly and effectively to the situation, and keep the competition off balance requires management controls, communications, and intelligence of the highest order.

It is one thing to *say* that innovative strategy, plans, and tactics are required to manage in a global environment. But *how* these innovative strategy, plans, and tactics are developed and executed is quite another. However, if the competitive landscape is effectively analyzed and opportunities are recognized and selected properly, the competitive advantage required for maximum profitability and brand integrity will be there.

Using a nonlinear business strategy such as brand integrity management is no more unique than what FedEx did to change perceptions about package delivery or what Southwest Airlines did for air travel. Changing the existing business model to create internal benefits for the company puts the competition at a disadvantage. It also creates new opportunities for profit improvement, increased operational effectiveness, and employee participation in brand management. Top companies often get that way by changing the rules of the game. This is exactly what brand integrity management does for the company. It is not an overlay of tools or techniques that add to the existing ways of doing business. It is rather an embedded approach based on a philosophy of protecting the product and putting the product first in every decision made by management.

What is the result that management is seeking other than maximum profit for the longest period of time from each product or brand? There is really very little else that matters. Consequently, if the specific goal is to manage the business from the perspective of each product or brand, the result should be that all corporate energy, focus, and resources should be organized to achieve that goal. Even in companies that have brand management practices in place, managers are very often responsible for little more than marketing, sales, distribution, and, in some isolated cases, manufacturing. The information required for identifying market risks, product problems, attacks against product integrity, gray market sales, or patent infringement is not central to day-to-day management of the brand.

The following considerations also need attention from senior management when determining how much effort should be expended in establishing a brand integrity program:

- *Fiduciary responsibility.* Is management "watching the store" effectively, ensuring due diligence in its actions and decision making and making prudent financial decisions to maximize shareholder value?
- *Social responsibility.* Is the company following international conventions regarding child and sweatshop labor, paying fair wages,

and participating in all applicable organizations as a good corporate citizen?

- *Ethical considerations.* Are controls in place to ensure compliance with all legal and ethical standards of conduct such as FCPA, FCRA, AA/EEO, SOX 404, and OSHA?
- *Margin improvement.* Is the business being managed to obtain increasing profits from products and brands through the application of sound and innovative practices?
- *Best practices.* Does the company use the same techniques throughout its operations that industry leaders employ to improve processes and practices?
- *Case law.* Is legal kept up-to-date on current case law related to key aspects of business operations, and are changes applied to improve profits, reduce risks, and create opportunities?

There are various levels of brand integrity applicability, the most basic element of which is the protection established for each product. The protection might be a trade secret, such as the formula that Coca-Cola has successfully used to add to carbonated water and caramel coloring for the past 75 years. It can be the unique crown symbol that Rolex uses to identify its watches or the advanced circuitry of an Intel or AMD microchip that is very difficult to copy and manufacture. In other words, it can be anything that is integral to the product that makes it unique, or hard to copy, or easy to identify, or easy to distinguish in some way.

Security executives often tell people that they are in the moving business. They move crime from their company to somewhere else. Most criminological studies also indicate that very little crime is really prevented, merely displaced—transferred to somewhere else. If your building is more secure than your neighbor's, he gets burglarized. If your car has a better alarm system, your neighbor's car is stolen. If you aggressively prosecute people who steal from your company, thieves are less likely to want to work for you. Aggressively prosecuting those who do attack you will affect the desire of the next person looking your way. Appear to be a hard target, be a hard target, and take a hard line on enforcement to lower the risk of an attack. However, once an attack takes place, aggressively investigate and litigate.

The most common types of product problems are related to patent infringement, the gray market, and counterfeit products. All these problems have common information requirements, but somewhat different elements of information need to be collected. So identification of the problem to be investigated is the first step in the process. Managing the risk for attack requires a strategic approach.

GET AHEAD OF THE RISK

What you are trying to do in risk avoidance is to encourage "good" business and discourage "bad" business while avoiding risks and threats to product and brand. This can be done by using good business practices such as:

- Knowing your customers
- Maintaining good pricing and margins
- Keeping customers satisfied
- Delivering products on time
- Responding to customer requirements
- Keeping products out of the gray market

As previously discussed, the six types of responses that are necessary to lower risk are:

- Pricing
- Promotion
- Packaging
- Policy
- Information
- Enforcement

Each response forms one layer of your brand integrity program; collectively they reflect how much value you place on your products and brands. All are present in a well-thought-out program. The extent to which each one is relied upon will, however, vary with the risk and threat perceived.

Pricing

Pricing is an art form that must conform to the profitability requirements of the company. It is often used as a weapon to attack a competitor's market share, establish a market position for products, or reflect social and economic conditions, governmental requirements, and so on. If product prices are considered too high and your product is unique, people will pay the price but buy less, search for alternative products, find alternative sources for your product, or be attracted to imitation products. Knowing where the price point is that will attract but not create market opportunities for gray or counterfeit products is crucial. Once equilibrium can be established for pricing, it must be maintained, adjusted, and controlled as required.

Case Study

The motion picture and recorded music industries are constantly battling "no-cost" music-sharing Web sites and counterfeit CD and DVD products that sell for 10 percent of the price of the original products. Sustaining premium pricing in the U.S. and E.U. markets, while difficult, is possible because of strong enforcement and packaging controls. Most of the attacks are based in Asia, where production is inexpensive and quality reasonable. Low prices attract many potential purchasers of real products. Since pricing is a core issue, many alternative methods of distribution and differential pricing are being established to encourage potential customers of nonauthentic products to buy the real thing. Along with pricing efforts, packaging and recording technologies are being used to lower risks; also, public education is being conducted to encourage real product purchases, and aggressive enforcement and litigation are used to protect property rights. Even with all the other layers of protection in use, demand is strong, prices are high, and nonauthentic products flood the market. Selling downloads at low prices, selling single-song recordings at low prices, and lowering original prices all erode the attractiveness of nonauthentic products and increase the desirability of products sold at the "manufacturer's suggested price." The rebalancing of pricing, enforcement, and education for films, music, and video games is a constantly evolving management concern. Multipronged strategies using price as a major component will dominate this product area.

Not all industries have the intensive pressure from nonauthentic products as the ones in the above example, but the same issues are present if even one product is attacked. Getting the balance right between price and value minimizes the risk posed from nonauthentic products. It does not, however, deal with gray market products, especially if differential pricing is present.

Promotion

Marketing programs build brand recognition, develop awareness of the value of product authenticity, and create demand. Creating demand and strengthening recognition are key to getting customers to buy the product. Supplying enough products to the area market is equally important since unfulfilled demand can generate copies and encourage nonauthentic products to enter the market.

Also, if counterfeiters see that a product is being marketed extensively, a good portion of their marketing work is already being done with your dollars. Staying ahead of counterfeiters during a new-product launch requires that as little time as possible be available for the nonauthentic product to be produced and sold before or during the new-product launch. It is critical to keep secret the plans, the country selected for the introductory launch, and the launch details to minimize the lead time counterfeiters have to capitalize on your marketing budget.

Case Study

Our daughter had just completed the Swiss Hotel School and was working at a five star hotel in Hong Kong. One evening she brought home a document she had found in the lobby of the hotel and asked what she should do with it. The document was titled "Strategic Investment & Acquisition Plan (1999–2004)." It was for a major multinational telecommunications company. She called the company office in Hong Kong and reported that an important document had been left in the hotel, but she was told to just "throw it in the trash."

I called the company's director of security and told him the story. Within half an hour he had one of his staff at our home to retrieve the document. He later told me that the employee my daughter had spoken to thought that because another, newer version of the plan was circulating, the earlier version was not important. As a result, an awareness brand risk training program was conducted for all senior staff in the office, and tighter document controls were established.

Packaging

Packaging involves brand image, product identification, required product information, warnings, bar code and POS data, RFID tagging, security features to deter counterfeiting, and numerous other data sets and layers of film, paper, cardboard, foil, and the like. All these features and pieces of information are placed on the product to guarantee authenticity, ensure safe delivery to the customer, fulfill legal requirements, identify price and place of manufacture, certify date of production, and so on. Each packaging layer, data set, and security feature provides consumer and producer alike with tools to ensure authenticity and value until the product is purchased.

The decision process regarding packaging and marking is product specific and should be based on risk, cost, threat, supply chain management considerations, and marketing requirements. Again there is no magic bullet for picking the "best" or "right" approach; it must be based on an analysis of what needs to be done to get the product to the consumer with a high probability of authenticity and at a competitive price. This is "frontline" product, brand, and market-specific BI decision making.

Policy

Sales, product handling, and production policies are significant areas in which attacks can take place and require careful development and management efforts. Policies that specify contractual terms for third-party manufacturing are essential to control the supply chain and product specifications effectively. Where, by whom, and how much product is produced is vital information. The supply chain distribution policy must be tightly managed. Sales terms and conditions, customer qualification standards, and credit terms are likewise significant issues for management controls. Policy must be developed for all major risk areas in the company.

Information

Market intelligence is essential in developing marketing plans and programs as well as understanding the nature of the risk and threat against brands and products. For example, if you know that gray marketers often restrict the range of activities to limited types of products, you can begin to identify who they are in your area of business. Electronic brokers tend to stay with electronic products, and medical products tend to be sold by people who understand that business, but consumer goods can have dozens of subspecialties. Good market intelligence can provide information for determining and monitoring distribution channels, documenting shipping and transshipping methods, and identifying the wholesalers and retailers and possible employees or ex-employees involved. If counterfeiting is an issue, you may even be able to locate production facilities. Remember, the idea is to collect good information about your products in the market and about those individuals who want to take advantage of them. Understanding the nature and substance of the threat allows you to fight back with marketing plans, enforcement actions, product repackaging, sales promotions, and consumer education programs based on actual market conditions. By responding to the threat, sometimes you can avoid an actual attack; other times you might catch an attack early, thus lowering losses, and take enforcement action before nonauthentic products get into the market.

Enforcement

Taking enforcement action is a recognition that your systems have failed and someone has attacked you or is ready to do so. Enforcement is conducted for administrative purposes, criminal actions, or civil litigation. Enforcement activities take place when a problem is identified in the market and sufficient corporate resolve is present to carry it forward. Good intelligence must exist to discover the activities of counterfeiters, diverters, or repackagers. Intelligence gathering must begin as soon as the problem is identified, and enforcement actions should be taken only when sufficient information is developed to be successful.

Each type of enforcement has specific legal requirements that must be met. The objectives of the investigation must be clearly formulated; for example, "Identify the source of counterfeit products, seize them, and prosecute the counterfeiter." Who will actually conduct the investigation, what is its timing, and who will coordinate the investigation are all matters that need to be specified in advance in the investigative plan, as well as who will coordinate with the U.S. and foreign governments to manage the investigation. Liaison with local police agencies and management of any Foreign Corrupt Practices Act or SOX 404 issues need to be addressed in the investigative plan.

Counterfeit investigations are a continual process that requires marketplace intelligence and a strict enforcement policy: wherever a counterfeit product is found, it will be eliminated—no question. There must be aggressive actions to curtail, control, and eliminate it. There must be internal monitoring of markets.

The identification of a counterfeit product is a critical element in taking effective action. A positive identification system is essential. Investigators must be able to quickly and accurately identify a product from the field. Special or secret coding or marking is important, and many systems are present to provide this capability and should be used. If necessary, the assistance of an analytical laboratory or engineering firm must be available. If raids and seizures are considered, they must strictly follow local legal requirements. Confidentiality before the raid and seizure is paramount, as is coordination with local counsel and the police. In some countries it is necessary to make sure the police can be trusted with the information about the raid. Even where some level of trust exists, surveillance on the raid site should be established by the company before and after the raid to monitor it for project security purposes. It is also prudent to install undercover operatives into or near the site who can monitor the operation before and after the raid.

Most counterfeit and gray market investigations and enforcement actions take place away from your corporate headquarters. That is just one of the numerous issues to contend with in getting good information. Others include:

- Being geographically distant from the problem
- Grappling with political and legal problems
- Dealing with corruption
- Having forgetful and "lost" witnesses
- Getting reliable local assistance
- Obtaining good information
- Convincing people to talk to you
- Securing prosecution, restitution, or employee termination
- Maintaining control over the investigation and the enforcement activities
- Maintaining control over the budget
- Getting pushback from business units that are worried about their financial results

Since investigations and enforcement actions are clearly not a "business as usual" environment, someone you trust must assist in handling the matter. Investigations and enforcements are time consuming. You need good legal advice and must be willing to spend money. Investigations can be very expensive, especially if conducted in multiple countries, which is not unusual in counterfeit and gray market cases. It is therefore extremely important that investigative goals be carefully defined, remembering that sometimes political considerations may be more important than criminal content.

Once the investigation or enforcement starts, set the ground rules immediately, review all reports made by local sources, and enforce strict adherence to established reporting and investigative timelines. Make sure to understand local requirements for conducting the investigation before beginning. Last, make sure to communicate with customers when the case is done so that they know the outcome directly from you, rather than reading it in the newspapers.

Defensive Strategies

Taking a product to market and keeping it secure requires the efforts of many people. To compete successfully, an even more focused coordination of brand integrity is required from a wider circle of employees, distributors, subcontractors, vendors, and customers. To maximize both profits and market share, control over the property rights inherent in the product needs to be maintained from the time of inception until the useful life of the product is completed.

Much like insurance risk management, brand integrity management is organized around two basic issues: (1) what will it cost you (in liability, insurance premiums, threats, and attacks) if you don't use it? and (2) what is the direct economic value of establishing a program? Or put more simply, "If X happens to your company, it will cost Y." How can having a brand integrity management program reduce this risk?

Protecting the strategic interests of the company against gray market products, trade secret theft, patent infringements, and counterfeit products is central to company profitability. Providing effective IT security to ensure that sensitive data are moving correctly "in the pipe" is likewise essential. Monitoring the marketplace for intelligence that provides warnings about threats to products or operations should be a daily activity. Becoming a part of the decision-making process to manage corporate risk and threat using the unique perspective of corporate brand integrity is not only desirable but also essential if the protective program is to be continually responsive to the changing global environment.

STAGES IN COMPANY PROGRAM DEVELOPMENT

There are specific steps in building a company brand integrity program that must be followed if the efforts are going to be successful in moving attacks to somebody else. These steps involve understanding and developing what is required to establish a program, building a high level of internal acceptance of the concepts, creating the structure and tools to operate the program, and then operating it to achieve the desired level of financial results. These steps form the basic blueprint for establishing a program.

Building an Approach
- Require brand integrity throughout the life cycle of products.
- Make the protection of reputation, image, products, and information a strategic focus.
- Create programs that respond to each brand and product individually.
- Remember that threat follows value.

- Ensure that programs enhance bottom-line performance.
- Require companywide participation—it is essential to the process.
- Use brand integrity to keep products alive in the marketplace.

Commitment

- Identify key assets critical to the company.
- Ensure a commitment of time and money by senior management.
- Develop strategic approaches to brand integrity.
- Focus actions to identify risks and threats from both company processes and the marketplace.

Getting the Pieces Together

- Focus corporate energy and resources.
- Provide tools to identify risks and attacks against brands.
- Develop internal responses.
- Educate staff on how they protect the brand.
- Create benchmarked strategies for managing brand integrity programs.
- Blend policy reviews and development with marketplace monitoring and crisis management.

Making It Work for You

- Develop and implement ongoing processes to identify key brand assets.
- Establish, coordinate, and manage brand integrity strategies.
- Conduct ongoing audits to review programs.
- Provide support services to business units.
- Monitor marketplace and competitive products.
- Develop incident response protocols and crisis management programs.
- Institute employee and customer awareness programs.
- Implement brand integrity in the company.

Metrics

- Develop market-driven programs.
- Build competitive advantage into the process.
- Establish product- and brand-focused operations.
- Improve profitability, market share, and margins.
- Maintain customer confidence, and ensure authenticity of products.

- Minimize nonessential corporate expenses and staff.
- Establish employees' stake in program effectiveness.

HOW TO PROCEED

Specific steps need to be taken to ensure that a business can operate effectively in the global marketplace against both government-supported firms and firms in the private sector. The process begins with understanding what needs to be protected. While this sounds simple, it is quite complex. How, for example, do you establish market leadership, licensing agreements, or strategic plans based on a realistic assessment of how much of the company's future profitability you risk by sharing key technology or development programs with high-risk partners or in high-risk situations? These high-risk situations include:

- Working with geopolitically risky firms or countries
- Protecting against attacks targeted toward technology at home
- Establishing a fresh perspective on both defining and protecting key assets
- Protecting against predators focusing on product lines or processes
- Establishing effective anti–gray market pricing policies
- Maintaining global marketplace surveillance over key products
- Aggressively defending brand image, reputation, authenticity, and reliability

Developing a BI strategic plan as a part of the product planning process will go a long way to focus efforts on key risk and threats. Figure 6.1 provides an example of how one company described its BI objectives and corresponding strategies.

In reviewing these strategies and their measurements, it is possible to characterize the operation of this program:

- Based on company values
- Process not program
- Individual and corporate values at the heart of the recommendations
- Matched BI prevention and organizational norms
- Based on a realistic appraisal of needs
- Broad employee involvement in the goals and process

FIGURE 6.1   Product Planning Process

Objective			
To ensure our customers and business partners are supplied with appropriate brands of the highest quality throughout the product life cycle via cross-functional global collaboration			

Goals			
• Reduce diversion and counterfeit while mitigating its risk. • Reduce WW diversion impact to product margin by 10% • Institutionalize regional / functional alignment and compliance with BI program			

Strategies			
Drive brand integrity into all phases of the product life cycle	Develop global / regional legal and regulatory framework to combat BI issues	Improve supply chain integrity and transparency	Create systems and metrics to provide actionable market insight and information to prevent BI issues

Tactics			
• Ensure risk of diversion is mitigated with new-product design and launch • Optimize pricing / portfolio strategies while minimizing diversion • Proactive communication of BI expectations and accountability with internal and external stakeholders	• Take action against offenders of brand integrity • Ensure legal agreements are written with robust BI terms • Create a legal BI template and plan for regional implementation • Audit and enforcement of BI terms	• Identify offenders of brand integrity • BI to influence global supply chain procedures • Develop and apply due diligence criteria to current and future distributors • Internet surveillance and enforcement	• Divert alert software improvement • Create global BI risk matrix • Training on BI issues

Measurements			
• 100% BI sign-off on design and launch of new products • Package authentication by Q4	• Plan milestones achieved • 100% counterfeit & diversion radar screen cases investigated • Use of regional dashboards	• Completion of mail-order pilot by Q4 • U.S. distribution compliant with BI training and WI by Q2 • BI position paper intro by Q2	• Global diversion risk matrix by Q1

The program also establishes a close link between the business strategy and the BI strategy for specific products.

An analytical effort must also be conducted within the company to determine risks, threats, and vulnerabilities for each brand. A global brand

---

POLICY GUIDE: WHAT THE KEY STRATEGIES FOR THE BI EFFORT MIGHT LOOK LIKE

2007 Key Strategies

- Improve supply chain integrity and transparency.
- Move BI into all phases of the product life cycle.
- Develop a regional and global legal framework to manage BI issues.
- Create data systems and metrics to improve BI activities.

integrity program developed and operated at the correct levels must be put into practice. Senior corporate executives must strive to develop a level playing field within the international arena by lobbying for assistance from the government. Remember that while a company can establish an effective brand integrity program, if the key assets are either not properly identified or used as gambling chips to assuage stock analysts, neither the government nor effective internal policies can save the company.

Developing a method to identify what is important to protect is as essential as protecting all technology or activities. It may be costly and may also inhibit the flow of information inside the company, but it is essential. The role of the BI executive in protecting information while ensuring a seamless flow of activity is most important. The development of effective IT and corporate security policy for information access and protection is an essential part of this process.

Collecting bits of information, while useful to a commercial predator, is not as valuable as being able to identify the collected, analyzed, and "approved" locations of information in a target company. The greatest value comes from determining who understands what the information means, how it can be used, and what the company plans to do with it. Consequently, protecting corporate "wisdom" and corporate knowledge is more important than protecting the day-to-day flow of data that comes in and goes out of a company via modem or laptop computer. Few predators have the time or resources to spend casting a big net to collect everything that comes through the modem. Clearly these data sources require protection, but the significant efforts must, of necessity, be focused on the collected, synthesized, refined, and strategically important data that drive the company.

Protecting brand and product assets in a global business environment is the most basic function of senior corporate management. Maximum profitability cannot be achieved unless brand and products are their primary focus. Brand integrity must be a part of the everyday responsibilities of the company executives responsible for product and brand management.

The objectives of a brand integrity program are to retain or improve margins, maintain consumer confidence in products, ensure authenticity of products, and keep the brand alive in the marketplace. The strategic focus of brand integrity for products should follow company profit goals and objectives and use the protection of key brand and product assets to enhance all other management activities.

Implementation methods require the blending of strategic and tactical management with brand integrity in all aspects of daily company management. These programs require product risk reviews, management systems, marketplace monitoring, and crisis management. A regular and ongoing audit program to ensure compliance with strategic plans is essential. Programs should be tailored to the uniqueness of each brand and product and should be designed to enhance bottom-line company financial performance.

If a brand or product is worth something to you, it's worth the same or more to someone else, whether it's your current competition or a new player. If it's not worth anything, don't protect it. If it is, how much is it worth to you? Are you protecting it at an appropriate level of worth and importance?

BEST PRACTICES

- Focus on the most important aspect of the business—keeping the product safe in the market.

- Don't lose sight of what's important—total results, not just quarterly performance.

- You can't maximize profits if you lose daily opportunities to improve results.

- Restructure product life-cycle thinking.

- Analyze the various risks in the product life cycle.

- Develop systems to manage product risks and opportunities.

- Motivate and provide incentives for employee participation in the process.

DASHBOARD QUESTIONS

1. Are our products and brands hard targets?
2. Do we have product protection plans in place?
3. Do we know our product losses?
4. How many product attacks have there been this month? This quarter? This year?

CHAPTER 7

YOUR OWN PRODUCTS
ARE OFTEN YOUR
LARGEST COMPETITORS
FOR PROFITS

Let the seller beware!"

Variation on an old theme

When your own products end up in the gray market, they compete directly with your products, and you end up competing with yourself. Why compete with your own products? Every advertising dollar you spend is helping unauthorized sales as much as yours. There was a time in China when Procter & Gamble determined that 50 percent of its consumer products were counterfeit. By cutting marketing budgets and using those funds for increased enforcement activities, this rate was cut in half within two years.

No company wants to compete with itself. And yet, unfortunately, it is done every day because of poorly designed sales and marketing programs, weak or nonexistent sales controls, and lack of market intelligence. Best-practice programs reduce opportunities for loss, help increase margins and profitability, provide business intelligence, and channel monitoring and decision-making support. To understand what is happening to your products, it is essential to focus best practices, coupled with penetrating gray market operations, on your products.

What should you be trying to do with any antidiversion or gray market activity? Very simply put, the answer is *encourage "good" business and discourage "bad" business*. How do you prevent goods from getting into the gray market? By taking the first-sale rule very seriously. Use the first-sale rule, which essentially says that you cannot control a product after you sell it, as a barrier to prevent gray market products from leaking out of the company. Form the barrier by doing all you can to protect your product *before* you sell it. When this barrier is established, the following will be used to control product leakage:

- Vetting companies early in the relationship
- Monitoring customer activities in the marketplace
- Developing controls to prevent shipping orders to questionable customers
- Providing custom pricing based on "good conduct"
- Instituting worldwide pricing programs

There often is a difference in distribution levels and access to products in large-volume sales. Who makes the deal is again critical to watch, as the first-sale rule applies here as well. The current order approval process for who sells the product to end users and resellers becomes the barrier that needs to be protected by careful vetting.

DO YOU KNOW THE RISK?

Many companies don't have a clear understanding of how bad their brand integrity problems and risk are and don't know what actions to take to protect themselves. Those that have initiatives often don't have a clear understanding of whether or not their brand integrity efforts are working. There are a number of contributing factors that make gray market and diversion a fact of global business and hard to quantify. They include:

- Differential pricing
- Sales incentives based on sales volume
- Sales forecasts that are too aggressive
- Greed
- Lack of employee ethics
- Lax enforcement
- Legal protection

The gray market also has common elements:

- Product arbitrage
- Borderline legal definition
- Margin loss to the product manufacturer

- Distribution problems
- Customer satisfaction
- Pricing problems
- Problems caused by internal factors

The key is not to give away margins but, instead, to return the highest possible long-term shareholder value.

GRAY MARKET PROBLEMS

If you have a gray market problem, do you tell your customers? In most cases it is not necessary, as your customers will probably know it before you do. They will see low prices outside of your normal distribution channels and wonder if the products are real, and not just priced more cheaply than normal. You will also learn about these problems from your regular distributors, who are losing sales to the gray marketers and complain about your pricing. You may also experience more warranty work than sales might otherwise justify, as well as more rebates going out for more products than were originally sold to a distributor—assuming your sales reports can generate this type of information.

In order to lower distribution channel risk from the gray market, it is essential to understand and continually respond to several key issues in sales and marketing and in distribution:

Sales and Marketing

- Understand the background of a customer and the customer due diligence process.
- Understand and qualify the details of an order.
- Understand the consequences of price and terms (e.g., discounts, special orders).
- Understand the end user and how the product is being used.
- Recognize and handle authentic versus nonauthentic products.
- Provide answers that deal with customer questions and issues.

Distribution

- Understand current tracking and tracing technologies.
- Recognize and handle authentic versus nonauthentic product returns.
- Understand the guidelines of the distributor agreements.

- Deal with distributor questions and issues.
- Understand the due diligence process on distributors and distributor audits.
- Understand transportation and delivery controls and logistics.
- Report incidents.

DIFFERENTIAL PRICING

"Everyone loves a bargain"—that is, except the company whose goods are being sold off-price. Gray market products are a serious problem for every type of product and in virtually every market around the world. The problem of the gray market is often thought of as purely a domestic U.S. problem, but it is not. The flow of products is global, not only because of offshore production, but because of the development of markets around the world. Most companies have differential pricing for products based on such factors are government regulations, import duties, cost of living, tariffs, and consumer pricing. Prices tend to be higher in developed countries than in Asian, Middle Eastern, and Latin American countries. Products sent to these countries often are sold for lower prices than in the United States or the European Union to reflect local economic conditions. When these genuine products are reimported into the United States or the European Union, they can consequently be sold for below prevailing U.S. or E.U. prices. The E.U. market encourages parallel importation, but the European Union causes difficulties in managing pricing in other parts of the world.

If we put aside the legality of this reimportation, having the product introduced into the U.S. market creates a dilemma for the manufacturer. Authorized supply chain distributors have prices that are set within the United States for their products. When an authentic product enters the market from unauthorized distribution channels, the price is going to reflect the lower sales price given to distributors outside of the United States. This price may be significantly lower than wholesale prices given in the United States. Reimportation at prices much below the wholesale distribution price in the United States allows products to be sold at retail for prices at or below the legitimate wholesale prices. This means that customers get a *bargain*, but everyone in the distribution and manufacturing supply chain loses significant margin. Large discount retail stores such as Costco often make large purchases of these products, and consumers love it!

Case Study

A large computer peripheral manufacturer sold 200,000 pieces of hardware to the Chinese Ministry of Education in 1999 to equip secondary schools in a large province with computer integration. Within days of the first shipment, identical equipment appeared in gray market channels in the United States at extremely low prices. The Chinese special price was $27 per unit, or approximately 50 percent below the U.S. distributor price of $52 per unit. The gray market products were being sold at retail for $37. The gray marketer sold all the units within days, made a $2 million profit, and went away. It took several months for the U.S. market to stabilize, while both the distributors and manufacturer lost several million dollars in margins.

In 1999 it should have been obvious to company executives that China did not have enough computers in schools to justify this sale. The numbers just did not make sense. Had senior management been concerned about protecting margins, this problem would have been stopped before it began.

It is necessary to have pricing that reflects economic realities around the world. It is not necessary, however, to sell products to people you don't know, at prices that hurt margins, and for purposes that are unclear. It is absolutely essential that brand integrity become a part of the pricing process for the company. Brand integrity is essential around the product, the company, the deal, and the market. Without all four of these dimensions being managed effectively, the risk of price arbitrage, reimportation, and all the related opportunities for loss of supply chain integrity is dramatically increased.

A major side effect of having gray market products is the potential it creates for introducing counterfeits of your products into distribution channels. Off-price authentic goods provide a profit margin for the distributors. If counterfeit products can be added to orders, the margin increases substantially.

Case Study

A well-known prescription medication is produced at a plant in France and sold in the United States and the European Union. Government-controlled selling prices in the European Union created a price differential with the U.S. price of about 35 percent. A gray marketer in the European Union made large purchases of the drug and shipped it to a U.S.-based wholesaler. This wholesaler was approached by an Indian company that claimed to manufacture a generic version of the drug, which it sold for 70 percent off U.S. prices. The Indian company offered to repackage its generic drug in genuine packaging. The wholesaler agreed and began mixing real and generic products in shipments to U.S. pharmacies. After several patients began complaining about the performance of the drugs they were taking, an investigation revealed the scheme and the fact that the purported generic drug had no active ingredients in it.

If the "generic" manufacturer had added a small percentage of active ingredients rather than none, the scheme might have continued for a much longer time. Several cases of this "reduced-strength" scheme have been uncovered in the past three years. Mixing real and nonauthentic goods have been used for dozens of years by distributors.

Case Study

We can remember a case in which airport shops in Asia and Europe were victimized by employees taking real goods from inventory, selling them to friends, and replacing them with knockoffs purchased from stall markets and street vendors. This problem came to light when defects appeared in the products, prompting a significant increase in the volume of customer complaints for airport purchases. The company investigated the problem and uncovered the scheme. The quality crisis—which took its toll on brand image and the company's reputation—was quickly handled by arresting the guilty parties, letting customers exchange their products for genuine ones, and having the company issue a public apology. This was very expensive in time, money, and reputation.

An additional problem that is caused by differential pricing is employee loyalty. The opportunities to make money both as an employee and, in a second career, as a gray marketer place considerable pressure on a sales and marketing executive. Financial expense for the company to replace staff as well as lost margins is a serious problem that can be minimized by closely monitoring employee activities and the market.

Case Study

A large cell-phone manufacturer had a large sales and marketing force in China. A letter alleging unethical behavior by the vice president of marketing was sent to the

U.S. headquarters. An investigation was undertaken to discover if he was receiving kickbacks from customers as alleged in the letter. During the review of the VP's activities, it was determined that he was receiving money from his staff. His staff was getting the kickbacks!

One of the VP's roles was to approve special pricing and OEM deals for his sales staff. He made an arrangement with his staff, of nine sales executives, that they could negotiate special deals with customers and take a percentage of the saving for the client below standard pricing. They would average about 7 percent on each deal. He required them to pay him 2.5 percent of all the money they received. From bank records it was determined that his share for the 2002–2003 year was over US$400,000. He was fired and charged by the local police. The other sales executives were replaced. Lost margin was estimated to be in excess of $20 million.

Differential pricing problems are less likely to take place where the market and participants are really understood. If you know the size of a market, it is unlikely that you are going to approve an off-price sale that ships a 10-year supply of diapers to Darfur, or containers of pantyhose to Liberia. The deal just does not make sense!

Case Study

We investigated a case in which a gray marketer had received a very low price for a "special deal" to ship 20,000 laptop computers for a "secret government project" at the U.S. Pentagon. He had set up a telephone number using a Pentagon extension, and a secretary answered the phone "Special Projects Office." It turned out that the computers were being sold to another country. The gray marketer had made similar special pricing deals with three other computer manufacturers, but none of the other companies had questioned the deal or his credentials. This represented a $10 million loss to the manufacturer. The gray marketer was arrested by the FBI and was charged and convicted of fraud because our client did the proper due diligence.

People make the decisions on special pricing and differential price structures. Make sure that those responsible for these decisions have the interests of the company foremost in their minds. Knowing whom you are doing business with and what they are going to do with your products is vital. Check them out closely before you sell them anything.

Preventing Goods from Getting into the Gray Market

While there are no guarantees, there is a series of best practices that will lower your risk of becoming a victim of the gray market. You will be attacked, but if you follow the first-sale rule and its barrier protection, you will not be a victim. The first-sale rule basically says that once you sell a product and the title transfers to the customer at this point of *first sale*, you no longer can control what the new owner does with it. Figure 7.1 diagrams how a gray market distribution scheme works. Sales are made by the XYZ Corporation to ABC in China, which in turn sells to the DEF Holdings Company, which then sends products to a variety of companies.

The first-sale-rule barrier is between those who make the deal and those who sell the product to end users and resellers. It is therefore critical that any actions you take to prevent your product from entering the gray market take place before this "trigger point." Figure 7.2 provides the organization chart for a simple gray market operation that looks much like an ordinary corporate structure. Vetting potential customers early in a relationship is the single best thing you can do to make sure you know to whom you are going to be selling your products. Develop controls to prevent orders from being shipped to questionable customers, and continually monitor customers' activities in the marketplace. Figure 7.3 provides a flowchart that illustrates how BI controls fit into an approval process.

You want to stop orders before delivery to bad customers. You should provide custom prices based only on good conduct and eliminate employee

FIGURE 7.1   Example of a Gray Market System at Work

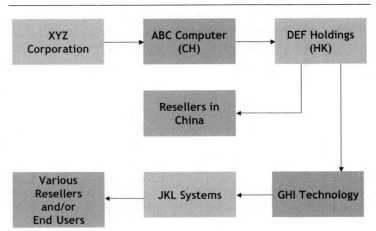

FIGURE 7.2   How a Gray Market System Operates

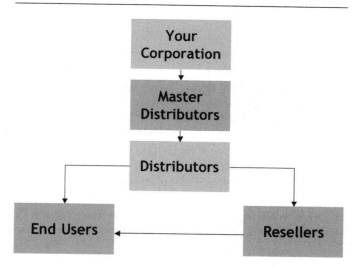

incentives to falsify sales. All these techniques provide checkpoints and alarms along the way between order and delivery. However, the single best way—the only sure way—to avoid any products getting into the gray market is to establish worldwide pricing and vet the deal.

FIGURE 7.3   How Brand integrity Can Fit into the Approval Process

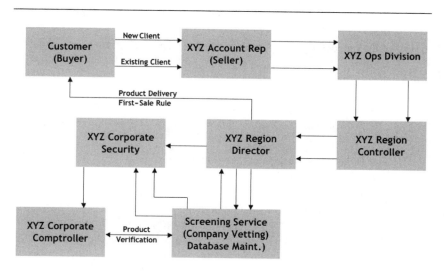

Case Study

Company B makes contact with Company A, or directly with a Company A employee, expressing the desire to either place an order or become a distributor, OEM, or PC builder. Company A assigns Company B a salesperson to handle the account.

The Company A salesperson will meet with the Company B representative, if possible, and get the basic background of the company. In addition, the Company A salesperson will ask the Company B representative a number of yes-or-no questions. The purpose of these questions is to decide if Company B fits a predetermined profile of a company possibly involved in the gray market.

If the answers to the questions show that the company may be involved in the gray market, then the following course of action should be taken:

1. If Company B is placing an order, the Company A salesperson will explain to the potential client that before the order can be shipped, the client has to:
   a. Fill out a company biographical data sheet (bio sheet). This form will provide Company A with a complete background on Company B.
   b. Provide Company A with a preprinted annual report and/or company profile, if available.
   c. Return the bio sheet to the Company A salesperson assigned to the client.
2. The Company A salesperson will then forward the bio sheet to her supervisor for approval.
3. The Company A supervisor then sends the bio sheet to an investigator to conduct a limited background check on Company B and its principals. (Time frame: three days maximum.)
4. The Company A supervisor will either approve or deny the order based on the criteria agreed upon by Company A's upper management and the report provided by the investigator.
5. If the supervisor gives the approval to Company B, then the order can be shipped.
6. If the supervisor does not give the approval, then the order is denied.

If the answers to the yes-or-no questions show that Company B is most likely not involved in the gray market, then the following course of action should be taken:

1. The Company A salesperson takes the order.
2. The company biographical data sheet is given to Company B with instructions to return it, completed, within 10 days.
3. The order is sent to the Company A salesperson's supervisor for approval. The approval or denial of the order should be given within 24 hours. The supervisor will make a decision to approve or deny the order based on the criteria agreed upon by the company's upper management.

COMPANY BIOGRAPHICAL DATA SHEET

Name of company

Address

Phone number

Fax number

Number of years in business

Dunn & Bradstreet listing

Dba's or fictitious business names

Key personnel:

   Owner

   Directors

   Managers

Branch Offices: ❏ *Yes*   *or*   ❏No

   Address

   Phone and fax

   Person in charge

Subsidiaries: ❏ *Yes*   *or*   ❏No

   Address

   Phone and fax

   Person in charge

Brief description of business

Estimate of quantity of product to be ordered per year

Sales for the last five years (per year)

Estimated sales for this year

Estimated sales for the next five years (per year)

Referred clients and customers

Let's take a look at the effect that differential pricing has on the various aspects of brand integrity. Using our brand integrity model of product, deal, market, and company, let's follow a product through the distribution supply chain.

Case Study

Computer peripherals are a hot commodity around the world. Networking computers are required everywhere, and manufacturers are often pressed to produce enough products. So pricing is an issue, and differential pricing has become a major issue for all companies in this market.

The salespeople for CNC (the company in our case study) were compensated for volume of sales in their geographical regions. Production was done in four major facilities around the world. Discounts for OEM use, large-distributor discounts, institutional discounts, special pricing deals for large installations, government contracts, and so on, were all in use globally. It very quickly became apparent to CNC executives that their products were becoming available in the U.S. and E.U. markets at very low prices, causing distributors and direct sales products to lose their competitive edge. Sales program patterns became known to distributors, who waited until the end of the quarter and pushed sales executives for greater and greater discounts. The salespeople found ways to comply so that they could make their sales goals. Former sales executives resigned to become distributors and became wealthy manipulating the sales program. Clever arbitrage became a way of life for these commodities to the detriment of CNC.

To meet the demand for products, several third-party manufacturing contracts were initiated to get additional products for distribution. As these third-party facilities began producing, a flood of very low-price goods began inundating the market in the United States, European Union, and Asia.

An investigation was conducted to develop a picture of how the products were getting into these low-cost sales. It was determined that the products were being sold to companies and individuals that had learned how to "game" the sales programs, discounts, and rebate offers. In 2001, $200 million in lost margins could be attributed to these attacks during one quarter alone. The demand that these low-price sales created for low-price goods spawned a very aggressive Asian counterfeit market for CNC products. At the peak of the problem, there were five price structures for CNC products: authentic, refurbished, nongenuine, nonauthentic, and counterfeit. Prices depended on how close to the real functionality of the genuine CNC product the crooks wanted the product to be! Customers became confused and could not tell real from nongenuine products, causing massive drops in sales. Even CNC salespeople couldn't distinguish real from nongenuine products.

It took a massive revision of pricing, production, and distribution controls to correct these problems. Investigative costs topped several million dollars and resulted in hundreds of arrests, numerous civil actions, and destruction of counterfeit goods. The problem of enforcement was made very difficult by the use of third-party manufacturers as it became increasingly difficult to positively identify CNC products: different factories were using different components, and components had no identification markings.

LESSONS LEARNED

Product

A successful product will continue to be successful only if it is carefully managed during its initial growth. Too many price levels, too many special deals, and compensation based on sales rather than profits are all counterproductive to long-term profitability. Keeping control over production and establishing uniform specifications for products, wherever they are produced, are both essential.

Company

The company was slow in recognizing that it had a problem. Once it did, it acted quickly to identify the root causes and change operating systems, controls, and production standards—but, unfortunately, not before a serious loss of revenue, image, and reputation occurred. The company discovered that while it was interested in making and selling a quality product, it had become a target for exploitation by people who wanted all the company's profits.

Deal

Pricing deals were the root cause of CNC's problems. They were compounded by market forces, exploitation of control systems, and clever businesspeople. Sales and credit executives were concerned about making the sale and getting the prices approved by internal systems and controls. As long as goals were being met, they saw no problems. Gray marketers, by the dozens, were, however, looking for increasingly creative ways to squeeze additional profits from deals. Nobody inside the company was focused on these attacks, while an entire industry was arrayed against the company, trying to steal its profits.

After the investigation, the products were no longer sold outside of tightly controlled channels, special pricing was extremely difficult to have approved, and end-user verification was conducted on all sales.

Market

It took a long time for the magnitude of the problem to become known at the executive levels in CNC. The market was happy until authorized CNC dealers were having their preferential pricing undercut by the gray market. Once a monitoring program was instituted for the market, price disparities were available daily, anomalies in product availability in gray market channels were recorded weekly, and the product source was traced quickly. Gray market sales slowed dramatically, and so did nongenuine sales.

While this example is from the electronics industry, we have handled a wide range of products, including diapers, cigarettes, drugs, alcohol, agricultural chemicals, industrial paints and coating, aircraft components, automobile parts, cosmetics, and more. All industries have similar problems and economics. All distribution channels are susceptible to gray market products and consequently counterfeit goods. Some products are, however, more prone to being counterfeited just because demand is great and counterfeits can be produced more cheaply than buying the authentic product and reselling it.

DIFFERENTIAL PRICING—A FACT OF BUSINESS

Differential pricing is a fact of business: different prices are required in different markets. What is important to remember is that an attractive product will be analyzed by the market to see how a profit can be made by manipulating distribution and sales programs. Since it all comes down to margin, how many pricing levels you have and what the price spread is between the highest and lowest price will determine your risk to arbitrage. Margin expectations are different in each business, and so how these prices are set will signal your vulnerability.

How Do Programs Work?

A comprehensive sales management program will lower gray market risk and the associated introduction of counterfeit products into channels. The key features of this program require you to:

- Know the customer.
- Understand the deal.
- Monitor the marketplace.
- Enforce your policies.
- Manage sales and marketing activities.
- Establish product identification and control.
- Share information with others.

Know the Customer   Simple and effective measures can identify questionable customers. These three steps will quickly provide a "go–no-go" test for a potential customer.

1. Do basic due diligence reviews and charting of all associated persons and entities to confirm the real identity of the potential customers.
2. Check the names against known diverters and restricted buyer lists.
3. Verify "ship-to" and "bill-to" data, and investigate anomalies.

Obtaining legal histories and conducting site visits should also be done before the first order is shipped. If you have all due diligence data available, it is very helpful to use a relational database and a link analysis program to cross-check C.O.P.E. data (C.O.P.E. is explained in a section below).

Case Study

We had a client company that used link analysis for checking all new orders for its products. The vice president of sales would not sign off on a special deal or a new customer without seeing a "spaghetti chart." In fact, he seldom wanted to see the written report of our findings, preferring to visually understand the relationships of any entity that the company was planning to have as a channel partner. Often the relationships shown didn't make much sense to us, but very often they provided the aha! moment for the client when he saw how a potential customer was trying to hide a relationship in a deal.

Case Study

A new client became very concerned about its sales program when it discovered that its single largest competitor in three key markets was its own products sold on the gray market. The company estimated that it was losing about $35 million a quarter in lost sales! How did this happen? Very simply: the sales staff was compensated on the total sales revenue, not margins produced. Aggressive sales forecasts put pressure for sales that were so high that selling to discount brokers became essential for salespeople to make their sales quotas and meet Wall Street expectations. They had no concern about the effect these sales had on other sales regions in the company. They were able to make their numbers, and that was what mattered.

Understand the Deal   Verify the ability of the potential customer to use the product for the purposes stated. Are meet-the-competition pricing, special deals, and other pricing valid for this customer? Do rebate programs operate as designed, and are your incentive programs carefully monitored? Could your customer use 100,000 computers for a school in China? Can you install 50,000 converter boxes in Lagos? If the deal does not sound right, it probably isn't!

Monitor the Marketplace   It is essential to track shipments from the production facility to the end users to verify the supply chain. Monitor the Internet for products and price anomalies to identify gray market products that quickly appear in the marketplace. Take prompt remedial action. Purchase sample products from Internet sources considered questionable so that you can determine their source and authenticity. Continually collect intelligence about customer mergers, acquisitions, and new ventures.

Covert penetration of gray market operations often requires "front" purchasing companies around the world that are viewed as a part of the gray market system and trusted by the bad guys. It is essential that these front companies get on the lists to do business and get requests from the bad guys to buy products. These penetration activities permit the front companies to collect intelligence as well as purchase your products. This global "honesty shopping" provides real-time tracking of product movement and activity. The front companies also monitor the Internet for product distribution and pricing intelligence. The data they provide can be incorporated into a database of active gray market players and pricing trends.

Enforce Your Policies   Conduct training and awareness programs about diversion and gray market prevention activities for company sales staff as well as OEMs, customers, and distributors. Covertly purchase your products on a regular basis from the diverter–gray market community. Use stings, buy-and-bust, and deception operations against known gray marketers. Lastly, take civil or criminal legal actions, request customs seizures, and demand differential price repayments from diverters.

Manage Sales and Marketing Activities   The first step in getting and maintaining control over the sales program is to review sales procedures and contract language and remove "gray market–friendly" language. Restrictions on where goods can be sold, conditions for sales and resale pricing, and so forth, all lower risk and increase chances for recovery of margins. Tighten controls and procedures for programs involving large discounts, and check for fraud and or misrepresentations by employees and customers.

Review all your sales procedures and contract forms. Train staff to use due diligence inquiries for all new customers or unusual deals with existing customers. Monitor staff actions and customer information and dealings for fraud or misrepresentations. Ensure that employee compensation programs, rebate programs, and discounts do not encourage fraud or abuses leading to gray market goods. Lastly, introduce ethics programs for staff, along with enforcement of all employee conduct standards.

Establish Product Identification and Control   Enforcement of ownership rights is not possible without your being able to positively identify products. Establishing a clear marking, coding, and tracking system is essential, along with maintaining tight controls over product quality and adherence to design and manufacturing specifications. This is especially important for rebate claims associated with special pricing deals. The ability to identify the real product from clones and unauthorized but licensed products is extremely important. If not already in place, establish and enforce security standards and controls for the contract manufacturers.

Case Study

A Japanese client was producing chips in a Malaysian manufacturing plant. It encountered quality problems with one batch of chips and scrapped them (but kept a list of the serial numbers). Instead of the chips being crushed as required, some employees falsified the destruction records and sold the chips to a counterfeiting ring. The chips were included in counterfeit motherboards that were sold to an OEM as genuine equipment from another Japanese firm. Very soon after they were sold, a high failure rate of the product was noted by the warranty department. In addition, there were several production shutdowns in manufacturing facilities caused by the failure of this critical component. Several insurance claims were filed for lost production time traced to the defective product.

We determined that employees had stolen the defective parts, and we obtained admissions of their involvement in the scheme that violated company QC standards. The list of serial numbers for the products that were supposed to be destroyed, but were not, was a crucial factor in placing blame where it should be, not with our client.

Share Information with Others   If you belong to an association or trade group dealing with gray market and counterfeit problems, it is essential that information about new attacks, known diverters, and tactics be shared with other members. The method used for sharing must be consistent with state and federal regulations covering information sharing, restraint of trade, and privacy. Public relations and advertising campaigns to end users as well as distributor education and involvement are essential. Training employees based on real-time data and giving high visibility to aggressive prosecution of violations of compliance and product diversion matters will highlight your image as a hard target.

C.O.P.E.

Sales Controls Using the C.O.P.E. Program

Over the years we have developed indicators that identify gray market risk. They relate to the following factors involved in the sale of products:

Company
Order
Person
End user

Company Indicators

- The company is unknown to you.
- It has recently been established.
- It has recently changed its name (but has the same ownership).
- It has recently changed ownership.
- It has recently changed ownership and changed its name.
- It has one or more subsidiaries (local, national, and global).
- It has recently set up subsidiary companies.
- It shares an address(es) with other companies in a similar industry.
- It has links to another company or companies *not* through ownership, or it shares employees (family).
- Its market is primarily international (it is looking to acquire products at cheaper rates).
- Its facilities do not justify the ordered products.

Order Indicators

- The first order for the company is unusually large.
- The company ordered only one specific product.
- The order does not make sense (e.g., too large for the claimed purpose).
- The company requested special pricing.
- The company required immediate shipping.

Person Indicators

- One or more of the directors of the company is a director of one or more other companies.
- The company has directors, owners, and/or employees with relatives working at your company.
- The company's directors, owners, and/or employees have personal relationships with employees of your company.
- Some of the company's employees are former employees of your company.

End-User Indicators

- The company is a subsidiary of a purchasing company.
- The company is located in a country other than the country in which the order was placed.
- The company is a government agency; and even though it has never bought your products before, it is placing a large order.
- The company is a reseller and claims that the end user is confidential or that the product is for a confidential project.

C.O.P.E. Questions

Detailed questions about each of these indicators have also been developed to help highlight inconsistencies or anomalies. Developing the specific indicators that trigger questions about your particular products is up to you. Read through these lists, and ask the questions. In fact, all these questions should be resolved before you ship to anyone.

Company

- Is the company in your database?
- Has the company profile been completely filled out?
- Who are the directors?

- When was the company formed?
- Does the company have subsidiaries or branch offices locally, nationally, or in other countries?
- Where are the company's primary markets?
- What are its channels of distribution?
- What shippers does it use?
- Has the company ever been involved in any civil or criminal litigations or proceedings?
- Has the company provided your company with a recent financial statement?
- Who are the company's clients and customers?
- Has there been a change of ownership within the last year?
- Has the company changed its name in the last year?
- Would the company report to you anyone who approaches it to provide gray market goods?
- Would the company be willing to use a preselected group of shippers?
- Would the company agree to a biannual audit by your company?
- Would the company agree to a visit at its offices and facilities by a representative of your company?
- Would the company be willing to reimburse you for products sold to it that are found on the gray market?
- Would the company object to a background investigation?
- Has the company moved to new facilities within the last year?

Order

- What is the size of the order?
- Does the order make sense for the customer?
- What product is being ordered?
- Are the bill-to and ship-to information the same?
- Are there questionable shipping instructions, shippers, or forwarders?
- How will the company use your products?
- Does the company want your products because of the price or because of their quality?
- Is a new freight forwarder being used?

Person

- What interest (ownership, directorship, employee) does the company itself and everyone in the company have in other companies?

- Does the company have ties with or are any employees in the company related to anyone who works at your company?
- Do family members or any of the employees work for the company's competition?
- Are any of the company's current employees former employees of your company?

End User

- Would the company object if you verified all orders over X number of products?
- Has the company verified the end users' ability to legally use or acquire products?
- How will your products be used?
- Does the company meet your compliance department's standards and qualifications to purchase the product?

Ask lots of questions even if you think you might not like the answers. Stopping an order before it is shipped might seem counterproductive; you're losing a sale. But not asking the questions can cause you to lose your market completely. Monitoring inside your sales program is as critical as monitoring the external marketplace. The more information you have specific to your products, the more informed a decision you can make about pricing, production, and customer requirements.

Protecting products and brands starts and ends with you, your approach to the market, and the amount of risk you are willing to take. While the risks are certainly present in the market, the tools are available for you to set up programs and protect your brands and products. The decision to do it is yours.

BEST PRACTICES

- Institute a customer screening process.

- Understand risks to your products in key markets.

- Establish product identification criteria.

- Monitor your products in the market.

- Take aggressive enforcement actions when your products are attacked.

- Use the C.O.P.E. process throughout sales and marketing.

DASHBOARD QUESTIONS

1. Are C.O.P.E. questions used in the sales process?
2. Are pricing and product analysis data collected from the market?
3. How many gray market attacks did you suffer this month? This quarter? This year?
4. What was the value of gray market margin loss this month? This quarter? This year?

CHAPTER 8

CONTINUALLY MONITOR THE MARKETPLACE TO LOWER RISKS AND INCREASE PROFITS

You don't know what you don't know.

Anonymous

Each type of product being manufactured has inherent marketplace risks that need to be identified and prioritized. These major risks include:

- Life safety (drugs, food, chemicals, aircraft parts, medical devices, etc.)
- Product safety (cosmetics, baby products, automotive equipment, fire-resistant clothing)
- Products that are outdated (old products, past expiration dates, returned or scrapped products)
- Counterfeiting (reputation risks, poor quality, good quality/low price, etc.)
- Gray market traffic (off-price authentic products, nonauthorized sources, etc.)

Monitoring for each of these risk categories requires that you be able to:

- Track your own products in the global marketplace. What's happening to your stuff?
- Understand your own supply chain. How is your supply chain working?

- Understand the open market for competitive products. How are your products being treated by the competition?
- Track your products in the virtual market. What does the cyber marketplace do with your products?

A monitoring program may be required for each of these categories, depending on what a risk analysis of your products, supply chain, e-commerce, or marketplace indicates is necessary. The techniques for marketplace monitoring can be adapted to any of these risk categories.

Take the initiative and operate your business as though you are constantly under attack by a determined opponent—because you are. In the *Art of War*, Sun Tze bases much of the success of a commander on understanding the nature of the opposing forces, the battlefield, and the state of the opposition's readiness. A business executive who does not have a system for continually collecting reliable, timely, and competitive and marketplace information is going to be attacked without warning and is at a great disadvantage.

KNOW YOUR MARKETS

Competition is everywhere, markets are everywhere, and the farther away from your headquarters you are, the more likely someone is trying to find a way to sell your products without your knowledge. It is essential that you know where your markets are, how they are treating your products, who is selling and distributing your products, who the ultimate users are, and what prices are being charged in the market and on the Internet.

Monitoring the market can be a big or small job, depending on the number of products, the geographical distribution, the history of abuse or attacks, and the attitude of management toward understanding the opportunities and risks present. You can do it yourself, hire consulting firms to conduct market surveys, use investigative firms to purchase products to test for authenticity, conduct continual market surveillance programs, and/ or hire others to surf the Internet and gather information from employees. Internet surveillance is often essential to understanding how your trademarks, names, and products are appearing. Visiting buying sites such as eBay and Shopping.com and closed sites used by gray marketers is often an integral part of these programs. There are numerous options for marketplace monitoring that include:

- Electronic commerce monitoring (e-shopping)
- Trademark, name, product, and logo searches
- Targeted purchasing of products from e-sellers
- Market monitoring firms
- Bounty hunters
- Electronic commerce and field purchasing
- Targeted purchasing programs
- Private investigation firms
- Honesty shoppers
- Market research firms
- Internal market research departments
- Business intelligence departments
- Market monitoring for competitive products
- Employee tips and information

How much or how little you do is often determined by how much you either want or need to know about your product in the market. Market surveillance is often done on an ad hoc basis by sales executives either talking to customers or distributors who have a vested interest in knowing how your products are being sold or responding to disgruntled customers who purchase problem products and complain. This basic approach to marketplace surveillance works well if the risk is perceived to be low and there are no issues on the horizon. Information about competitive products is often obtained through those these channels as well. At the other end of the spectrum is a comprehensive competitive intelligence staff working with R&D, marketing, and strategic planning to provide real-time threat and opportunity information.

The difference between a *threat in* the market and a *treat for* your sales staff is not just the letter *h* representing *hope* (as in things will turn out OK) or *haphazard*. It represents *hard data*. If you "don't know what you don't know," it is difficult to collect the hard data needed to turn threats into treats or prevent what are thought to be treats (a high sales volume to a gray marketer) from turning into a threat (to your margins).

When a distributor complains or a defective product appears, the basic approach may not be sufficient to develop a comprehensive picture of the market situation. How much time and effort is put into market surveillance is directly related to how much pain the company is willing to accept before spending time and money for a specific surveillance program. The amount of loss from out-of-channel products must usually reach a certain threshold before programs are developed. That threshold is a moving target and is often determined on a case-by-case, product-by-product basis.

Case Study

A customer from Florida returns a partially used bottle of shampoo purchased at a large discount store to the Consumer Complaint Department with a note that says "This shampoo is too watery." The Quality Assurance Department tests the product and determines that it is counterfeit and is contaminated with bacteria. An investigation was initiated to identify where the product was purchased and how it got to that discounter. During the investigation it was determined that thousands of cases of this same product were shipped continually from China to a well-known gray market drug and cosmetic distributor in the United States using false importation documents. The counterfeit shampoo was seized by customs, and the factory producing the shampoo was located in southern China, raided, and closed down. Since this counterfeit posed both an economic and a public health risk, a continual monitoring program was established to get early warning of any new attempts to counterfeit and distribute shampoo products.

GET SOLID MARKETPLACE DATA

If you decide that good marketplace data are needed for your business, how do you get the data at the right volume, quality, and price? Like any other business requirements, you must first analyze what data you need to understand the forces arrayed against your products and operations. "How much information is enough?" is a classic problem of all intelligence and investigative agencies. The National Security Agency collects so much data that it is difficult to find what it is looking for without extremely sophisticated computing power and software. The CIA, DIA, and Homeland Security collect extensive information that must be analyzed against risk and threat objectives and program goals. A business also needs to know the competition, the market, and sales data. How much information is enough?

Intelligence agencies closely guard their sources and methods for collecting information, as exposing these provides clues about what they think is important to monitor and where they are getting their information. Reliability of the data is also very important in order to have confidence in the information that is collected. Consequently both overt (open source) and covert (secret) collection methods are used. Business data collection must follow the same model if a company wants to be successful. The difference is that business collection relies more on open sources than on covert collection, although the manner in which the investigation is done can make a significant difference in the quality of data.

There are several business operation areas that require good information:

- Market research on an existing product
- New-product development
- Competitive intelligence
- Business processes such as credit, deal-making and end-user verifications, and compliance with government regulations
- Attack mitigation such as counterfeit and gray market investigations
- Legal enforcement such as patent infringements and trademark violations

Each of these has specific goals and objectives for the data, and for each, there are often well-defined methodologies for information collection. Getting reliable information in areas where there are deliberate attempts to mislead or subvert standard business practices requires more aggressive techniques than those normally used to obtain comparable information in the course of day-to-day business operations. For example, if a gray marketer poses as a legitimate distributor and claims to have a warehouse but operates from a small home office, this might not show up on a normal credit report. You can find this out only by sending someone to the location and physically inspecting it. If OEMs say that they are producing 10,000 computer towers per month, only a visit to the factory will give an accurate assessment. Taking the extra information-collection step, although adding cost to a business process, will, more often than not, save lost margins to the gray market.

One of the key results of an effective marketplace monitoring program is to narrow the time a nonauthentic product is in a global trade channel before being identified by the owner of the original product. The quicker nonauthentic products can be found, the lower the risk to reputation and customer safety. If the products being sold in the gray market are authentic rather than counterfeit, out-of-date, or improperly labeled products, finding them quickly will lower the erosion of margin loss.

Case Study

A major supplier of surgical products received a call from U.S. Customs that it was holding a shipment of its products in a Miami customs warehouse for collection. Since no products were made outside the United States, an employee was sent to the warehouse to look at the merchandise arriving from Russia. It was soon determined that the products were counterfeit and had been mistakenly addressed to the original company rather than the intended nonauthentic market channel by a worker in the counterfeiting plant in Russia.

   An investigation quickly identified the maker of the product in Russia and the intended seller in the United States. Both were shortly put out of business, at least for that product line. The entire situation was resolved in less than 30 days.

Case Study

The manufacturer of automotive aftermarket products learned that an unidentified company in the Middle East had for several months been selling containers of brake fluid that contained water instead of the original fluid. Rather than initiating an immediate investigation and possible recall of the fluid, the legal department wrote a letter to the U.S. Chamber of Commerce in the capital city of that country and asked if it could help identify the source of this counterfeit product. The problem continued for several months while letters were sent back and forth with no results. When this approach proved fruitless, an investigation took place. Within a week the source was identified, and the local police raided and shuttered the plant. Fortunately there were no known reports of accidents or injuries. As in most cases of this nature, the use of a chamber of commerce for resolving counterfeit cases is just not effective. It can sometimes assist with governmental relations but not problem solving.

Case Study

A small company in the southwest part of the United States was the sole producer of a pump used in oil well operations. In 1999 it received an inquiry about its product from a company in China and sold a sample to it for field testing in advance of a sizable order. Since each pump sold for in excess of $250,000, it was not an unusual request to buy just one for testing. The U.S. company never heard back from the Chinese firm, but in 2001 it noticed a major drop in sales in Europe and the Middle East. By 2003 its sales *almost stopped completely. It could not understand what had happened until one of its old customers sent in a pump for repairs and refurbishing and the company discovered that the pump was a counterfeit. Once the company discovered that pump, it began investigating and found that the Chinese company had stolen its design, had set up a European company with a name similar to the original one, and had been selling the pumps at a steep discount for the past four years. By the time the company identified the problem, the only work it had was repairing the counterfeit pumps and could not continue operations. The owners subsequently closed the company and began another, unrelated, business.*

Authors Note: As it was closing the plant, another Chinese company tried to purchase some "samples" of a key component from it, claiming that the original was defective. This was one of the components that had not been functioning properly in the pumps that had been returned for servicing. Apparently that component had not been copied properly, and the Chinese company was trying to get another "good sample" to complete a better-quality copy!

INDUSTRY GROUP INITIATIVES

Some companies try to do everything themselves, while others band together into industry groups to collect information and solve problems together. Groups such as the Business Software Alliance (BSA), the International Anti-Counterfeiting Coalition, and the Anti-Gray Market Alliance (AGMA) all attempt to deal with information collection and enforcement for specific industries or issues. While collective groups can provide some assistance, it is still an individual company's decision to determine how much and what kinds of data are specifically required.

Business Software Alliance

The Business Software Alliance is the foremost organization dedicated to promoting a safe and legal digital world. BSA is the voice of the world's commercial software industry before governments and in the international marketplace. Its members represent one of the fastest-growing industries in the world. BSA educates consumers on software management and copyright protection, cybersecurity, trade, e-commerce, and other Internet-related issues. Established in 1988, BSA has programs in more than 80 countries. BSA can be reached at www.bsa.org/usa/.

Anti-Gray Market Alliance

The Anti-Gray Market Alliance was established by a group of major high-technology firms to analyze the adverse effects of fraud and unauthorized product diversion on brand integrity and consumer confidence and to develop or maintain information that permits individual companies to easily identify these activities and, ultimately, to ensure the delivery of high quality and value to the consumers who purchase and use their products.

Manufacturers and sellers of high-technology products (and, by extension, consumers of these products) continually fall victim to fraud and unauthorized product diversion. For example, certain companies and individuals present false information or false documents to order fraudulently obtained discounts on high-technology products. Fraud can also take the form of sales of counterfeit products or products configured or designed for uses different from those for which they are ultimately sold by certain third parties. Problems with unauthorized product diversion—sometimes referred to as the gray market—arise because of this fraudulent activity.

U.S. Government Piracy and Counterfeiting Initiatives

The U.S. copyright industry estimates that global losses from piracy overseas amount to approximately $30–35 billion per year. Copyright piracy is most prevalent in the area of music CDs, movie videos, VCDs and DVDs, business software and some illegal copying of books and other printed materials. The parties responsible for this piracy are often organized crime groups with ties to many other nefarious activities. The State Department's Office of Intellectual Property Enforcement conducts anti-piracy efforts on its own and with other U.S. Government agencies involved in combating piracy and counterfeiting, such as the Copyright Office (part of the Library of Congress), the U.S. Patent and Trademark Office, and the Departments of Justice and Commerce. The State Department also works with many U.S. industry organizations such as the Recording Industry Association of America (RIAA), the Motion Picture Association of America (MPAA), and the International Anti-Counterfeiting Coalition (IACC). Anti-piracy efforts include assisting foreign governments in drafting copyright legislation, training of foreign officials charged with enforcing laws to combat piracy, assisting judicial officials in prosecuting pirates, disseminating information on the prevalence and repercussions of piracy, coordinating IPR training efforts, supporting public awareness campaigns and educational efforts and training State Department officers overseas to be better advocates on IPR issues.

U.S. Department of State, 2006

There are several models that can be used to collect, process, and analyze information: do-it-yourself is one, purchase of services is another, and then there is a combination of the two. There is no good method to help determine what will work best for you. Some Fortune 500 companies "do it themselves," while others purchase 95 percent of the services they need, and still others have collaborative relationships with investigative and research firms. No matter the model, the same issues must be confronted:

- Market availability of products in geographical areas, on Internet sites, and in distribution channels
- Pricing by geography, distributor, reseller, end user, or the Internet
- Verification of data for distributors, end users, and resellers
- Product purchasing and supply chain integrity testing

There may be situations in which all these issues are relevant to your company, but in normal day-to-day operations, elaborate programs are not required. The elements included in comprehensive programs can be modified and either purchased or done jointly. Most are better not done alone.

INTERNAL STAFF POSITIONS

Some companies have established internal positions to monitor the marketplace. The major purpose of such a position in a large company would be to monitor company products in worldwide markets to ensure that the products reach customers at established prices through authorized channels. An ongoing program to monitor the effectiveness of brand integrity programs in the marketplace is essential. It should coordinate and manage a centralized marketplace monitoring system. Outsourced investigative and other monitoring services will likely be used to carry out these activities.

The following components are necessary for a comprehensive plan to collect information in regard to pricing, channel distribution, and gray market activities:

- At least two people are required to monitor all available open sources and routinely report their findings in spreadsheet form to the applicable company management. Sources to be checked would include broker sites, flyers, Internet mailings, and buyers. Also, these people would purchase products from targeted companies and might also make purchases should any special pricing deals arise.
- Additional purchasing should also be made by two other covert buyers on a regular basis.
- Various shipping locations should be utilized as drop-off points for the purchases, and these buyers should be responsible for checking on the returns and recording serial numbers.
- Brief background investigations or end-user verifications must be done on all new companies. All other investigative work is commenced only as directed by company staff.

A minimum number of purchases should be required each quarter to adequately test the various channels under review in a region. This number is to be established with each company so that purchasing plans can be established for each "buyer." This will also require that covert buyers be provided with updated price information, as well as information about special orders for the products to be monitored, any special relationships that member companies have with the resellers being tested, and any new customers that should be tested during the quarter.

Comprehensive Purchasing and Market Surveillance Plan

The example discussed in the following policy guide describes part of a comprehensive purchasing and market surveillance program that was conducted over an extended period of time for a major electronics manufacturer with a severe gray market and counterfeit problem. This portion of the investigation was to determine the extent of the gray market activity with respect to specific SKUs. Another targeted investigation was conducted to determine the source of the counterfeit products.

POLICY GUIDE: GRAY MARKET MONITORING PLAN

The purpose of the project was to collect data and intelligence concerning channel distribution and activity related to designated products for the company's World Wide Compliance Group. A systematic and ongoing purchasing program focused on distributors, brokers, and resellers that advertised and sold company products without authorization and that were suspected of being involved in gray market sales. This purchasing project was strictly for information gathering and not for any type of enforcement action.

Data were collected from open as well as closed sources, bulletin boards, reseller networks, and personal contacts that were established within the reseller community. Information on product availability, advertised pricing versus actual pricing, and "street intelligence" were collected.

Comparable data were also collected on similar competitive products in the marketplace. The additional information provided reference points for determining the impact of the special pricing deals, discounts, and rebates requested by sales and marketing staff.

Operational Plan

Companies were selected quarterly, either by region or because of past activity. The company's World Wide Compliance Group provided its target list to the investigator. Occasionally, new resellers were identified as "targets of opportunity," and they were approached by the investigator's buyers. Additionally, other sources known to the company were from time to time added to these lists for data collection, purchasing, and market analysis actions.

Purchases from the targeted companies were made on a systematic basis during each quarter. Repetitive purchasing allowed each product buyer the opportunity to develop a relationship with the company and also gave them the appearance of being legitimate brokers. Since many of the gray market sources work only through personal contacts, relationships were maintained throughout the year to keep the flow of information positive and minimize the likelihood that the investigator's activities would be uncovered. Continual contact with the resellers also enhanced data and intelligence collection and provided real feedback not available with one-off purchasing.

Reporting

The spreadsheet in Figure 8.1 presents a sample of the type of information provided to the company using the investigator's data collection program. This spreadsheet may require adjusting from time to time to accommodate

FIGURE 8.1 Gray Market Tracking Spreadsheet

Person	Account	Date	Item Purchased	Price	Quantity	Total, US$	Comments
Herb	Com Micro						
Dolph	XYZ Computer	21-Oct-99					Hatch quoted $50
Dolph	XYZ Computer	22-Oct-99					Negotiated buy at $49
Jason	XYZ Computer	25-Oct-99	3C905-TX-M	$49.00	100		Issued formal purchase order, obtained bank check
Dolph	XYZ Computer	28-Oct-99					Got shipment from receiving point. Included 100 sets of 2 floppy disks, packed in a separate carton
Dolph	XYZ Computer	29-Oct-99					Processed shipment and reshipped to client at UPS office
John	CDE Plus	06-Oct-99					Roh quoted $52/60 $50/100 $46/500 since they are a direct distributor of The Company
Dolph	CDE Plus	21-Oct-99					Contacted
Kris	CDE Plus	22-Oct-99					Negotiated buy at $49
Dolph	CDE Plus	25-Oct-99					Followed up with CDE Plus reshipping
Dolph	CDE Plus	26-Oct-99					Follow up
Jason	CDE Plus	28-Oct-99					Follow up
Dolph	CDE Plus	29-Oct-99					Follow up
Dolph	CDE Plus	02-Nov-99					Follow up phone calls
Herb	LAN Plus	03-Nov-99					Follow up phone calls

new information or changes that are necessary to provide information that is timely, valuable, and important for company decision making.

A pricing survey was completed weekly by each agent buying for the investigator. The data were provided to the company weekly so that adjustments to the program could be made swiftly in accordance with the data collection needs of the company.

Data Provided to the Investigator

The client provided the investigator with the following information:

1. The World Wide Compliance Group supplied a list of distributors and companies to be targeted during the quarter. If contact numbers and background information about the company were not available, a brief background investigation was conducted. It was important for the investigator's buyer to know something about the company and staff if a new relationship needed to be developed. All information obtained during this inquiry was given to the company.

2. The products to be purchased were also identified by the company, and the investigator was advised of any special requirements or information related to these products that would affect the buying process. The investigator reported any unusual considerations discovered while purchasing. Such considerations included sudden high volumes of products being available, changes in demand for products, attitudes of resellers, suspicious behavior, and offerings of refurbished products, clones, and special promotions by resellers.

3. Information was supplied about the current street price of each identified product as advertised by the resellers. The actual purchase price was often different from the listed price, depending both on the ability of the investigator's buyer to negotiate and on the quantity of goods being purchased.

4. The client also shared information about the availability and location of the product. Resellers frequently listed the product as being available, but once a sale was discussed, the reseller would often have to locate the product. The product might also be free on board (FOB) at designated international locations. Product inventory lists were also available to some of the investigator's buyers, and the buyers were able to access this information on a routine basis.

5. Information collected on competitive products was provided, but no purchases of competitive product were made unless the investigator was directed to do so. Flash reports were forwarded by the investigator as necessary with sensitive data or information requiring immediate action by the company.

Expenses Related to Purchasing Data

There are three areas of expense associated with purchasing data collection: intelligence collection, purchasing of products, and returns and shipping.

Intelligence Collection   Time is required to monitor Web sites, chat with brokers, review bulletin boards, and do whatever else is needed to look and act like other resellers. A considerable amount of raw data comes from these activities and is essential for the long-term reliability of the data collected. Relationships also need to be established with broker networks, and the mounds of data available daily must be sifted, organized, and read. There is usually an hourly cost associated with the activities of the agents assigned to monitor broker networks and provide weekly reports on pricing and channel activity to the company. This fee is determined in advance and used to charge collection time against the project.

Purchasing of Products   To be effective, the actual negotiations for product purchases and sales must be done on a regular basis. This allows the buyer to establish a relationship with the reseller, facilitates ease of a sale, and provides intelligence that would not be available through straight online buying. Many of the gray market resellers are suspicious and do not want to sell unless they know the customer.

With a new reseller, it may take time to establish the relationship. Often the company will require background information and bank details of the purchaser. The length of time necessary to get set up and registered as a buyer varies by company. However, once this is done and the agent (buyer) has established a working relationship and credibility with his salesperson, the speed of a transaction is minimized. When these companies sometimes have a turnover in personnel, more time is needed to connect with the new salesperson.

To maintain these relationships, it is necessary to continue making minimal purchases on a periodic schedule rather then use just a one-shot approach. Once the buyer becomes a good customer, that buyer may be put on the "special" pricing list and receive all Internet notices that the gray market company sends out. This helps agents (buyers) in their negotiations so that they can get the best price available, and it also makes the buyers look legitimate.

It is very difficult to make single or very small purchases. When possible, it is easiest to purchase in the smallest unit packs, or better to purchase 100 or 200 SKUs for more than five items. The agents (buyers) should try to keep the cost to a minimum, with the understanding that at times it is necessary to make larger purchases. These purchases also need to be made with a fast turnaround. To expedite the purchasing process, it is essential that the company provide the agents with weekly target prices and preferred products and quantities. Thus, the agents can work independently and spend less time purchasing; and it also makes them appear legitimate.

The majority of purchases are usually paid for by either a cashier's check or a wire transfer. All agents must have their own company and their own company bank accounts. Paying by wire transfer is preferred by the sellers, speeds up the purchasing process, and makes it much harder to trace. However, this does require that each buyer have funds that are instantly available.

The most successful agents used for these projects are retired intelligence officers and retired high-tech executives. All buyers should be trained by company staff on purchasing practices and procedures and should be very knowledgeable about the products that they are purchasing.

Returns and Shipping   Once the product is received by the buyer or at the drop-off location, all information on the boxes and all materials inside, including the serial numbers, are recorded. It takes time to collect serial numbers and process the returns, especially if a large number of SKUs are involved or if the packages require unpacking and repacking. The information is forwarded to the company, and the product is returned to the requested company location.

Case Study

We were conducting a long-term market surveillance program for a high-tech client and were sending a product back to our client's manufacturing plant in Ireland for technical inspections. Only one manager was to know about the source of the returns and have knowledge that a buying program was being conducted. The manager had a family emergency and was not in the plant when some returns were received. Another manager opened the shipment. He discovered the gray market products and sent memos around the company telling about what he had found. Before the CFO could get the problem under control, word had leaked out to the gray market distributors that gray products were being returned to the plant. The distributors were able to trace back the purchases to one of our buyers. Several threats were received before he could convince the gray market community that he had sold them to another broker who must have been the "real source" for the product returned to the client's plant.

Case Study

In another case for this client, a staff attorney told a gray marketer that she had a product that was found in the market in violation of a sales agreement. The gray marketer asked who had provided the product to the company. Although there was no obligation to do so, the attorney gave her a copy of the purchase order sent in by our agent. Several death threats were made against him. Shortly after these incidents, we terminated our contract with the client, as the client was not able to keep the buying program confidential and so put our staff at unnecessary risk.

Shipping costs for returns depend on the number of purchases made, the products involved, and the location of the product. The agents try wherever possible to avoid paying value-added tax (VAT) and to keep shipping charges to a minimum. However, in some situations it is not possible to eliminate VAT or freight-forwarding charges if the purchase is to be made with targeted brokers where VAT payments are required.

One avenue that can be explored with the purchased product is to have the agents put limited amounts of the product back onto the market for sale once the serial numbers have been recorded and the decision has been made not to use the product as evidence. This would allow the agents to look and act as if they were real traders. This can also eliminate some of the costs for returns and shipping.

It is essential that the company's receiving department understand the need for secrecy and that all products being returned to the designated address do not end up in the hands of the sales staff or anyone who will have the ability to blow the cover of the operatives.

Counterfeit Monitoring

The parallel market surveillance for counterfeit products often involves more direct field investigations. This type of investigation is normally done for enforcement purposes and litigation. The following policy guide presents an example of investigative plans.

POLICY GUIDE: INVESTIGATIVE PLAN (ASIA)

The purpose of this investigation was to develop information usable in any legal or corporate proceedings involving the unauthorized distribution of XYZ Company's agricultural products by BAD Chemical Co. in Taiwan.

Nature of the Problem

There were indications that an unauthorized "same-as" product was being produced and distributed by a company in Taiwan. This investigation was launched to (1) determine the nature, extent, and methods by which the product was being manufactured, distributed, warehoused, and sold to end users; (2) identify those responsible for the losses, and possibly, in conjunction with XYZ Company, retain counsel; and (3) develop a case for prosecution as well as recommendations for internal company action. It was reported to the investigator that a probable source of this product was BAD Chemical Co. (Taiwan).

Operational Plan

There were two major aspects to the investigation: Phase 1 consisted of interviews, a field investigation, and identification of the sources of the product in question. Phase 2 focused on the identification of any and all sources established to sell the product in the market coming from BAD Chemical's distribution and sales. An additional phase 3 included the possible coordination of an enforcement action in conjunction with legal counsel and local authorities.

The investigation was conducted in a discreet manner and used covert surveillance and information collection techniques. Information about the existence of the investigation was limited to the senior management of the company and legal counsel. The investigative environment in Taiwan is difficult, and accidental disclosure of the investigation could have proved detrimental to a successful completion.

Coordination with outside legal counsel was required after detailed information about suspect company operations was developed. If necessary, these meetings were to be coordinated with the exact requirements needed for a successful enforcement action based on XYZ Company's legal advice.

Information to Be Provided by the XYX Company

The following information was requested from XYZ Company to guarantee cost-effective conduct of the inquiry. The information was to be provided at the start of the inquiry along with a briefing for the investigation company's field manager assigned to the project.

1. Details regarding the suspect company and all available information already collected
2. The names of the suppliers and dealers currently purchasing legitimate XYZ Company products
3. Leads developed to date by XYZ Company
4. Background information related to the products
5. Samples of real labels and packaging
6. Photographs or samples of questionable XYZ products

Phase 1. Interviews and Fact-Finding

A variety of interviews were conducted to determine the source of the same-as product, those involved, the methods used, and the distribution methods. In order to do this, an investigation was conducted to collect and identify the following information:

1. Source(s) involved in the distribution process
2. Outlets and buyers of the product and the volume being sold
3. The ultimate source of the product and the methods by which it is being brought into Taiwan
4. The methods used to distribute the product
5. The warehousing and shipping system
6. Potential sources to provide information about questionable operations

It was estimated that this phase of the investigation would take no more than 10 working days. Reports were submitted as soon as enough information was available. Meetings with legal counsel and company management determined the follow-up investigative requirements.

Phase 2. Ongoing Investigation and Litigation Support

A field investigation was conducted to determine the marketing methods being used to sell products in Taiwan. To gather evidence of the sale of BAD Chemical products to end users, a controlled purchase of the products was arranged. This involved the establishment of a potential customer relationship by a "controlled" source. All conversations were recorded and/or videotaped to ensure that all possible background information was obtained. A sample purchase order was made and collected before any legal action was commenced.

The investigation extended over a two-month period in Taiwan to develop comprehensive information about all aspects of the operations. Phase 1 was expected to obtain sufficient information about the distribution, marketing methods, and volume being sold. Phase 2 involved a broader look at BAD Chemical's activities in Taiwan and outside Taiwan as well. If the suspected activity was part of a systemic marketing activity carried out in countries with weaker patent protection of same-as or other competitive products, it was important to identify and restrict the activities in all the countries.

Phase 3. Litigation Support

Coordination with the XYZ Company's outside counsel was necessary. It was accomplished along with planning for raids, enforcement actions, and seizures. Ten working days were required by management and operatives for the investigator on the project. Staff was provided at each facility to be raided, coordination of last-minute information about product location and status was provided, and guidance was given to enforcement officials on-site.

Time and Budget Required

The initial investigation required two weeks to ensure that there was little likelihood that anyone was aware of the investigation.

Phase 2 was estimated to take an additional two months in Taiwan and whatever other countries that might be identified. The cost for this inquiry in Taiwan included direct costs plus associated out-of-pocket expenses. If inquiries were needed in other countries, the cost for those would be determined after a review of the facts and requirements.

The phase 3 budget would be determined based on what, if any, ongoing assistance was needed with legal proceedings, raids, or actions.

Reporting

Findings were reported on a biweekly basis for phases 1 and 2, and a final report was issued when the work was concluded. All information was collected in a manner that would allow XYZ Company to use it for any legal proceedings in Taiwan. Efforts were coordinated through regular meetings with the XYZ Company manager responsible for this project, XYZ Company legal counsel, and outside counsel retained in Taiwan.

WHY IS IT NECESSARY TO VET COMPANIES?

Every day in the United States and Europe, all kinds of products find their way into the gray market. Gray market problems arise because of parallel importation by an authorized distributor or importer or by an unauthorized importer. The only means of ensuring that companies and individuals do not obtain products through deceptive or illegal means is to thoroughly vet each person and company that is a current or potential customer. If that is not possible or realistic for whatever reason, then a company should at least investigate those companies or persons that it has questions about.

WHY IS END-USER VERIFICATION NECESSARY?

There are two simple reasons why end-user verification is essential:

- There is no control over the gray market.
- The end users are unknown.

The end user of a product or technology is as important as, and in some cases more important than, the person who is actually purchasing the product. End users often establish separate companies, or use a company with whom they have a close relationship, to purchase a product that they are not able or willing to purchase themselves. Verifying the end user is a vital step in ensuring the legality of a transaction when goods restricted from sales in certain countries are involved.

All U.S. companies are, for example, required to comply with various governmental regulations that prohibit the sale of restricted products from general sales to any customer. The Department of Commerce and Department of State require that customers and end users be identified for these categories of products. These regulations ensure that U.S. national security interests are advanced by enforcing economic sanctions against hostile regimes and international criminals and by preventing the export of sensitive and dual-use technology to inappropriate destinations.

Every corporation must ensure that it has conducted a thorough examination of all customers and can validate their representations regarding how the product will be used. This is a huge responsibility and can be very costly should a fine be imposed. Not only must you be 100 percent certain of your customers, but you must also be responsible for gray market goods that can easily end up in the hands of unacceptable end users.

Issues and Concerns

To require a sales force to conduct this type of detailed vetting can be viewed as totally opposite to the objective of any sales organization. Sales staffs are either unable or unwilling to conduct rigorous vetting, often feeling that an overly restrictive customer screening program will adversely affect their sales capabilities. Requiring this activity is also often contrary to how an effective sales unit is measured in terms of success and failure. More often than not, the methods needed to obtain the requisite information fall outside the professional expertise of a sales unit staff.

Due to the worldwide presence of product sales and distribution, the process of vetting in other countries—with their varied political and governmental systems, record keeping, and openness to public scrutiny of business and other financial records—is a varied and complex one.

SUSPECTED VIOLATIONS

If questionable transactions are suspected by an existing customer, a specific investigation can be conducted, and the information developed on that customer will be included in the database.

Investigations of gray market products can be time consuming and expensive to conduct properly. Absolute confidentiality is essential. Only key management should have knowledge that the investigation is being conducted. Premature disclosure of the inquiry can be both detrimental to a successful outcome of the investigation and possibly dangerous as well for the investigators.

Information Collected

Companies generally need to be worried about two categories of companies or individuals:

- *Authorized distributors, OEMs, and VARs*—companies that are selling your product(s) and that you should have some amount of control over
- *Unauthorized distributors, OEMs, and VARs*—companies that are selling your product(s) in the marketplace without your knowledge or approval

Both these categories contribute to the gray market, both need to be monitored, and all pertinent information regarding the companies and individuals must be collected.

Authorized Distributors, OEMs, and VARs

A comprehensive questionnaire or data sheet should be developed for these companies and should contain the following information:

- Complete identification of company ownership
- All directors, officers, key management, and shareholders
- Locations of all subsidiary companies
- Relationship(s) to restricted organizations, individuals, and entities

Based on the information obtained from the questionnaire and information collected from other sources, it might be necessary to conduct further due diligence investigations to obtain an accurate profile of the company or individual.

Unauthorized Distributors, OEMs, and VARs

Limited information on these companies can be collected through a number of different means:

- Monitoring of the Internet
- Intelligence from salespeople
- Internal business intelligence division
- Market surveys

The above sources usually reveal only limited information about a company or individual, such as address, phone, fax, e-mail, Web site, type of products the company deals in, and price. In order to obtain as much information as possible about a company (owners, directors, subsidiaries, relationships, etc.), it is necessary to conduct a complete due diligence investigation. (Asking for and filing the results of a Dunn & Bradstreet report filled in by the company in question does *not* constitute an investigation.) A due diligence investigation should include:

- Market surveillance
- Product purchasing
- Database utilization

BEST PRACTICES FOR PRODUCT CHANNEL INTEGRITY VERIFICATION

Product channel integrity verification is a system used to monitor actual marketplace transactions. This system includes making marketplace purchases to determine the source of a product and its legitimacy on the open market. Due to the extreme sensitivity of the process and the need for information collection and documentation for possible legal action, extreme care must be taken in conducting this activity.

In general, the verification process should include the following steps:

- Identify resellers from authorized sellers.

- Establish rapport and a good working relationship with the reseller's representatives.

- Obtain information about the reseller wherever possible—for example, where it sells and to whom, its best product line, a description of its best customer, annual turnover—and make notes to include in monthly general reports to the client.

- Attempt to be placed on the reseller's mailing list to receive product catalogs, price lists, price changes, company newsletters, and the like.

- Note any changes regarding the reseller's sales personnel, and try to identify what company they may have moved to.

- Maintain an audit trail of all transactions, especially financial. Keep records of all bank deposits, check registers, purchase orders, shipment invoices, and such. Maintain a separate file on each reseller, containing hard copies of all correspondence exchanged, including e-mails, faxes, and so forth.

- Provide expeditious reports to the internal client.

Checklist

Develop a Profile of the Reseller

- Establish a list of clients and competitive products handled by the reseller. (This can be conducted at the reseller's Web site in many cases.)

- Identify pricing and quantity information if possible (*Note:* Web site information normally does not reveal the best selling prices.)

- Determine, where possible, shipping and handling information.

- Establish what documentation if any is provided with the product at the time of shipment.

- Identify what software and product support are provided at the time of shipment—and at what cost.

- Obtain a warranty and the returns policy if available.

- Try to identify reseller relationships (other resellers) via Web links.

Initiate Contact with the Reseller

- Identify as many reseller's interfaces (sales personnel) as possible by name.

- Seek to identify names of management personnel to complement the reseller profile.

- Determine a full list of client products handled by the reseller. (Web sites often do not list all products.) The focus is on products of specific interest to the client.

- Obtain pricing and quantity information on products of interest while at the same time pressing for the "best" price.

- Determine shipping and documentation requirements of the reseller.

- List the product documentation provided automatically by the reseller.

- Obtain data on what software is automatically provided by the reseller for the product.

- Determine whether additional documentation and software can be obtained from the reseller at no cost or at what additional cost.

- Identify the financial requirements (the reseller agreement, bank financial statements, etc.) of conducting business with the reseller. For international requirements. include the need for wire transfers, letters of credit, and so on.

- Ascertain the reseller's policies on product warranty, returns for repair, and the like.

Place a Purchase Order with the Reseller

- Create an order position with the reseller (develop quantity of buy and at "best" price), and confirm your intent to purchase with a confirming fax, e-mail, or letter using the buyer letterhead.

- Create a purchase order draft, including shipping and insurance charges where appropriate. Include a statement of documentation and software provided as part of the purchase agreement.

- Identify where and to whom shipment is to be made and by what type of carrier, for example, UPS or FedEx.

- Forward the purchase order to the reseller via UPS, priority mail, FedEx, or other means, and enclose a cashier's check where appropriate.

- Confirm the expected shipment and receipt date to the reseller.

- Provide an audit trail on all transactions that result in a purchase.

- Maintain a copy of all correspondence exchanged with the reseller—e-mails, faxes, letters, and notes on telephone conversations. Always send the reseller a confirming e-mail following a telephone conversation.

Shipments

- Request tracking numbers of all shipments.

- Track shipments using the UPS or FedEx Web site to determine the origin of shipments. Maintain copies of the tracking information (print out, in detail, the data provided by the tracking system), and keep them in the reseller's file.

- Prepare to receive and expedite the record of shipments.

Receive Shipments

- Receive shipments from the reseller, and note the date and time of receipt.

- Record all shipping container information, for example, a description of the container, label information, serial number information, and special markings.

- Make note if the container is original or repacked.

- Remove the contents from the shipping containers.

- Record all product serial numbers, the country of manufacture, and other pertinent information.

- Prepare a content report with pertinent label information, serial numbers, and any other markings or special container information.

- Forward the report to a designated person at the specified client location, and include a copy of the report with the reshipment. Maintain a copy in the reseller's file.

- Confirm to the reseller that the shipment was received.

Reshipment of Goods

- Repack the contents as received.

- Place a copy of the shipment report inside the container on top of the product to assist in identifying the shipment's origin and to aid tracking.

- Prepare a label for shipment, addressing it to the specified client location and identified representative.

- Make reshipments via UPS or FedEx surface where possible, unless special shipping instructions are requested.

- Obtain tracking numbers for all shipments and number of containers in each shipment.

- Prepare notification to the client that reshipment has been made and to what specific destination. Provide tracking information and the expected date of arrival.

DASHBOARD QUESTIONS

1. Are marketplace data available to measure our products' channel performance?
2. Are attacks against products being found via purchasing programs?
3. Are market prices in line with established company pricing?

CHAPTER 9

BRAND INTEGRITY AS A BASIC MANAGEMENT TOOL

The trouble with following the herd is stepping in what it leaves behind.

Cowboy philosophy

Having well-designed policies to manage the BI process is essential. How they are implemented depends on senior management's commitment to the philosophy.

It is often said, "We behave as we believe." If, for example, you believe you are a holding company, not an operating company, certain values will be stressed rather than others. If you believe that the only constraint to growth is financial, not human, people will not be valued. If you believe that the long term doesn't matter as much as short-term EPS, the long term doesn't matter. If you don't believe in BI, it won't work. If you believe in BI, force the issue as participative management, or it will not be valuable. If *you behave as you believe*, that is how employees will manage your brands, and, the hope is, they will also believe.

MANAGING THE BI PROCESS

Brand integrity programs are established when a company focuses on maximizing the value of key product assets. That means:

- Protecting the product(s)
- Protecting image and reputation
- Protecting the brand
- Providing maximum product revenues and profits
- Minimizing production costs

In order for these assets to be protected and the BI concept to flourish, it is necessary to have a corporate policy that establishes BI as a major corporate objective. Policies to support the development, introduction, and operations of key programs are essential. Implementation procedures corresponding to established company strategies should be used. It is then possible to revise any organizational structure as may be required. Best practices for BI implementation and program operations should be followed. All program efforts must be based on changing behavior throughout the organization to increase employee involvement, participation, and acceptance of BI as an essential part of day-to-day business activities. Awareness of BI values and individual employee ownership of the process will improve financial performance while reducing at-risk behaviors that cause losses.

Three areas related to effective program operations are fact-finding, marketplace monitoring, and crisis management. Because of the sensitive nature of the activities involved, close senior management oversight is required. The use of fact-finding for mergers, acquisitions, due diligence, litigation support, corporate and competitive intelligence collection, and the handling of product-related crisis situations is extremely sensitive. The ethical use of these management tools is essential to ensure a flow of high-quality, untainted information for business decision making, strategy development, and product management.

The interlocking parts of a BI program make theft of intellectual property and intellectual capital (business know-how) less likely, lower the risk from elicitation, and limit leakage of sensitive data. A BI program provides the company with employees who understand that they must protect products to protect the company and their jobs.

Can a BI program prevent a determined attack against a brand or product? Can it prevent access to R&D information or to sensitive manufacturing facilities? Can it stop employees from stealing intellectual property or intellectual capital? The answer is no, but it can make it much more difficult for these things to happen. It can also provide early warning if something does happen, so that remedial actions can be taken quickly.

In thinking about brand integrity as a management tool, there are basic brand integrity concepts to remember:

1. Losses are due to management problems, not security issues.
2. Risks are best controlled by those responsible for operations.
3. Trade dollars for time delays and barriers.

4. Losses are lower when there is increased involvement, greater personal interest, and a close parallel between company and personal goals or viewpoint.
5. Those with the most access can cause the most serious problems—this is a basic impediment in BI efforts.
6. A balance is required between BI and business objectives; neither should be subordinate or superior to the other. There should be a blend of the objectives that is just right for the environment.

Case Study

A major high-tech company sent several scientists to China to present technical papers at symposia that were held at three different prominent universities. After each presentation, question-and-answer sessions were conducted with university students and academics. In each city, representatives from a government ministry posed as students and asked questions. The questions seemed innocuous individually but were carefully orchestrated to elicit needed information. Key data were inadvertently disclosed, because the scientists were naïve and not concerned about disclosing information. During a post-trip debriefing, it became apparent what had transpired. While the genie could not be put back into the bottle, the nature of the loss was identified, and steps were taken to minimize the potential loss to the company.

Case Study

A lead scientist on an aerospace development project abruptly quit his job at a major manufacturing company in the United States. He claimed a family emergency in Taiwan and resigned to return home. One year later, a company sales representative identified a new product being marketed that appeared to be very similar to a product scheduled for release in the United States within six months. Samples obtained by a private investigator were analyzed, and it was found that the product was an exact copy of the new product to be released for sale in the States. The company producing the copy was investigated, and the resigned scientist was identified as a major shareholder and advisor.

The U.S. company's legal department conducted an evaluation and determined that the scientist had not executed a confidentiality agreement and had not been given an exit debriefing regarding nondisclosure of proprietary data. The delay in getting the product to market was a function of management changes in the company and budget cutbacks for new staff. Consequently, no action was taken against the scientist and the company with the stolen technology. The new technology was never released in the United States.

IMPLEMENTING BRAND INTEGRITY

There are really only five brand-related concerns that need to be protected: products, information, reputation, shareholder value, and margins. If they are protected and the company operations are managed to ensure long-term value from them, a brand or product integrity program is proving its value. Managing these assets is the ultimate goal of a brand integrity program. Deciding how best to introduce and manage the concepts in day-to-day operations requires follow-up on analytical and leadership skills.

At its most basic level, brand integrity can be described as the prism through which all activities in the company are viewed. What is viewed through this prism is what brand integrity does for the company.

Embedding the BI culture in the company, much like embedding BI into the products themselves, ensures that cost-effective protection is a part of all aspects of company operations. Product BI and brand management are the two vital layers that provide operational protection to products and brands in global commerce.

BI is not a part of the business process—it *is* the business process.

BI Is Not a Traditional Corporate Security Function

The operations of the company and its employees need to be secure from risks and threats. Traditional corporate security and IT security provide the tools to guard against everyday risks; they can also provide support for global BI efforts. As deterrents, however, they cannot be expected to be as cost effective as managers with day-to-day responsibilities for understanding the marketplace and the strategic risks faced by their brands and products. Neither can management that is not involved with the product or the brand have the intimate knowledge of alternative measures that can lower risk, increase product attractiveness, and lower overall protective costs. Corporate security and BI, where they are separate functions, are support services for the main business of the company, protecting the company's key brand and product assets. Management using BI principles in daily operations protects the cash flow from products into the company; nothing is more essential. Protecting against terrorism, employee violence, and theft are important but do not ensure the day-to-day flow of revenue into the company. BI does.

Providing incentives to employees to actively participate in BI pays high dividends. Including BI responsibilities in all employee performance evaluations further stresses the company's commitment to and value anticipated from BI.

Making BI a part of all strategic plans, new-product development, acquisitions, and IT systems development further infuses BI into the company's culture. It is going back to basics in managing the company: focusing on the product and making sure that customers are protected and that geography, product lines, supply chains, and brands are secure.

Benefits to Your Company

Shareholders demand that the maximum value be provided from their investments in a company. Value cannot be provided if brand value, market share, and margins are eroded due to a lack of consumer confidence in products caused by authenticity issues such as gray market problems, counterfeiting, parallel importation, or improper manufacturing practices by subcontractors. Loss of margins caused by predatory gray marketing of products damages distribution channels, lowers the value of brands, and disrupts manufacturing schedules. Dealing with the causes of these problems can be a time-consuming but profit-enhancing experience if done properly.

When companies can maximize their profits and find their way through the maze of market and supply chain information, understand the sources of their problems, and eliminate them through cost-effective application of BI principles, a strategic advantage can be realized.

STRATEGIC USE OF BRAND INTEGRITY

Physical protection of people and operations is only one dimension of protecting company operations, and while essential in order to have continuity of a business, it does not address vital product and brand protection issues related to the "business of the business." BI costs, programs, policies, and activities directly enhance the bottom-line performance of the company over time and for a specific product or brand throughout its life cycle. BI programs respond to the needs of each brand and product when attuned to corporate strategic plans and brand management requirements. Consequently,

BI has multiple strategic uses and organizational structures, depending on the requirements of each company.

Companies using BI principles differentiate themselves from those using more traditional models. The way in which their products are viewed by customers and competitors will likewise be different. Oakley Sunglasses, for example, has an aggressive BI program to ensure that customers will purchase authentic products, Cisco Systems closely monitors markets to minimize product attacks and maintain product integrity, and the Motion Picture Association works with numerous governments to lower the risk of piracy and to take enforcement actions. These companies differentiate themselves in image and authenticity by aggressive patent and IP protection, enforcement of property rights, crisis management, and anti–gray market programs.

How BI philosophy drives company program development and how it structures organizational approaches will vary by company. How programs are embedded in the everyday business process also will vary. The tools used to make programs work follow basic BI concepts. These tools include:

- Public relations
- Intelligence collection
- Fact-finding and enforcement
- Policy, BI programs, and employee involvement

Corporate BI focus is also required in the following key areas:

- Loss prevention of intellectual property and intellectual capital
- Prevention programs at each stage of the life cycle
- Employee participation at each level of the company's operations
- Auditing and monitoring of business processes
- Timely intervention when problems are identified
- Effective communication of program results

SUGGESTED BI RESPONSIBILITIES AND ACTIVITIES

Establishing BI in day-to-day business requires involvement at all levels of management. Many of the responsibilities in the following lists may already be part of current job descriptions. Where they are already in use, emphasizing their direct BI value to highlight senior management support is essential. Where they are not currently part of executive responsibilities, they should become part of dashboard questions in regular performance reviews.

Executives

- Avoid brand damage by applying adequate measures to monitor licensing, manufacturing, and subcontractor contracts.
- Ensure that the monitoring of manufacturing and licensing relationships is adequate for the degree of risk allocated to key products.
- Complete product risk evaluations.
- Establish strategic product protection plans.
- Tie executive incentive plans to brand and product integrity performance.

CEO

- Undertake fact-finding before entering partnering, production, or alliance relationships to ensure that representations are accurate.
- Request a confidential analysis of information protection within the company, facility, or country or on a specific product line under development.
- Verify that the executives being hired are representing their background, reputation, and skills truthfully.
- Initiate sensitive internal investigations into allegations of questionable executive behavior or the misuse of company assets, funds, or information.
- Establish an independent review of distribution channel product protection.
- Provide crisis management support for product extortion or contamination problems or counterfeits that harm product reputation and credibility.
- Include BI dashboard questions for all business plans and strategic reviews.

CFO

- Establish independent testing of distribution channels for compliance with sales policies, rebates, and discounts.
- Investigate fraud, theft, and product diversion problems.

- Support internal auditors in reviewing instances of questionable ethical conduct.

CIO

- Review the IT systems for compliance with established security standards.
- Support the development of internal security policies, procedures, and standards to protect sensitive company information.
- Provide computer forensic support to investigate attacks against or losses caused by compromise of the IT system.

Brand Managers

- Develop product and brand risk assessments and BI plans.
- Ensure that products are being sold at proper margins and that fraudulent transactions are not affecting sales, rebates, and discounts.
- Monitor markets around the world for specific products to check for pricing, unauthorized sales, and availability.
- Check the reputation and reliability of new customers, distributors, resellers, and end users.
- Purchase products from the Internet to verify source and pricing.
- Investigate counterfeit products, product contamination, and extortion.
- Investigate suspected kickbacks; unauthorized rebates, discounts, or returns; theft of returned products; or selling of rejected products to consumers.
- Investigate contract manufacturers that are producing unauthorized products and selling into the market, conducting the investigation in a way that will support legal actions against them.
- Identify substandard products being sold as regular quality rather than seconds, and provide support for litigation.

Compliance Managers

- Ensure compliance with all export control regulations for end-user verifications, denied parties list, transshipments, and customs-related investigations.
- Monitor labor practices for foreign contract manufacturing.

General Counsel

- Investigate questionable business practices, FPCA concerns, and ethics policy compliance questions.
- Investigate violations of patents, patent pending matters, and copyright infringements.
- Investigate theft or suspected theft of trade secrets.
- Investigate compromises of proprietary information from foreign or domestic facilities.
- Review information security programs and IT security systems for unauthorized access, adequacy of controls, and system integrity.
- Provide investigative support for general litigation for theft, infringements, fraud or loss of intellectual property as well as work in process, or finished products anywhere within corporate operations.

Security and BI Professionals

- Support the development and operation of the BI strategic planning process.
- Provide corporate support to BI program development efforts for brand and product management.
- Support the development of product and brand risk profiles.
- Provide investigative support for due diligence, fraud, trade secret theft, and related types of loss or risk situations around the world.
- Perform security reviews of facilities or operations, provide employee security training and awareness programs, and develop information security programs.
- Support crisis management programs, and provide specialized risk-reporting and outsourced management services in global and high-risk markets.

STRATEGIC PLANNING AND PROGRAM DEVELOPMENT

Corporate management is responsible for reviewing emerging critical external and internal BI issues and their implications that can affect the achievement of corporate and operating strategic objectives, goals, and plans. Management should develop and communicate those strategic BI goals having companywide implications. Business unit management must both monitor local marketplace trends that have potentially significant impact and develop programs responsive to critical BI issues.

BI Program Components

Taking a product to market and keeping it there requires the efforts of many people. To compete successfully, focused coordination is required by a wider circle of employees, distributors, subcontractors, vendors, and customers. To maximize both profits and market share, control over the property rights inherent in the product need to be maintained using BI processes from the time of inception until the useful life of the product is completed.

Each stage of the product life cycle is characterized by different degrees of risk, threat, and vulnerability. Companies that wish to minimize brand-related risks should have all the following components effectively operating and integrated within their business to ensure that they control their products and brands:

- Ownership rights secured and maintained
- Legal filings for patents, trademarks, and copyrights completed and maintained
- A system to handle trade secrets
- Physical controls in place
- Policy and procedures developed
- Management systems
- Supply chain management
- Manufacturing plant BI preparedness/operations
- Subcontractor and contract manufacturer controls and monitoring
- Brand integrity awareness training for all employees
- Enforcement of ethical standards
- Human resources management (background investigations for new employees, etc.)
- Ongoing product, market, and brand risk evaluations
- New-product launch readiness
- Effective insurance programs for products and intellectual property
- Coordinated brand integrity activities throughout the company
- Aggressive legal action against attacks on brand integrity
- Crisis management plans to deal with brand-related problems

Each of these components must be managed using established policies, procedures, and structures to operate a BI program for each of the five key areas in the company. While there is a close correlation between the activities for protecting brand, products, image, information, and reputation, each has unique characteristics that need to be addressed by brand- and product-specific policy, procedures, and organizational structure.

Philosophy

The basic philosophy of a BI program has the following characteristics:

- Recognizes the responsibilities of the business unit and brand management
- Is objective driven
- Requires centralized development of objectives, policies, and standards
- Encourages flexibility of implementation
- Utilizes line resources
- Provides training
- Identifies key, definable elements
- Builds in continual assessment and improvement
- Is compatible with corporate security policies and ethical codes

The objectives of a BI program are to:

- Minimize the probability of loss or damage caused by a brand or product attack.
- Limit the loss or damage if an attack does occur.
- Provide capabilities to recover rapidly from loss or damage resulting from an attack.
- Verify and improve an organization's ability to achieve program goals.

Policy

The establishment of a corporate philosophy for brand integrity is the first step in the process. This philosophy should become part of the existing strategic planning process of the company. Product risk-reduction goals should then be used to enhance whatever profit objectives are currently being used. The key elements for the policy should be:

- Identify key BI objectives.
- State that key brand and product assets must be protected.
- Focus on brand, reputation, image, and shareholder values.
- Structure compensation and rewards based on BI principles.
- Use BI principles to evaluate financial and product performance.
- Require a BI component for all business plans used in the company.
- Audit BI performance on a regular basis.

Procedures and Structure

How the BI program is implemented depends on the unique requirements of each company. The procedures for implementation of the program will be based on those requirements. They should follow the best practices for operating a program, the risk profiles for the products or brands identified in the development stage, and the structure used in the company. Let's look at a specific application of BI related to structuring a product protection program.

PROTECTING PRODUCTS IN THE MARKETPLACE

Getting the product into the market requires the development of a low-BI-risk product and an effective market surveillance program. This gets the product ready for sale. BI provides specific support during the R&D process and in maximizing brand identity and policing the marketplace. BI programs in R&D ensure longer new-product lead time until legitimate competition enters the market. It lowers the risk of illegal competition and product counterfeiting or cloning. It also assists with maximization of brand value by reducing the impact of counterfeits. High-profile advertising with slogans such as "You can be sure if it's Westinghouse©," "Coke's the one©," and "The one and only©" do not help sell products if significant low-quality, defective copies or nongenuine products are in the marketplace. BI programs that police the marketplace are useful to build image by assuring customers that when they "Care enough to send the very best©," they are, in fact, sending the *very best* greeting card, not a copy.

As we have already seen, policing the marketplace is more than sending people into the market in a foreign country to see if counterfeit products are being sold. Global commerce allows products to be distributed around the world within days rather than weeks or months. The Internet as well as discount channels, flea markets, foreign markets, volume dealers, product brokers, electronic bulletin boards, and electronic multilevel selling groups must be monitored. How much monitoring and which sources will yield good marketplace intelligence vary with products, country, price points, availability, distribution restrictions, and so on. All these activities might be required or only one or two; it depends on the particular characteristics of the product. High-tech consumer products often require more worldwide Internet monitoring than consumer goods that are geared to local consumption.

Different Approaches for Each Product and Brand?

BI involvement in marketing efforts has several valuable purposes:

- Makes it hard for unauthorized channels to get the product
- Monitors markets for below-price products
- Supports conclusions about how markets are operating
- Identifies counterfeit and gray market products in channels and markets

In working with marketing activities, the BI focus should be on supporting the corporate requirement to protect profitability and margins for each product. BI should provide management with comprehensive services and tailor-made programs that manage risks to the product as well as to corporate profitability from theft or loss of trade secrets, gray market products, patent infringements, counterfeit goods, and untrustworthy customers and suppliers.

Complete product protection packages are often required. Comprehensive support programs that lower risk, strengthen security, minimize margin losses, and increase credibility to key products are essential for the marketplace.

Providing for a secure manufacturing site and where and how a new product is launched are two issues that can directly affect the ability of a company to protect new and high-value products. How the security of the manufacturing site is developed will differ from the process used to introduce the product into the market, but both are key to robust product BI. For example, in new-product launch readiness, new products are often put into the market while legal filings are in process, such as when patents are pending. These products frequently require specific additional plans to ensure product integrity until the final patent approvals are granted.

Facility Preparedness

When establishing new production facilities for company products, it is essential to take BI into account during site selection, design, and operation. In doing site selection, it is equally important to consider product and political risks to avoid needless exposure for new products in high-risk locations. The use of a product-specific checklist is essential to gather complete data.

POLICY GUIDE: NEW-PLANT BI PREPAREDNESS CHECKLIST

I. Site Selection Risk

Risks associated with products and their manufacturing facilities have several basic dimensions related to political, economic, criminal, and geographical concerns, including:

- Location (country, state, city, address)
  - o Has the political risk and CAP-index report for the location been reviewed?
  - o Has a political risk report been prepared covering governmental stability, supply chain reliability, taxes, and import-export regulations?
- Government relations issues for the company (in the country)
  - o Has a liaison been established with local governmental officials including police, fire, and emergency services?
- Adequate insurance for facilities, products, personnel, and operations
  - o Have risk management and insurance provided evidence of required coverage for all construction operations?
- The identification of all reasonable and foreseeable threats to personnel and operations
  - o Has a country operational risk assessment been conducted by corporate security, risk-control service, or a similar service?

The site selection risks to be included in the plan are those related to the safety and security of the products to be manufactured, including:

- The location of a plant near other facilities that have a high risk for hazardous environmental impact on production
  - Has a review of all facilities with hazardous production (chemicals, explosives, biological) been completed?
  - Has contact been made with the local emergency service providers for evacuation planning?
- The location of a plant in a high-crime area
  - Have upgraded security features been incorporated into the site design, including access control, fencing, lighting, and guard patrols?
  - Has security been provided for all personnel and equipment during construction operations?
- The documentation of property ownership
  - Has verification of site ownership been completed with local governmental offices and planning commissions?
  - Has lease or sale documentation had legal review and acceptance?
- The availability of secure communications into and out of the plant
  - Has a study of all telecommunication support available to the site been completed?
- The availability of secure transportation to and from the facility
  - Has a study been completed for secure truck services to and from the site?
- The availability of an adequate labor pool
  - Has an HR workforce availability review been completed for the site, area, province, state, or country?

II. Operations Risk

Planning, building, and beginning operations in the manufacturing plant require the interaction of physical security, operating policy and procedures, trusted and well-prepared personnel, trusted partners, and secure communications and IT systems. Risk factors to be addressed in this part of the commissioning plan focus on operational, personnel, and information security.

Operational Security

Establishing the initial plant culture is critical for the long-term success and acceptance of brand integrity. For a high degree of brand integrity to be in effect, operating controls are needed for personnel, IT, and day-to-day management of internal and external relationships and processes. The risk factors in this area to be incorporated into the commissioning plan include:

- The designation of secure areas for high-risk-product life-cycle operations (such as R&D, raw materials storage, finished-product storage, shipping and receiving controls, and manufacturing)
  - o Has a risk analysis been completed for facility operations?
  - o Have high-risk areas been identified and designated within the facility?
  - o Have controlled areas (R&D, high-value materials storage, finished-product storage, raw materials storage) been designated?
  - o Have control procedures been established for the daily operation of the facility, including access control, ID procedures, shipping and receiving, returned goods, product destruction, and scrap and waste handling?
- The existence of brand integrity policies and procedures for the operating plant
  - o Has a brand integrity program been developed for the facility?
  - o Has training been conducted based upon BI plan requirements?
- The existence of policies for establishing and monitoring secure relationships with vendors and suppliers
  - o Have policies and procedures been developed for vendor and supplier vetting and relationship management?
  - o Have all supply contracts been vetted with the purchasing department for compliance?
- The documentation of product protection manufacturing standards
  - o Have product protection plans or controls been established for all products produced at the plant?
  - o Have manufacturing control guidelines been established for the facility in compliance with the BI plan?
- The documentation of product protection distribution standards
  - o Has a distribution standard for products from this facility been developed and tested, and have employees been trained in its use?
- The shipping controls for finished products stored in and leaving the facility
  - o Have shipping controls been established that are consistent with product protection standards?
  - o Have all transportation company personnel been briefed on access control, ID procedures, and product protection requirements?
  - o Have all product protection control requirements been included in transportation contracts with suppliers?
- The controls over packaging materials, containers, and finished products
  - o Have secure areas and controls been established for packaging materials?

    o Have secure areas and controls been established for finished goods?
    o Have secure areas and controls been established for all other product finishing materials?

Personnel Security

Personnel risk factors focus on the procedures associated with hiring and firing employees and with sales. These include:

- The employee screening process prior to HR hiring (for all employees)
  - o Have background investigation guidelines been established for all levels of employees to be assigned to the facility?
  - o Have all employees hired by HR been vetted according to established standards?
- The security screening for employees in all high-risk positions
  - o Have all employees assigned to or hired for high-risk positions (R&D, process control, shipping, distribution management, sales) been screened according to established standards before beginning work?
- The application of C.O.P.E. (customer, order, product, and end user) standards for all product-related operations
  - o Have procedures been established to apply controls for all positions that have access to the finished product?
  - o Have procedures been established to ensure that all sales and marketing personnel assigned to the facility use C.O.P.E. guidelines?
- The sales controls for products (if sales are conducted from this location)
  - o Have C.O.P.E. guidelines been applied to all orders being shipped from this facility?
- The employee termination procedures in place for information control
  - o Are termination procedures coordinated with security procedures?
  - o Have access to IT systems, account information, and system privileges been terminated?

Information Security

Information security risks emphasize the security, management, and access control of sensitive information and systems used in the manufacturing plant. These include:

- The compliance of IT logical and physical security with company security standards
  - o Are all facility IT standards in compliance with company standards?

- The classification and control of sensitive product-related information (such as formulations, production know-how, sales and financial information, and supplier data)
  - o Have brand integrity standards been developed for all product-related information?
  - o Have classification standards been applied to all product-related information?
- The production techniques and product formulation controls used for batch materials, placebo ingredients, and so forth to manage risk of loss
  - o Have sensitive product-related production and formulary information been provided with security controls?
  - o Have provisions been made to conceal sensitive product formulations and process engineering data?

III. Product Risk

Product risk focuses on the risks that products may be counterfeited or trafficked on the gray market. Product protection measures must be in place. These measures must be appropriate to the levels of product risk identified. The product protection factors that drive the assessment of brand integrity readiness in the manufacturing plant include:

- The identification of the product(s) to be produced, including ongoing product lines and new product lines
  - o Have all products to be produced at this facility been identified, and have risk assessments been completed?
  - o Have special protective requirements (if any) been identified?
- The expected scope of product distribution from this facility
  - o Are products being produced only for local (in-country) markets?
  - o Are products to be distributed worldwide?
- The processes used to document product risk profiles and the product risk profiles themselves
  - o Have processes been established to identify product risk?
  - o Have processes been established to control access to product risk profiles?
- The processes used to document product diversion profiles and the profiles themselves
  - o Have processes been established to identify product diversion risk profiles?
  - o Have processes been established to control access to product diversion profiles?

- The plans to protect products over their life cycle, including R&D, product development, manufacturing, distribution, and life extension
  - Are information security controls in place to manage product life-cycle planning data?
  - Are these plans in compliance with company security standards for protection of sensitive data?
- The security of destruction processes and the facilities used for scrap, waste, and returned goods
  - Have scrap and product destruction procedures been vetted by brand integrity management and security?
  - Are returned-goods procedures in compliance with brand integrity standards?

IV. Third-Party Risk

Third-party risk focuses on the risks associated with trade partners involved in sourcing materials and product components, third-party manufacturing, and third-party warehousing and distribution. The risk factors in this area include:

- The due diligence processes used for screening and selecting trade partners
  - Have due diligence standards been agreed upon and coordinated with brand integrity and purchasing to establish vetting criteria?
  - Have agreed-upon standards been used to initially screen all new trade partners and rescreen them on a regular basis?
- The control processes used to source and manage raw materials
  - Are approved processes used for the sourcing of all products?
  - Are only approved suppliers used for raw material sourcing?
- The control processes used to set, control, and monitor compliance with a third-party manufacturer's critical production requirements
  - Are only approved control processes used to monitor production by third-party sources?
- The security standards used to select, hire, and use distributors and freight-hauling contractors
- The standard agreement terms used with third parties, including terms of sale, rights to transaction data, audit rights, and authorization certifications
  - Are all standard agreements in compliance with purchasing standards and those of brand integrity and security?
  - Have C-TPAT standards been adopted by the facility for all transportation and shipping arrangements and conditions?
  - Are inspections conducted to ensure compliance with all C-TPAT terms and conditions?

V. Incident Management Risk

Incident management risk addresses the processes, systems, and controls in place to report and respond to counterfeit and gray market incidents on a timely basis. The factors related to this risk area include:

- The product crisis management plans that are in place
  - o Have crisis management plans been developed for all products produced and distributed by this facility?
- The incident reporting and management systems that are in place
  - o Has an incident reporting system been implemented at the facility?
  - o Has this plan been tested, and have employees been trained?
- The regulatory and law enforcement engagement and communications strategies and procedures that are in place
  - o Have law enforcement and regulatory agency relationships been established by the facility?
  - o Has a product recall communications plan been established?
- The product authentication procedures that are in place
  - o Are procedures in place to verify the authenticity of all returned products?
  - o Are procedures in place to have questionable products tested for authenticity?
  - o Are procedures in place to verify the authenticity of packaging?
  - o Are procedures in place to destroy expired and defective goods received at the plant, including returns, suspect goods, expired products, and defective products?

PRODUCT-LAUNCH READINESS

Releasing a new product to the market is an art form with unique characteristics. Making sure that the product is protected while conducting the launch requires the application of BI principles to the process.

Case Study

A major motion picture studio produced an action film starring a famous foreign actor. The film was set for release in a high-risk country with a history of film piracy. For marketing and cultural reasons, it had to open in that country. Instead of the normal release process, high-security measures were used to prevent piracy during the critical first few weeks of distribution. Audiences were forced to enter theaters through metal detectors, no cameras or cell phones were permitted, security officers were present in the film projection rooms during viewings, and distribution of the films was handled using high-security procedures.

The film opened to rave reviews and was not copied for many weeks. When it finally did occur, it was well after distribution was completed to all major markets. No significant revenue was lost due to piracy. This was the first time that a film opened in this high-risk country without early piracy taking place. Millions of dollars in revenues, over and above the incremental security costs, resulted from the application of a strict BI regimen for this film.

Patent Pending

Specific methodology for protecting products for a limited time until full patent protection is in force can be developed and applied. Comprehensive programs ensure that production security, site inspections, internal monitoring, and marketplace surveillance are in operation until the product has international patent protection in force.

Crisis Management

The basic concept in crisis management is to manage the predictable and prepare for the unpredictable. The key BI goals of crisis management are to protect company or brand reputation, public image, and customer confidence. Product and consumer safety, customer satisfaction, profit enhancement, and the minimization of liability are additional outcomes of a well-managed program. Most public relations experts advise corporate executives to get out in front of crisis situations with positive public relations programs, tell the truth, and always err on the side of being ethical in all dealings with the public. Sometimes, when a situation is sensitive, it may require that limited information be shared with the public immediately, such as in product extortion. Conversely, when a product safety issue is involved, speed, candor, and positive steps to resolve the situation are essential. Similar practices should be established for the related problems of product contamination and recalls.

CORPORATE AND SECTOR POLICIES

To get started, the development of BI policies, standards, and a review process is essential. A nominal number of BI policies are needed that should reflect:

- Corporate and business unit responsibilities for identifying risks to brands and products
- Methods for evaluating and measuring program effectiveness
- BI strategic planning based on the product and brand
- Protocols for responding to problems, issues, and crises

The overall goal of operating a BI program is to have the corporate organization provide expertise and policy, not program administration. Administration is provided by the business with the product. The development of rules and responsibilities for BI is managed by a very small and capable corporate staff or external consultants. They will primarily furnish consulting assistance, crisis management support, and fact-finding for the business.

BI is to be considered an equal partner to product managers or other corporate support functions. Overall BI will be improved by linking business BI plans to corporate strategic plans, letting more groups develop their own plans, and BI personnel acting in a consulting capacity, not a directing one.

WORKING RELATIONSHIP

Achievement of company objectives within a decentralized organizational environment is a joint responsibility of corporate and business unit BI management. Effective performance will require their coordinated action according to defined roles with respect to planning, establishing policy, developing and administering programs, and monitoring and reporting results.

Corporate and business unit managers must keep each other informed about their plans and activities, in particular regarding new BI issues that may arise. Corporate management must participate in major decisions in critical areas or in circumstances of special risk or potential legal liability and must provide a central reference for information of concern to all business units and to corporate management.

Both business unit management and corporate BI management must carry out continuing reviews to ensure that company policy in regard to BI management remains responsive to changes in the environment and will make continuing efforts to strengthen and improve programs and procedures. Major new programs or program features developed by a business unit should be discussed with corporate management during the planning phase prior to initial execution.

To the extent that it is necessary to summarize and compare performance at a companywide level, basic common performance reporting standards should be established by corporate BI management. This will apply, for example, to areas of regulation and compliance where adherence to government standards is necessary.

What is the corporate BI role? It is to:

- Develop broad BI policy, formulate corporatewide strategic goals, and serve as a resource to top corporate management.
- Ensure compliance with legal requirements through cost-effective programs and the development of performance standards and measurements.
- Review, recommend, and ensure consistent application of corporate BI policies, practices, and philosophy for managing people in the company.
- Ensure that the management of BI philosophy, approaches, *and* values is balanced and responsive to both business and customer needs.
- Ensure that corporate BI strategies, objectives, and programs reflect and are integrated with the short-term operating priorities and long-term strategy business objectives, goals, and product revenue plans of the corporation.
- Review emerging critical external and internal BI issues, and recognize the implications that can affect the achievement of corporate and operating strategic objectives, goals, and plans.
- Support management in the development of business unit programs and operating BI policy, and facilitate information exchange throughout the company.
- Provide consulting and problem-solving assistance where requested or required.

Policy Guide: Broad BI Policy Statement

Rich Benefit is a business enterprise dedicated to supplying goods and services of the highest quality to all of its customers worldwide, at the same time satisfying the needs of shareholders and employees. The fundamental goal of the company is to provide a reasonable return on the investment made by shareholders. By achieving this basic objective, the company retains the strength and vigor needed to promote healthy competition and fulfill social and moral responsibilities.

The company is committed to the highest standards of personal integrity in its daily work and pledges to respect both the letter and the spirit of the laws under which it operates anywhere in the world. Through constant dedication to these principles, it exemplifies responsible leadership in the business community and ensures the continued confidence of customers, vendors, and employees.

BI policies identify the basic principles that guide the day-to-day and strategic actions of all employees. The continuing challenge is maintaining an environment that promotes full support and participation in the company's activities. Thus the adherence to a product-based management style serves the company well.

Operating highly focused businesses requires flexibility, creativity, and shared responsibility. Anticipating market changes that are an integral part of global markets demands sensitivity and an entrepreneurial spirit. Management of the diverse changes, in a constantly changing environment, requires a thorough understanding of and commitment to the company's BI philosophy. Creative risk taking requires sound product controls that are a part of each manager's responsibilities.

Each person contributes to actually running and controlling the business. Central to close involvement with the overall success of operation is an acceptance of the basic principles of the BI responsibilities that are demonstrated by the company and its employees. The company is committed to the full and creative use of the skills and abilities of its employees. This commitment is contained in the following brand integrity policy statement.

Broad BI Policy Statement

We believe products are the key to protecting the company's future. Their continuing market leadership can be best ensured in an environment that identifies risks and opportunities and supports creating long-term product stewardship.

We support a management climate that allows BI decision-making authority to be as decentralized as is practical and encourage employee involvement in the setting of job-related goals.

The future success of the company depends on employees successfully participating in BI activities. To the extent that the management of this process is effective, company success with strategic goals is assured.

The following specific policy statements will guide relationships between all parties in the company.

It is the policy of Rich Benefit:

1. To protect all company products and brands against the effects of marketplace forces by actively promoting widespread participation in product risk assessment and BI planning efforts
2. To provide a work environment that encourages personal responsibility for BI
3. To provide an environment that encourages two-way communication for the identification of BI issues, concerns, and solutions
4. To provide planned BI training and development activities that enable employees to successfully attain their goals and assume additional responsibilities consistent with their own interests and abilities

RISK REVIEWS AND DEVELOPMENT OF A NEW BI POLICY

The integrity of the supply chain is essential to an effective BI program. If the integrity of the supply chain has not been tested, it should become a priority to do so for ensuring quality throughout company operations. The following example provides an approach for measuring current program strengths.

POLICY GUIDE: SUPPLY CHAIN RISK ANALYSIS FRAMEWORK (ASIA)

A company is considering the development of a third-party due diligence process to review the continuity of its major worldwide manufacturing operations. The current international locations for manufacturing are Singapore, China, Malaysia, the United Kingdom, Italy, Mexico, Brazil, and Argentina.

The analytical process should produce risk and vulnerability data and offer recommendations for high-quality alternatives where significant concerns are identified. Furthermore, the process should be designed to provide ongoing follow-up for both local and senior management to identify and manage changes in the risk profile for a specific product line, facility, or country.

The investigator has developed a proprietary system for analyzing the risk to specific brands or product lines in each stage of a product's life cycle: research and development, manufacturing, distribution, and marketplace. The analysis process used for the manufacturing portion of the life cycle includes the following factors:

- Political risk in the country where significant manufacturing takes place related to terrorism, extremism, crime, and governmental stability
- Risk-related industry regulations
- Labor stability or social activism
- Weather and natural phenomena (earthquakes, etc.)
- The stability of alliance partners in regard to business reliability, reputation issues, and commercial practices
- A review of the alliance partners' use of subcontractors in the manufacturing process and a review of the subcontractors' facilities, operations, and reputation
- The physical plant integrity and controls
- Product integrity reviews related to unauthorized production, control of IP, infringements, and gray market activities
- The reliability of the transportation and electrical and communications systems
- The risk for the company personnel resident in the country

The analytical process and the techniques used for conducting the reviews included both statistical weighting and best practices to present and document the risk profiles. Both on-site reviews and investigative fact-finding were used to collect information from company executives and alliance partner sources and to gather independently collected information.

POLICY GUIDE: SUPPLY CHAIN RISK ANALYSIS ACTION PLAN (ASIA)

Problem Facility

Develop a process for conducting due diligence investigations and analysis related to selecting and using supply chain contractors in the company business units. The process should be integrated into business unit decision making to ensure product protection and integrity of the manufacturing process and to minimize production continuity problems.

Basic Due Diligence Process

The following four steps have been identified as essential to developing a comprehensive risk analysis for supply chain decision making within the six business units of the Parts Group:

1. *Geopolitical risk assessment.* An overall review of local and regional political, economic, and social conditions that support the business. Areas subject to review are the stability of the government, rates of inflation, demographics, labor laws and practices, regulatory and environmental issues, public utilities infrastructure, transportation, public safety, and medical facilities.
2. *Background investigation.* An in-depth analysis of public records and confidential inquiries to verify the reputation of the company and ascertain the honesty and integrity of potential business partners. Areas subject to review are records that reveal past or pending criminal charges, judgments, liens, and corporate affiliations that could present a conflict of interest or otherwise affect any decision to do business with a particular person or company.
3. *Security and environmental health and safety risk assessment.* Where applicable, an on-site inspection of the physical and operational security procedures of the company to ensure they meet the company's security standards. Among the areas subject to review are access control, protection of intellectual property, IT security, environmental health and safety issues, and adequate employee background investigations.
4. *Business continuity planning.* A review of the processes, systems, and technology to respond to critical incidents; an evaluation of the areas of emergency response, crisis management, and business resumption. This process also involves assisting the business in the identification and preliminary vetting of additional local or regional resources that have the ability to step in and restore production in the event the principal supplier experiences a long-term business disruption.

THE DELINEATION OF THE CORPORATE ROLE IN BI

Both centralized and decentralized management styles can accommodate the implementation of a BI strategy. The achievement of company brand integrity objectives within a decentralized organization is a joint responsibility of corporate and business management. Effective performance requires coordinated action according to defined roles with respect to policy formulation and compliance, planning, program development, and administration and monitoring. Effective BI management also requires the kind of information flow that keeps corporate and business unit management informed both of major issues, problems, and opportunities in critical areas and of significant program innovations occurring at all organizational levels as well as in the markets.

Organizational Responsibilities

Specific behaviors and actions are associated with the delineation of BI responsibilities in a company.

The corporate responsibilities include:

- Developing broad policies and guidelines in which principles are firm
- Developing strategic goals that have enterprisewide implications
- Ensuring that all corporate fiduciary responsibilities are met
- Providing consulting resources to business units, brand managers, and corporate staff groups
- Developing and providing performance standards for functional BI activities
- Managing the policy and guideline process for all applications in the company

Business units and brand managers are responsible for:

- Developing business-specific BI strategies within broad corporate guidelines
- Creating programs to deal with BI issues
- Implementing and administering all BI programs
- Seeking relief from the policies and guidelines when necessary
- Coordinating and communicating with corporate BI support functions as appropriate

The introduction and operation of a BI program can follow one of several models of the process development life cycle. It can be integrated into an existing strategic planning process as it is being developed, or it can be developed as a separate stand-alone process and integrated after all development work is concluded. A starting point can be a single product within a brand on a test basis, and then it can be followed up in a standard company format after it has been "field-tested." However, for practical considerations of company operations and business, the following BI principles often apply.

Brand Management

- The basic strategic BI direction for each brand and business unit is provided by the company general management.
- Capital investment decisions involving BI cost versus risk should be reviewed by the company general management. Brand and business unit management must be informed of cost-versus-risk decisions.

General Management

- The business unit general managers and brand managers provide tactical BI guidance for products, facilities, and operations in their business segments.
- Risk-versus-cost decisions are the responsibility of the business unit brand manager and the manufacturing manager.
- Risk management, security, and legal need to be informed of actions and decisions affecting risk versus cost so as to optimize insurance premium considerations, compliance with security policies and procedures, and any legal implications.

Brand or Facility Manager

- The establishment and maintenance of a cost-effective BI program is the direct responsibility of the brand or facility manager.
- A specific individual can be assigned as a BI representative (manager).
- If appointed, the BI representative reports directly to the brand or product manager.
- BI representatives shall be guided by the corporate BI standards and policies.

BI Policies and Standards

- BI policies and standards adopted for brand or facility usage must be in accordance with corporate policies and standards.
- Not all standards apply to a given brand matter or facility; those that do should be evaluated based on their usage.

Program Rationale

BI is a management responsibility and a part of each person's job. The company must develop systems to identify needs and establish plans for key brand asset protection. BI planning must be integrated into the over-all strategic product plans and yearly business planning cycles. The plans must establish accountability at the product, brand, facility, business unit, and geographical level within the company. There must be coordination of corporate support for program development and maintenance as well as coordination of support services for incidents with significant brand or product impact or exposure. Lastly, training and development of BI skills to increase the levels of personal involvement throughout the company is essential for long-term program effectiveness.

Policy Formulation

Corporate management carries the primary responsibility for developing broad BI policies and guidelines that identify strategic corporate objectives. Each business unit adapts and extends these policies, applying strategies to fit the unit's individual BI circumstances within the parameters of the corporate policies and guidelines.

BI policies and strategies have some common elements that are important to ensure when they are being developed for the company:

- Prevention rather than response is paramount.
- Brands and products are the basis for programs.
- The focus is on key business revenue assets.
- There should be a minimum number of policies.
- Standards can be applied flexibly.
- Reporting requirements are kept to a minimum.

During the transition to a BI model, there will be a time of reorganization. At this time it is essential that policy guidance be available for all levels of management. A policy should contain the following elements:

1. All current security and loss prevention policies are in effect throughout all the business units of the company.
2. The company is to provide cost-effective physical security and protective services for all company personnel, operations, activities, assets, and facilities.
3. The protection of brand assets is the major goal of the program.

4. The primary responsibility for the establishment and maintenance of a BI program lies with product, brand, or business unit management.
5. Corporate staff (security, IT, legal, HR) provides detailed guidance, support, and expertise as required.
6. BI policies are reviewed by the business unit general management as required, but it should be done at least once annually as a part of the strategic planning and goal-setting process.
7. The security procedures and controls related to information technology are to be developed by the corporate staff.
8. IT security requirements are reviewed with business unit management before implementation.
9. The technical information controls for R&D activities are developed by the appropriate R&D personnel with support from the corporate staff.
10. The technical information security requirements should be reviewed with the business unit general management before implementation.

Policy Compliance

To the extent that it is necessary to summarize and compare performance at a companywide level, basic common performance reporting standards must be established by senior company management. This will apply, for example, to areas of regulatory and legal compliance where adherence to government standards is necessary. Business units are responsible for developing and implementing programs that will meet both corporate compliance and fiduciary responsibilities.

Benchmarking

By applying a variety of techniques, it is possible to coordinate the benchmarking of each process or issue that is addressed by the strategic analysis team concerning copyright licensing and enforcement, infringement investigations, and so forth.

In order to make the best use of the brand management staff and minimize costs, the active participation of key management is paramount. It is anticipated that the company brand management staff will work with the company legal, licensing, security, and other key executives to identity important issues, collect background information, and develop strategic approaches.

The Development of Best Practices

The development of best practices for brand integrity is still evolving. There are numerous organizations that have established and shared practices, others are internal and not shared, while still others are considered trade secrets. The following lists are not exhaustive but are based on our professional practice, internal audit standards, and a review of the following sources:

- Committee of Sponsoring Organizations (COSO) (American Accounting Association)
- Criteria of Control Committee (Canadian Institute of Chartered Accountants)
- Cadbury Commission (United Kingdom)
- Malcolm Baldrige National Quality Award Criteria
- ISO 9000 and 14000 Series Standards
- E.U. Standards

Some of these standards are very specific on how controls over assets are to be maintained in various operational settings, while others identify criteria that should be applied. However, in all cases, identifying key assets, establishing local practices that can be audited, and assigning risk levels are essential to establishing effective loss control programs. The practices espoused in this book are a combination of approaches that appear to work for our clients and other major corporations. They might not work exactly as written in a specific situation and may need some tweaking to get them right. That is your responsibility. The following best practices are provided as examples of what might be done to begin operations of a brand integrity program.

Guiding Principles Underlying BI Best Practices

1. The operating philosophy, policies, and procedures must be compatible with those of the company.
2. The evaluation criteria must be multidimensional and acceptable to the company. The criteria must be attainable and quantifiable and bear some relationship to the structure of the BI program.
3. Expectations must not exceed the capabilities of the BI program. If they do, it can only lead to frustration and failure.
4. Expectations must be linked to the actual performance of the BI function.

5. Expectations must be assessed in light of management and technical capabilities of the BI staff.

6. BI programs must have a level of performance and accountability comparable to that of any other corporate function.

BEST PRACTICES

Program Design and Development

1. A BI goal-setting, measurements, and review system is established and maintained, with managers accountable for obtaining results.

2. A communications program is developed and implemented in support of the corporate BI strategy.

3. A BI program that conforms to the corporate model and guidelines is developed and implemented.

4. Competitive information for industry, products, and competition are gathered and maintained.

5. Training programs for units are conducted to ensure competent internal BI expertise.

Incentive Plan Design

1. The incentive plan is designed to stimulate behavior that leads to the attainment of significant well-chosen BI goals.

2. The plan is extended to those individuals whose duties and responsibilities give them the opportunity to have substantial impact on the achievement of BI goals.

3. The incentive levels are fully integrated with salaries, benefits, and perquisites in a way that supports the compensation strategy of the business unit.

4. The plan is coordinated with business unit performance targets and a range of performance targets for BI goals that are appropriate for the unit.

5. The size of the individual awards is based upon attainment of measurable, preestablished goals in support of strategic BI goals.

6. The plan is designed, communicated, and administered with corporate approval, consistent with compensation policy and strategy.

Each of the key management areas—fact-finding, marketplace, and crisis management—have specific best practices that increase value to the company.

Fact-Finding

Due Diligence

- Review all acquisitions candidates, alliance partners, contract manufacturers, major customers, and distributors.

- Verify the representations made by end users, prospective partners, and investors.

Background Investigations

- Investigate all job candidates at all levels in the company.

- Investigate customers asking for a credit line, a loan, consignment inventory, or special pricing.

When to Stop an Internal Investigation

- When management wishes to stop inquiries

- When all documentation has been collected to support findings

- If an admission or confession has been obtained

- If intuition anticipates that nothing more will be gained by more work

- When public law enforcement is called in to handle the situation

When to Start or Continue an Internal Investigation

- When there is an actual or suspected violation of law, policy, or an ethics directive

- When directed by company management

Marketplace

Best Practices for Dealing with the Gray Market

- Conduct due diligence on deals, customers, and end users.
- Monitor the market.
- Review compensations programs.
- Base bonuses on margin as well as sales.
- Establish a universal pricing program.
- Discourage special price deals.
- Be able to track products and pricing.
- Be able to identify products.

Best Practices for Understanding the Deal

- Verify the ability to use the product for the purpose stated.
- Ensure that "meet-the-competition" pricing, special deals, and other special pricing are valid for this customer.
- Be sure that rebate programs operate as designed.
- Check to see that incentive programs are carefully monitored.
- Verify ship-to and bill-to data, and investigate anomalies.
- Conduct due diligence reviews, and chart all associated persons and entities.

Best Practices for Dealing with Monitoring the Marketplace

- Purchase products from Internet sources considered questionable.
- Track shipments from the production facilities to the end users.
- Identify gray market products quickly in the market, and take prompt action.
- Monitor the Internet for product and pricing anomalies.

- Collect intelligence about customer mergers, acquisitions, and new ventures.

Best Practices for Enforcing Your Policies

- Conduct training and awareness programs concerning diversion and gray market prevention activities for company sales staff as well as OEMs, customers, and distributors.

- Make undercover purchases of products on a regular basis from the gray market to gain acceptance in the gray market–diverter community.

- Use stings, buy-and-bust, and deception operations against known gray marketers.

- Take legal actions, request customs seizures, and demand differential price repayments from diverters.

Best Practices for Managing Sales and Marketing Activities

- Review sales procedures and contract forms.

- Train the staff to use due diligence inquiries for all new customers or unusual deals with existing customers.

- Check for fraud or misrepresentation by employees.

- Check for fraud or misrepresentation by customers.

- Ensure that employee compensation programs, rebate programs, and discounts do not encourage fraud or abuse leading to gray market goods.

- Establish ethics program training, and implement enforcement.

Crisis Management

Best Practices for Dealing with Product Extortion

- Respond to the specific situation, assess the damage, and contain the problem.

- Establish a crisis center and staff.

- Contact the K&R (kidnap and ransom) insurance carrier immediately.

- Activate the crisis management committee.

- Establish contact with the appropriate governmental agencies.

- Manage the incident following established internal policies.

- Use an active PR program as the situation dictates.

- Communicate with the public as required for public safety and image enhancement.

DASHBOARD QUESTIONS

1. Does a BI policy exist?
2. Has a BI planning process been initiated?
3. How does BI performance affect compensation of executives?

SETTING UP AND MANAGING A BRAND INTEGRITY PROGRAM

Form follows function . . . that has been misunderstood. Form and function should be one.

Frank Lloyd Wright

The structure of the global BI program should reflect the requirement to extend product life in the marketplace, minimize the erosion of revenue from margin loss and counterfeit product attacks, narrow the exposure to safety risks and hazards caused by these attacks, and enhance the reputation of company products and brands.

Executive leadership must set the organizational requirements for establishing BI as a key component of the strategic planning process, executive compensation reviews, and product management. Senior management must encourage the effective management of products, brands, sensitive information, and margins using best practices:

- There is a strategic focus on key business protection issues for the brand, for the profitability of the product, and for the corporate reputation, image, products, and information.
- Program objectives ensure market share, retain or improve margins, maintain consumer confidence in products, ensure the authenticity of the products, and keep the brand alive in the market.
- Implementation methods include a blend of policy reviews, development, ongoing internal audits, marketplace monitoring, and crisis management.
- Programs are tailored to the uniqueness of each brand or product and are designed to enhance bottom-line company financial performance.

TYPES OF PROGRAMS

Currently, multiple global organizational models are in use that employ brand integrity as a management tool. In some companies BI is structured as a process to improve parts of corporate operations, in others it is a function performed by either full- or part-time staff, while in many situations, commercial services are called in to solve intermittent BI problems. Companies clearly have many choices in establishing the approach that can be most effective in managing enterprisewide BI issues.

The size of the company, in either sales revenues, number of employees, or number of geographical locations, does not affect the type of BI structure used. Some relatively small companies with high-risk products have a strong functional BI department, whereas some large organizations do not have a department, assigned staff, or any BI process in place.

Companies that produce high-risk products often have organized their security resources to protect their products and operations. It is not uncommon for a pharmaceutical company to spend 85 percent of security/loss prevention staff time on product-related BI matters, while a company with a lower-risk product line, such as automobiles, may assign only 25 percent of staff time to these tasks. In still other companies, a noncounterfeit product–related issue may never be reported to corporate security, nor would the security department have any significant role in other BI decisions.

Case Study

The security director of a major clothing manufacturer was investigating a counterfeiting problem involving products originating in Asia. During the investigation, he learned that the vice president for manufacturing was selling excess products into secondary markets in Hong Kong. A significant portion of these products was being mixed with the counterfeit products that were being investigated. The security director took the evidence of the VP's complicity to senior management.

The security director was subsequently informed that the VP was spoken to about the problem, that it would not occur again, and that no further action would be taken against the VP. The security director protested the decision. Because of his actions, several people who provided information had already been arrested in Hong Kong and several lower-level employees had been terminated for their involvement in the counterfeiting problem. The security director was then told that the VP was too important to the company and that he would not be terminated for this breach of ethical behavior. The security director found a new position and resigned. The VP continued to work in

Hong Kong—but not with that company. Shortly after the incident was squelched, the VP found another position with a larger clothing manufacturer, where he became the VP for Asian operations.

Not only was product integrity overlooked for short-term profits, but by keeping the VP, a good employee trying to protect the brand integrity of the company was forced out of the company.

Case Study

A clothing buyer for a very large U.S.-based retailer traveled to Hong Kong several times a year to purchase lines of clothing. He had tight schedules for visiting factories, selecting designs, and negotiating contracts. A confidential letter to company management said that the buyer was taking kickbacks from the manufacturers in China, and an investigation by the corporate loss prevention department began.

On the buyer's next trip to Hong Kong, his activities were monitored. It was quickly determined that while his schedule was very tight, he did not follow it exactly. Instead of going to the suppliers' factories, the factories brought their samples to his five star hotel room. Instead of visiting with buyers, they were providing him with young women— daily. Through inquiries within the Hong Kong manufacturing industry, evidence was obtained revealing that the buyer had an arrangement that provided him a 1.5 percent commission for each order placed through the firms he selected. The commissions were paid into a Hong Kong bank account that the suppliers had established for him. He collected a portion of this money during every visit.

In order to keep the prices competitive and provide him with a commission, the suppliers were forced to partially manufacture the clothing in China rather than produce the products solely in Hong Kong. The relabeling of the garments, which was not in accordance with U.S. customs regulations, came to light when smugglers were caught bringing the goods into Hong Kong for finishing and labeling. Unfortunately for the buyer, a Hong Kong television station filmed the arrest and showed the name of the buyer's company on the evening news.

The evidence obtained by the company and the Hong Kong investigators was provided to federal prosecutors in the United States. The buyer was convicted and sent to federal prison. The contracts with the clothing suppliers in Hong Kong were terminated. All the bank accounts owned by the buyer were seized.

In this case, the company was aggressive in investigating allegations of wrongdoing; and as a result, it was able to avert a public relations disaster since it had already completed the investigation and actions were pending with the U.S. attorney. The investigation, arrest, and conviction of the buyer sent a strong message to the employees, vendors, and general public that BI was a serious concern of the company and that strong actions would be taken to protect the company and its customers.

APPROACHES TO BI

Three approaches to brand integrity are currently in use around the world: product centric (*We do something when we find a counterfeit product!*), business process (*Let's identify the root cause of the attack and develop a process to prevent it from happening again*), and enforcement (*Raid the counterfeiter, seize the products, and sue him!*). These approaches have previously been discussed in some detail, but how these approaches are structured and incorporated into operations varies widely among companies.

The usual starting point for implementing a BI approach is some type of product attack ("We found counterfeit products in Nam Sam market in Seoul"), a drop in revenue for a specific product ("Sales are off by 75 percent in the United States on this SKU"), or a suspicion triggered by unusual orders ("We just sold 150,000 computer networking cards to the Nigerian government"). As might also be expected, progression to using some type of BI approach varies by company and type of products, but usually starts with an incident of some type.

A range of approaches for BI activities is available:

- Nothing formal
- Embedded process
- Single dimension
- Product protection plans
- Multidimensional
- Specialized support staff
- Specialized functions
- Coordinated by corporate security
- Coordinated by the legal department
- Commercial services
- Alliances and associations

Nothing Formal

This is the most common type of BI approach. It tends to be reactive and often relies on legal protection rather than risk-based activities. Smaller companies and those that have not experienced BI issues often take this approach. The response is almost always after a product or brand has been attacked.

Embedded Process

Various aspects of product and supply chain management have best practices for the control of products, distribution, physical security, contract terms, and so forth. BI is not used as a business process to manage products across product life cycles.

Single Dimension

A single-dimensional approach most often develops in response to a product being attacked. The response focuses solely on managing the incident. For instance, when a counterfeit product is found, the decision is made to redesign packaging; or when gray market products are discovered and are traced to a distributor, the sales terms in the distributor's contract are tightened or sales incentive plans are changed to reflect margins as well as volumes for bonuses. Each of these examples is a single-dimensional approach to brand integrity.

Product Protection Plans

Specific product features such as RFID, track and trace, packaging design, control of IP, and trade secrets are common. Detailed product risk reviews, risk assessments, or new-product prelaunch BI planning is not included. Risk plans are most common when there are potential life safety issues such as might occur with food, pharmaceuticals, aircraft parts, and so on. This is followed by product safety issues caused by counterfeit products, unauthorized refurbishment of old products, and the like. Single-product or single-brand companies with trade secrets for IP also tend to exhibit a higher standard of care in product BI planning.

Multidimensional

Multidimensional BI programs include several options such as marketplace monitoring and contract modifications based on investigative findings. This approach could also involve covert product purchasing and enforcement measures against counterfeiters. Supply chain controls, contract term changes, and product security enhancements are also used without being tied to an overall approach. These approaches, while multidimensional, stop short of establishing a comprehensive BI program.

Specialized Support Staff

In many organizations there is a "go-to" person who handles BI issues. This may be an auditor who specializes in BI problems, a manager in sales operations who tracks questionable sales deals, a security manager, an investigator, a manager who handles counterfeit cases as a specialty, a patent attorney who handles legal actions and seizures, or an executive who took an interest in BI problems and is considered, on an informal basis, to be the person responsible for managing BI issues. In all of these organizational settings, the problems get addressed as either "one-off" issues or are considered to be "below the radar screen" of significant corporate problems and are handled as such.

Specialized Functions

These corporate functions are most often incident-based company responses to BI management. When incidents such as gray market trafficking demand a significantly high level of executive management time or financial concern, a manager or staff is assigned to handle the issue.

Coordinated by Corporate Security

In organizations where BI incidents are viewed as security problems, corporate security is put in the lead role for responding to problems. This is most often a reactive function, but it can evolve into BI preventative management, especially in large and global organizations.

Coordinated by the Legal Department

Many companies use the legal department to manage all BI issues, as BI issues are viewed as solely a legal matter. In these cases, without input from management, decisions are made for strictly legal rather than brand management considerations. The legal department's BI activities should be made part of a brand integrity plan and strategy. If patent, copyright, or trademark enforcement is the cornerstone of the BI strategy, rather than developing a more effective market entry strategy, the company will develop a defensive marketing strategy. If a patent registration program is coordinated with the marketing strategy, registrations will be filed in the right places, on time.

Commercial Services

Rather than develop internal staff to respond to problems or monitor ongoing marketplace concerns, some companies will hire commercial firms to provide BI support or specialized equipment (inks, tracking devices, etc.). The most often used services are investigative fact-finding, enforcement of property rights, and marketplace monitoring such as monitoring the Internet and purchasing products. Monitoring can include the company's own products, its supply chain vendors, its manufacturers and distributors, and the open market. Equipment for track and trace, Internet monitoring, packaging, labeling, inks, specialty products, and so on are also available and used in abundance.

Commercial security support can be provided along each step of the production process. Continuous protection of a product throughout its life cycle by commercial services is often less expensive than stopgap or ad hoc company efforts to address specific problems as they arise. When a new product is being introduced, security planning should be included, along with the commercial services identified to manage risk. A budget cost analysis can then be conducted along with the product risk profile.

Associations and Alliances

Some companies have determined that common industry problems such as the piracy of software, music, film, and other media are more effectively handled by industry associations and alliances. This approach often involves paying the association or alliance to handle various aspects of BI, such as marketplace monitoring and enforcement, rather than maintaining a large internal staff. For some companies this is a valuable approach, but for others it does little toward developing embedded company-based approaches to product risk planning. The cost for using outside services varies by company revenues and can be quite expensive for smaller companies in both actual expenditures and opportunity cost.

Company management often believes that when a service of this type is used, internal BI resources can be minimized. However, the converse is often true: if the problem is endemic in an industry, company-based efforts are often more essential than those of an association and should not be reduced. The costs for association support should be viewed as a necessary additional cost of doing business globally. But company efforts are essential and not supplementary to those offered by an alliance—an alliance supports company efforts.

Industry alliances do offer a wide range of services to member companies. Services range from investigations and enforcement to consumer education and government relations efforts to influence both the U.S. government and the governments of foreign countries to reduce counterfeiting, piracy, and the like. Several of these groups (see Chapter 8) are very active in the collection of marketplace intelligence as well as criminal enforcement.

CURRENT MODELS

There is a wide range of BI models in use today, but most of them have several common organizational origins within their respective companies—in either the legal or the security department. In fact, currently most companies that have a BI activity manage BI issues through either or both of these functions. The ways in which these functions operate vary greatly, depending on the vision for BI and its value to company operations, strategic use of lessons learned from past incidents, value to brand and product integrity, and impact on product stewardship.

Progression to a BI Function

While BI in most companies has its historical roots in corporate security, it also has evolved from compliance, brand management, legal, or audit functions. In some organizations, multiple approaches are being used simultaneously, with little coordination and little interdepartmental communications. As these efforts are frequently directed to specific product-related problems, it is not often recognized that similar problems are being managed independently within the same company. Unless and until a BI philosophy is set forth by senior management and a common approach is established, multiple approaches, initiatives, and structures will continue to be a common phenomenon. These multiple approaches are often found in business units that face BI issues such as gray market products and customer fraud. Counterfeit problems tend to get corporate security or legal involved more directly, and companywide policy will determine how they are handled. These pockets of BI management in brand and product operations can be more effective if they are coordinated, common methodologies are developed, and, when applicable, commercial services are employed.

Case Study

The corporate security department of a major pharmaceutical company hired an Internet surveillance firm to monitor products on various Web sites and auction sites. The pricing structure allowed significant price discounts for volume monitoring. Corporate security was servicing the request from one division's brand to look into gray market and counterfeit products. After the commercial service began yielding good results, corporate security contacted other business units and learned that they were also having similar problems. When other brand managers discovered that a shared service was available to look after their products, they requested support, and the full extent of all the brand problems emerged. There was no requirement that brand management contact security for what were identified as brand-related problems—such as margins lost from gray market attacks—but they did.

A new contract with the vendor was negotiated, and a 50 percent reduction in fees yielded a 150 percent increase in product coverage for multiple products rather than the single brand initially monitored. Questionable deals are now reported regularly, margin losses are declining, and brand integrity is being more effectively managed.

Case Study

A major high-tech company was experiencing a number of gray market incidents affecting its worldwide operations. When incidents of gray market trafficking were discovered, the corporate security department was given the lead to identify the parties involved and develop sufficient information to bring civil action against them. The volume of these cases became so great that outside investigative support was hired to supplement the internal investigations, conduct marketplace monitoring, and provide covert purchasing of products. The scope of the problem only increased.

During the investigations, a significant database was established by the outside agency. Using link analysis techniques, the outside agency found relationships among various dealers, distributors, and employees. It quickly became apparent that many of these attacks could have been prevented if a more thorough screening of purchase orders had taken place before shipment. Even more questionable orders, end users, and customers were identified as the investigation continued.

While the cost for having an outside agency was reasonable for providing services rendered, the success of this approach indicated that basic business processes within the company needed to be changed. Consequently, several company employees, including a senior security manager, were assigned to a business compliance function in the sales organization. Management of the investigation was brought back in-house. An outside agency continued to conduct the investigation, but management of that service was moved from corporate security to the sales organization.

This new function was responsible for several hundred million dollars in margin recovery during the first year of its operations. Several major civil actions were also concluded that returned an additional $100 million to the company.

Corporate security continued to have responsibility for managing counterfeit attacks against company products, but attacks caused by faulty internal business processes were handled by the business compliance function.

In most companies a counterfeit problem is handled by the law department and corporate security, with assistance from the business unit that controls the product being attacked. Gray market problems, however, may or may not rise to the level of being handled by either legal or security, as they are often viewed as product arbitrage by clever operators or as a contract enforcement problem, not a matter for investigation or criminal action. Unfortunately "you don't know what you don't know" about a situation until you look.

Case Study

A global multinational corporation had an operation in Italy. The vice president of sales was a star performer who exceeded his goals by 25 to 50 percent each year and was paid significant bonuses. The company wanted to reward him with a promotion and moved him to Asia to manage regional sales. His successor in Italy had trouble making his goals, as several key accounts stopped purchasing from the company. About the same time, some questionable rebate and return problems involving several Italian companies were being investigated by internal audit and corporate security.

The investigation concluded that the prior sales VP had been selling large volumes of products to front companies, usually at the end of a calendar year, that were then returned after company rebates were collected by the front companies. The investigation determined that the front companies were owned by an automobile dealer that leased cars to the company's operation in Italy. The sales VP had arranged for the auto dealer to get the company's lease business if he set up the front companies to support the product fraud.

Because the products entered the gray market, customer loyalty was lost. In addition, the company lost margins for the original sale, paid rebates on the deals, and refunded money for the returned products, all after paying the salary and bonus to the sales VP. Had a customer vetting program been in effect or had there been tighter controls on returns and rebates, the problem would never have happened or would have been discovered earlier.

Several large companies have redesignated their corporate security department as brand integrity departments, established brand integrity divisions within a corporate security department, or created stand-alone brand integrity departments. There are also a number of major corporations that have established positions with brand integrity manager titles in the legal, sales, or brand management department.

BI PROGRAM MODELS

The following examples show how various companies have approached organizational design for brand integrity. Frequently design is based on the type of problems: gray market or counterfeiting, and sometimes the size of the company determines the approach.

Gray Market Focus

- Company: High tech
  - BI based in the business compliance department
  - Global program
  - Worked closely with corporate security, legal, sales, and finance
  - Revamped pricing structure worldwide
  - Revamped distributor and sales agreements worldwide and standardized them throughout the company
  - Revamped the order approval process and standardized it throughout the company
  - Established awareness training programs for the sales and marketing staff
  - Active in order verification, product purchasing, intelligence gathering, market monitoring, and enforcement
  - Also very focused on counterfeit products
  - Executive-level backing
  - Team of seven to ten people
  - "Integrated" focus
- Company: Health-care products
  - BI based in the corporate security department
  - Global program
  - Works closely with the product and legal departments
  - Active investigation—monitoring, purchasing, and enforcement
  - Team of five to seven people

Counterfeit Focus

- Company: European aftermarket automotive parts
  - o BI based in the legal department
  - o Global program
  - o Counterfeit product and packaging issues
  - o Customer safety issues due to substandard products that can lead to accidents
  - o Active in investigation, market monitoring, enforcement, and packaging design
  - o Team of approximately five people
- Company: U.S. aftermarket automotive parts
  - o BI set up as a separate brand integrity department
  - o Similar to the above program
- Company: Consumer goods (China business only)
  - o Similar to the other identified programs but with more emphasis on counterfeit products
  - o Limited interaction with domestic divisions in the United States
  - o Conducts many raids on counterfeit manufacturers in China
  - o Reports to corporate security

Integrated Focus

- Company: Pharmaceutical consumer health-care products
  - o BI based in the corporate security department
  - o Global initiative
  - o Established as a separate team with executive-level backing
  - o Mission—to be proactive, with a focus on four areas: counterfeit, diversion, theft, and fraud
  - o Established coordinated response plans
  - o Set up a central database
  - o Established and implemented best practices
  - o Emphasizes technology solutions (RFID)
  - o Created a global supply chain security team
  - o Received C-TPAT certification in 2004
  - o Maintains close relations with government offices, including the FDA
  - o Companywide policy in place
  - o Involved in product design

    o Active in investigation and monitoring
    o Team of seven to ten people
- Company: Sports fashion
    o BI based in the legal department
    o Global program
    o Primary focus on gray and counterfeit products
    o Aggressive in investigation and enforcement
    o Emphasis on product design
    o Established and implemented best practices

Company-Size Focus

Small Small companies often have the most to lose—especially if there is just a single product. Senior management controls the BI process and most often relies heavily on legal protection. Single products are the most vulnerable to attacks unless product risk planning has been implemented and product design and protection features are intrinsic to the product. Those with trade secrets face special challenges to control access to their IP from their global competition while marketing or manufacturing their product. Ideally, an embedded BI process is a part of the day-to-day operations of the company. BI is a low-cost way of ensuring that all employees take care of the product in their areas of responsibility.

Medium Where single or multiple products or brands are produced, BI emphasis is most likely reactive and legally based. If a BI process is present, oversight of product management has been assigned to a senior executive, an executive of programs, or an operations management executive. Product protection plans are rudimentary and specific to a product, brand, or division. If the company has loss prevention and corporate security departments, they may have limited responsibilities for product-related issues.

Large Large companies that are multinational or global may have single or numerous products and brands at risk at any one time. The product and brand management functions often have the responsibility for developing and managing the BI programs. Legal and preventative programs are often used with both corporate security and specialized BI departments to manage risks, respond to product attacks, and operate risk-mitigation programs. Embedding BI processes is often a goal in order to obtain employee involvement.

Case Study

A major corporation identified gray market and counterfeit problems affecting several key products. The losses were deemed significant enough by senior management that a stand-alone brand integrity department was authorized and staffed. This new department reported to a senior operating executive and was given a corporatewide mandate to identify BI issues and establish a BI planning process, incident reporting, and product protection plans. It coordinated with the corporate security department for investigations of counterfeit products, but gray market remediation would not be handled by the BI department. (Figure 10.1 shows the organization selected.)

FIGURE 10.1   Organization Chart for the New BI Department

Program Design

Brand and product protection plans that are not tied to strategic business plans do more harm than good. They provide management with a sense that "someone is watching the store" when, in fact, "the lights are on but nobody is home." To make sure that someone is at home, the program must be designed to reflect key management concerns. The design of a strategic program requires a review of the following questions:

- What is the brand or product requiring protection?
- What are the risks and threats?
- What assets and resources exist for protection?
- What people, physical barriers, and processes exist for protection?
- What is the loss experience (current and historical)?
- What is the impact of the loss on the company?
- What is the current philosophy on protection (legal, executive, security, brand management)?
- What stage in the revenue life cycle is the product or brand?

Program levels may include corporate BI, product-line BI, and specific-product BI. Where a corporate BI function has been established, it will provide overall guidance and policy for BI operations across the company. It will set the tone and structure for BI programs and most often exists because of attacks against products that could not be resolved by actions of individual business units. Where a product line has a BI initiative, it often developed organically from brand-related problems within the business unit's operations. This might take the form of revising packaging, initiating a track-and-trace technology, or conducting a gray market investigation to solve a specific problem. When problems develop with a specific product in a specific market, actions might be taken to change the labeling, package design, terms of sale, distribution, or production contract terms. These measures are focused on resolving what is perceived to be a short-term or "one-off" problem.

Program implementation is often facilitated by using the above design process. In designing a program, it is important to remember that a BI program in all companies will reflect these six specific ideas:

1. BI programs involve virtually all organizational entities, departments, and activities in the company.
2. BI is an individual employee responsibility.
3. Because of the varying complexities of company products and operations, the application of specific BI measures will vary.
4. The applicability of programs will be the responsibility of the brand manager and the general manager to whom he or she reports.
5. Corporate staff services (security, legal, IT, HR, audit, etc.) are available to provide implementation guidelines and program development assistance to ensure support, technical assistance, and coordination.
6. A BI operating plan tailored to the specific requirements of that product, facility, or operation is used by each facility, product, or function.

BI PROGRAM OPERATIONS

When brand integrity is adopted for a brand or product, senior management must incorporate and promote this philosophy in its strategic plans, operating practices, and day-to-day operating style. Product risk and intelligence, brand integrity program status reports, and margin and market position improvements become part of executive performance appraisals, compensation plans, and business plans. Staff training in brand integrity is required for all new hires, and yearly refresher sessions should be held for all employees.

Improvement of Operations

BI operations are continually reviewed for effectiveness. The following factors may be used to manage the review process:

- An understanding of which brand assets are really important to the company
- A willingness to spend management time and money to develop strategic approaches to brand integrity
- Specific programs to identify risks and threats from the marketplace and within the company
- Well-developed crisis management programs to deal with mistakes, problems, and attacks against a brand
- Integration of protection plans into product life cycles
- Marketplace surveillance programs to detect, identify, and respond to attacks against your brand

Solutions to Be Considered

A variety of program options, both internal and external, can be used to improve BI operations and the scope and effectiveness of BI. They include:

- Technological solutions (electronics, track and trace, software, package redesigns, etc.)
- Communications (with customers, suppliers, the public, government agencies)
- Information sharing (within an industry)
- Private partnerships, alliances, public-private partnerships, and so on
- Public policy (advocacy of legislation, etc.)
- Transnational cooperative programs (programs with foreign governments)

Review of Existing BI Programs

The sole purpose of the company should be to produce, sell, and protect its brand and products while maximizing its profits. The design of the company for BI should in some very focused way embody this basic principle. Corporate services such as legal, security, HR, and IT are necessary to provide technical assistance to these efforts, not to manage them. The people with the most knowledge about strategy, and with the P&L (profit and loss) responsibility for operating the business, should control the BI efforts, as they are ultimately responsible for the success or failure of those efforts.

The design of the corporate structure to manage brand profitability should reflect the strategic focus on the brand by making the employees who are responsible for managing the brand and products directly responsible for strategic and tactical decisions and actions. The collection of information about risks and threats (including related program development), as well as about daily program operations, should be handled by these employees, possibly with technical assistance from corporate staff. Once all the legal requirements to establish ownership rights are in place, the primary BI responsibilities are to ensure product protection through design and risk planning and to establish operational controls throughout the useful revenue life of the product. Corporate security or BI can likewise assist with enforcement and some prevention activities, but the day-to-day control for products and brands rests with the brand and product managers.

Coordination of all enterprisewide efforts are the responsibility of the chief brand integrity officer or senior executive designated to handle BI responsibilities. Programs can be operated at the corporate level using corporate staff or at the operating unit level (business units) using dedicated staff, or they can be dispersed throughout the company using product management or be outsourced to commercial service companies. They are, however, still managed by those with hands-on responsibilities for selling them and growing the business. The tools necessary for successfully operating a BI program at any level in the company, under any organizational structure, are very similar.

Allocating Staff, Responsibilities, and Budgets

Allocating BI employees internally to brand integrity and to BI investigative work varies among companies. Several of the models previously presented focused solely on counterfeit products, others solely on the gray market, and some on both. Budgets for these areas of BI response or vulnerability management are set by business units based on specific criteria established jointly with senior company management. Assigning employees to specific

FIGURE 10.2   Brand Integrity Management

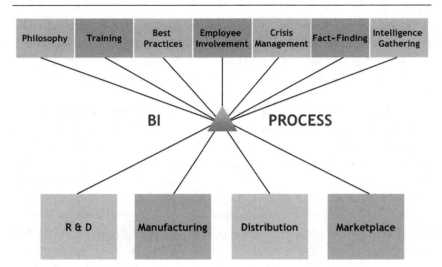

BI activities, selecting commercial vendors, or using company specialists should be done within established guidelines or standards. Figure 10.2 shows how all the pieces are integrated in the company.

Staff allocation is often a function of head-count authorizations, budgets, and the like. What factors will mitigate staff allocations? Major consideration needs to be given to the kinds of attacks, the products being attacked, the revenue recoveries anticipated, and where they are anticipated. Figure 10.3 provides a product attack summary for each part of the life cycle.

The allocation of resources for establishing programs can also take place at the facility, business unit, or product level in the company. If the program calls for this organization at the facility level, the following features will be present:

- Manufacturing BI programs will consist of a statement of activities, controls, procedures, techniques, and resources, both organized and coordinated.
- The BI program will include guidelines such as self-inspection checklists, self-audit forms, or other aids to assist the facility in a meaningful application of policy and standards.
- A plant or facility BI program will address the following major considerations and the associated risks:
  o Employee participation in BI efforts

FIGURE 10.3   Life-Cycle Attacks Chart

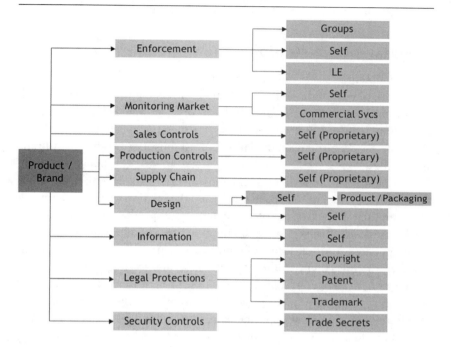

- o Physical security for the building and activities
- o Control features such as ID systems and surveillance
- o Proprietary process controls
- o Computer and IT systems controls
- o Information security
- o The protection of raw materials and finished goods

Program Innovations, Diffusion, and Consultation

Where a BI program is not yet established, corporate security very often has the primary responsibility for assisting with the assessment and communications of state-of-the-art practices and new BI-related information that has potential value to the business unit BI program. Corporate security often serves as a focal point for the exchange of innovative program ideas from all parts of the company, from industry, or from developing best practices. It provides consulting and problem-solving assistance to business units, staff groups, and brand management in particular areas of expertise. While corporate security is responsible for assessing local and industry BI practices and innovations, business unit management is responsible for sharing effective program strategies with broad application potential.

Program Administration

The implementation and administration of BI programs within the overall framework of corporate policies and guidelines is the primary responsibility of the business unit and of brand and product management. Business units also have the major responsibility for meeting specific areas of companywide BI performance standards and establishing product and brand risk profiles.

One of the underlying principles of brand management is that if employees are aware of the product risks and the relation to personal rewards for them, they will actively protect the brand and product, especially if personal rewards are involved. A key assumption of a BI policy calls for an active training program for all levels of employees in program principles, in the way the principles apply to their specific jobs, and in the personal value of participating in company BI programs. These programs become a part of the new-employee hiring process, provided on an initial basis for all employees, with follow-up training for specific company assignments. Refresher training and product risk-reduction meetings should also be held on a regularly scheduled basis.

Executive and Employee Evaluations

Evaluating executive and employee performance is a function of the specific goals and objectives agreed upon in advance to further BI practices in the company. These goals can be:

- P&L
- Margin maintenance
- Brand stewardship
- Social responsibility
- Shareholder value

Each of these goals has value for most organizations, but their relative value must be determined on a company-by-company basis.

P&L   Agreement of company management on P&L goals follows various formats to reach agreements on performance levels, revenue expectations, budget approvals, compensation and bonus plans, etc. BI expenses must be calculated and tied directly to strategic short- and long-term product protection goals during this stage of planning.

Margin Maintenance Margins cannot be maintained if variables caused by external forces such as channel distribution problems, product arbitrage, management irregularities, pricing variances, and the like, exist. Early warning that problems exist is essential to identify the problems before they affect margins. Margin maintenance must be a key aspect of a strategic BI program. Identifying a pricing problem related to unrealistic sales targets that will force sales personnel to make unethical deals—deals that result in gray market products flowing into distribution channels—is but one example of the importance of a strategic program.

Brand Stewardship Typical brand stewardship goals are to:

- Maintain product and brand value for as long as possible.
- Protect image, reputation, authenticity, and margins.
- Monitor attacks against products (brands) in a timely manner.
- Respond decisively to brand and product attacks.
- Maintain healthy employee attitudes toward BI principles.

Social Responsibility An important aspect of BI is having a good program for vetting contract manufacturers to ensure that they do not employ child labor, do not run sweatshops, but do pay fair wages for goods being produced. Being viewed as a good corporate citizen has many advantages in enhancing company and brand reputation and share value. Statements about the social responsibility stance of the company set the moral tone for both internal and external expectations by customers, clients, vendors, employees, and the public at large. The company must not only talk the talk, but walk the walk if it is to be believed and viewed as a company that people like to associate with, work for, and buy from on a day-to-day basis. BI programs help to monitor the global social and business climate to assist in adjusting policies and programs to support strategic goals.

Shareholder Value Share price, the maintenance of share value, and shareholder perception are all related to how well the company performs and to how company management is viewed to be running the business. In companies with a significant IP portfolio, it is important to commercialize what is not being used in daily operations. It is equally important to make sure that IP does not leak out into the market without payment. Likewise, significant counterfeiting of high-value products and gray market attacks need to be stopped before they rise to a significant level and require disclosure in annual reporting to shareholders.

It is not unreasonable to expect stock analysts to ask questions related to brand integrity when conducting their periodic performance reviews. The CEO or CFO who is asked about the company's BI initiatives may have some explaining to do if a comprehensive program is not in place and large losses occur. If an analyst has a copy of the key questions about BI management from this book, arming yourself with sound answers and statistics is a must.

Offering well-developed statistics on gray market losses and counterfeit losses, along with providing remediation plans, will defuse concerns that problems are not being effectively managed. Having a positive program to aggressively maintain brand integrity and product security can have a positive effect on shareholders and consumers. BI programs will extend product life and keep your products alive in the market longer.

Training and Development

BI programs are required for various levels of company operations including:

- Executive
- Marketing and sales
- Administrative
- Manufacturing
- Distribution
- R&D

The Brand or Product Manager

The responsibilities of the brand or product manager range from R&D to market management. The manager must:

- Maintain overall management responsibility for the product.
- Maintain overall product security.
- Oversee all efforts to reduce risks, threats, and attacks.
- Allocate budget.
- Coordinate response and support services.

Training Required

- Brand integrity executive training
- Brand integrity management training

Tools Required

- Incident tracking
- Asset tracking
- Risk and threat analysis
- Monitoring reports
- Audit reports
- Support services
- Response protocols
- Best-practices manual

Staffing

What about the staff required? In companies that have a BI manager who is operating at the company level and is responsible for building a comprehensive program, the definition of success will vary considerably. In most cases where a specific series of BI problems are identified, success is often seen as solving them quickly. When the measure of success is establishing an ongoing BI process to manage future BI problems, success is more elusive. Identifying how much staff is necessary constitutes a major concern.

One manager working on product risk issues within a specific business unit can be viewed as successful if product attacks are lowered as a result of changes to product protection technology. Another manager dealing with gray market losses may be less successful since he or she cannot stop these attacks quickly because of all the changes required to multiple business processes in order to lower product risks. How much staff is required to operate a successful program will vary depending on many of the factors presented throughout this book. One may be too many, whereas twenty may be too few.

Audits, Modifications, and Ongoing Refinements

Regular reviews of program operations and effectiveness are essential to ensure ongoing performance at a high and consistent level. Process audits are a central point for all aspects of BI operations.

Audits   BI system reviews can have both conformance and effectiveness dimensions. Conformance to established policies and standards have the following features:

- All BI programs are subject to review and audit.
- Manufacturing programs will be audited by the general auditor.
- A change of manufacturing management or changes in facility status should include a program review for BI implications.

Specific audit plans should be established to ensure that strategic program objectives are being served by BI activities. Strategic program objectives include:

- Program planning and ongoing refinements. Program planning involves the consolidation of product risk identification, the development of goals and the establishment of appropriate metrics.
  - o Identification of key products and brands.
  - o An understanding of the deals being made.

Effectiveness Issues

The key elements of brand management must be reviewed for value, impact, marketplace protection, and strategic program design and operations. These elements are:

- Control of IP assets
- Verification of representations by clients, customers, vendors, partners, and end users
- Product channel security
- Protection of the information supply chain
- Protection of product margins
- Protection of sensitive information
- Manufacturing security
- Distribution security
- Crisis management plans
- Due diligence process
- Compliance management

- Product protection including:
  - o IP
  - o Patents
  - o Patent pending
  - o Trademarks
  - o Copyrights
  - o Trade secrets
- Identification of gray markets and product diversion
- Counterfeit identification

Identification of Key Product and Brand Assets

To protect what is important to the brand, it is essential to focus on the answers to these questions:

- What is the major product?
- How important is the product to financial goals?
- How important is the product to the company's future?
- What are the future plans for the product?
- What happens if the company loses control of the product?
- Are there any brand or product issues in the marketplace?

Planning

The company business and brand units should complete a strategic BI plan and an annual operating plan (budget) each year, just as they do the budget and business plan. This document describes the long-range planning process and outlines implementation steps for BI. It serves as a reference manual for business units and brands that are new to the company, and it provides suggestions to existing businesses on improving their BI planning.

Each company business is usually responsible for its own long-range planning. Businesses and brands that do not have a strong base of information about their industry, competitive position, and market dynamics usually find a broad-based general planning approach most effective. Businesses that already possess a well-developed base of industry, competitive, and market information and have a clearly defined ongoing business strategy may choose to focus their planning efforts on one or two key BI issues. The long-range BI plan contains:

- An analysis of the competitive and market risk environments
- A statement of long-range goals and objectives

- A description of BI strategies and major programs
- An analysis of risks and trade-offs
- An identification of capital requirements and cash needs
- An identification of future operating assumptions and a most-likely-case financial scenario

BI Planning Guide

Given the increasing importance of BI management to accomplishing long-range goals, this guide includes several suggestions for strengthening this important component of brand management. Establishing and maintaining effective BI planning information is critical. Good decisions and superior performance come from a management team that can make plans and achieve results based upon a shared knowledge base of critical market, competitive, and operating information. (See Figure 10.4.)

FIGURE 10.4   BI Program Development

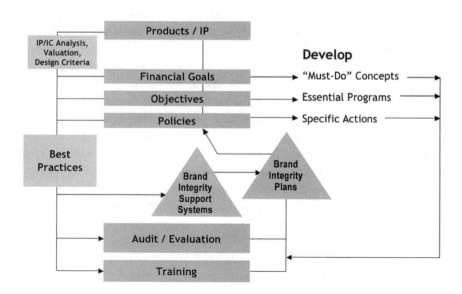

POLICY GUIDE: THE PLANNING PROCESS

The long-range BI planning process can be tailored to meet the needs of each product, brand, or business, provided it meets a corporate requirement for updated plan text and long-range financial projections. The following seven steps describe the general process.

Step 1: Target Setting

The process begins when the executive management meets with sector executives to set BI goals for a specific period, for example, from 2007 through 2012, and to discuss planning issues for each of the business units. The targets should help focus the operating efforts of each business on its fundamental products, brands, problems, or opportunities. These goals will be discussed with the general managers and brand managers and will become primary input to their planning efforts.

Step 2: Preparing for the Planning Meeting

During the planning period, each business will commit some time to long-range BI planning. For many businesses, the plan will evolve from an intensive product protection planning meeting. The goal of these planning meetings will be to discuss long-range product risk issues and options and to achieve management consensus on future strategies for protecting the products and brands. The planning meetings will require preliminary staff work in advance of the meetings.

Preparation for the planning meetings consists of assembling a planning database. A review should be conducted of critical factors affecting the business, its industry and competitors, and potential strategies. The business might assign each product manager responsibility for assembling data on one of the areas or issues to be addressed in the plan. The best place to begin preparation of this database will normally be last year's long-range BI plan. These preliminary planning databases should be circulated among all participants of the planning meeting in advance of the meeting so that a basic set of issues, facts, and information is shared beforehand.

Step 3: The Planning Meeting

Once the BI planning database is assembled, a planning meeting can be held. Participants at a typical planning meeting will:

- Discuss and elaborate on the data collected in the planning database.
- Examine critical factors affecting product and brand risks, including the product's or brand's competitive position, product maturity, competitive activity, and market risks.
- Review current BI performance against past plans.
- Identify emerging problems and opportunities.
- Discuss BI objectives, goals, and issues.
- Identify and evaluate strategic alternatives.
- Recommend a strategy for each product or brand for the next three to five years.
- Outline resource requirements and planning assumptions for implementing the proposed BI strategy.

The actual planning session is usually a two- or three-day meeting. The participants usually include the brand manager, business unit executive, representative from corporate BI or corporate security, and other key BI personnel.

Step 4: Finishing the Plan

The long-range BI plan is a summary of the conclusions of the planning meeting which communicates the strategic plans for the business for the next year.

Step 5: Initial Corporate Review

A corporate BI planning process normally will coordinate preliminary reviews of the business unit BI plans. The plans will be analyzed by corporate BI, security, corporate legal, IT, and other corporate departments, where appropriate. Following this staff review of plans, the senior executives may request discussion of specific issues.

Step 6: Executive Committee Discussions

The general managers and senior executives will discuss their long-range BI plans and address specific BI plan issues. The purpose of these meetings is to discuss the plans and to resolve any remaining planning issues.

Following the executive discussions, the businesses will receive feedback instructing them to implement the strategies as proposed or to modify the plans as instructed.

Step 7: Ongoing Implementation

Monitoring and reviewing long-range BI plans on a continuing basis should be integrated into the normal business routine. A critical component of implementing the strategic and operating plans is usually a part of the budget process. This process transforms the "agreement in principle" from the planning process into a specific decision to implement a BI strategy. The company should review all major BI expenditures to ensure that they comply with the strategic goals of the businesses and also capitalize on the best opportunities faced by the company.

BEST PRACTICES

- Identify key product and brand risks.
- Establish program goals to address identified risks.
- Set up staff and organization resources to manage the process.
- Identify performance metrics to demonstrate financial results.
- Involve all levels of brand and product management in the process.
- Provide executive-level support and leadership for the process.
- Focus policies and programs on product and brand integrity.

DASHBOARD QUESTIONS

1. Are BI plans reviewed during all executive program review meetings?
2. Has brand management established product BI plans?

QUESTIONS THE CEO
SHOULD ASK ABOUT
BI METRICS

You have to ask yourself, "Do you feel lucky?" . . . well do ya?
Dirty Harry

What you use to evaluate brand integrity depends on what is important to the company to show as value received for money spent. Value can be highly quantifiable or less so, depending on whether margin improvement, customer satisfaction, return on investment (ROI), higher-quality service, employee participation, or competitor analysis is the focus. This chapter reviews the 10 things the CEO needs to know about brand integrity metrics—what they are and a bit about the tools available to measure company performance.

10 Questions the CEO Needs to Ask about Brand Integrity Metrics

1. Did we look; did we find?
2. Are the lessons learned from BI incidents being used?
3. How much risk do products and brands have in the market?
4. Can we identify our own products?
5. Can we respond effectively to product or brand attacks?
6. Do we have reliable loss information?
7. Do we have anyone responsible for brand integrity?
8. Do we have brand integrity policies and procedures?
9. Are brand integrity costs justified by risks?
10. How do we compare to other companies?

DEVELOPMENT OF BI PERFORMANCE STANDARDS

The development of performance standards for brand integrity must follow those established for other corporate functions. These standards fall into three categories: *normative, prescriptive,* and *evaluative.* The normative standards are those that set forth a particular behavior or set of objectives that are compatible with those of the CEO or senior corporate management. Prescriptive standards are basically compliance parameters, formulated by senior management and strongly recommended to business units. Evaluative standards are those that are quantitative or judgmental types of statements regarding compliance issues. The brand integrity philosophy and policies that are promoted by senior management are going to determine which of these categories will be emphasized within the company.

Normative

- Designed to stimulate behavior that leads to the attainment of significant well-chosen business goals
- Designed to have aggressive business performance targets (stretch goals) and to organize performance around the target goals that are appropriate for the unit

Prescriptive

- Extend only to those individuals whose duties and responsibilities give them an opportunity to have substantial impact on the achievement of the goals
- Incentive levels fully integrated with compensation and benefits in order to support the strategy
- The size of individual rewards based upon attainment of measurable preestablished goals in support of larger strategic business goals
- Rewards based on unit performance versus targets and individual performance versus individual targets

Evaluative

- Appropriate measurements established for unit and individual performance against strategic objectives
- Brand value measurements established to measure performance against a specific brand or product

Standards of Performance

The various performance standards at each level differ for each part of the life cycle.

R&D

- Lower the product risk rating.
- Reduce IP insurance costs.
- Increase morale.
- Develop tighter controls.
- Produce more lead time in the market.
- Increase competitor lag time after new-product introduction.
- Provide more information on competitor product development.

Manufacturing

- Lower the counterfeit rates.
- Lower the unauthorized production rate.
- Develop better control over the supply chain.
- Lower the production costs for products.
- Develop employee support for the program.

Distribution

- Improve efficiency.
- Lower the losses due to waste, theft, damage, and the like.
- Support JIT.
- Narrow the window of opportunity for loss.
- Identify supply chain issues quickly.

Marketplace

- Obtain better market and competitive information.
- Reduce the number of counterfeit products in the market.
- Reduce the amount of gray market items, aiming for vastly improved margins.
- Reduce the warranty, rebate, and discount fraud rate.

The expected performance standards are different for each stage in the cycle. Some results are financial; others produce operational efficiencies, increase the quality of information, and improve human resources management. Perhaps changing to a direct distribution system rather than

FIGURE 11.1   Improve Controls

Controls Can Be Improved

Global sourcing, supply, and global distribution must have an integrated BI approach

SUPPLY CHAIN OPERATIONS

R&D	Procurement	Manufacture	Packaging	Logistics	Warehouse	Distribution

GLOBAL MARKETS

Points of Entry, Use, and Sale	Secondary Wholesalers/Distributors

using distributors may eliminate problems caused with gray market products or counterfeit products entering your supply chain. You must decide what options are on the table, and use the evaluative method most appropriate.

The bottom-line BI question is: "Is the chase worth the catch?" The answer is not simple, but if any of the following "Do you want to" goals are desired, the answer probably is yes.

- Appear to be a hard target.
- Have better information about internal operations and issues.
- Have better information about markets and competition.
- Improve margins in the market.
- Lower the risk to R&D lead time.
- Lower the risks in shipping and transportation of products.
- Improve controls over the manufacturing process.
- Improve employee and corporate accountability.

EVALUATE RESULTS

Value in BI efforts can be measured in margin recovery, cost avoidance (cost of loss), and improved incident management efficiency, as well as in prevention programs that enhance product and supply chain security. Both quantitative and normative factors can also be used for evaluation of BI effectiveness. Hard and soft analytical factors are both useful measures, depending on corporate requirements. Soft measures such as the following are secondary benefits that have intangible benefits:

- Being more responsive to customer requirements
- Being more competitive
- Supporting better communications
- Providing job enlargement opportunities
- Increasing personal involvement in the business
- Fostering innovation

While less precise than purely financial results, they constitute a significant factor in making BI successful. They must be taken into consideration in any final decisions made using the financial analysis results.

What we don't know very much about at the present time is how to relate product integrity costs to direct tangible benefits. Making a single product more difficult to attack—using, say, holograms or RFID tags—adds cost, but the deterrent value is difficult to measure precisely.

Many corporations use metrics of various types to measure financial and product-related risks. They measure the cost of risk by calculating:

- Return on capital employed (ROC/ROCE)
- Value at risk
- Risk-adjusted return on capital (RAROC)
- Earnings at risk
- Below-target risk
- Probability of ruin
- Expected cost of ruin

Additionally, the corporate security departments of large corporations often apply the following loss-related metrics to product- and brand-related losses:

- Investigative costs relative to recoveries or resolved cases
- Loss incidents on a year-to-year basis
- Dollar recoveries relative to costs
- Gray market losses as a percentage of total sales
- Background investigations relative to pass-fail rates

There are many very measurement-driven organizations where extensive metrics are used to measure the effectiveness of various financial and operational efforts. In those settings, security or brand integrity management using established company metrics is required to ensure that the measures are attuned to corporate strategy. BI must do this to be viewed as a value-added organizational tool capable of delivering services that correlate and align with company strategies such as growth, profitability, and customer market share—linkage to broader corporate goals is key.

Additionally, all capital investments by some large security and BI functions go through an ROI analysis to determine payback and return schedules. Basically, they have the same type of accountability expected of a business unit, but just don't generate revenue.

The use of a P&L-statement type of format to better demonstrate BI value added is not very common, nor are using cost avoidance and recovery types of measures to serve as a revenue equivalent. Likewise, the impact of indirect losses resulting from incidents has not been successfully demonstrated.

It should be anticipated that key business issues of the company would also be a major factor in evaluating BI activities. The following issues are often identified as being of significant concern to senior management:

- Earnings growth
- Revenue growth
- Return on capital
- Earnings consistency
- Expense control or reduction
- Product pricing
- Cost of technology
- Personnel costs
- Compliance costs
- Regulatory costs
- Operating costs
- Shareholder value

Being able to relate BI costs and value to these types of issues is essential. But getting good information about the state of brand integrity in the company can be difficult. Clearly responding to a specific loss situation from gray market margin erosion can return immediate margin improvement. Demonstrating continuing large returns will also be possible until significant amounts of opportunity are removed from sales and marketing processes. It will become harder and harder for BI to prove a negative. After all, how do you demonstrate that gray market trafficking did not take place because tight controls are in place? It will look like you are doing "good business," but unless continued vigilance is built into the processes using BI principles, you are bound to revert to just "doing business."

☑ *Question 1. Did we look; did we find?* You need good empirical data about what is going on related to product and brand integrity, but if you don't ask the question, nobody is going to volunteer the information. Making BI a key question on business reviews will raise its visibility and start the information flow coming. In many companies, there are pockets of information about losses and product-related problems. This information often does not surface at an executive level, as it is considered an operating problem and handled without significant reporting or oversight. *Ask for it.* The information could be very significant, as small losses become big very quickly.

Silos of Data and Experience

Product problems and solutions are found in various operating units, or they may be specific to a high-risk brand. Often this information does not get transferred to other parts of the company, as it is not considered worth sharing or is viewed as a problem that is not discussed outside the business unit because it does not affect immediate earnings targets, and so on. Also, these problems, and often their solutions, are not shared because they are viewed as a shortcoming of business unit management and are "fixed and forgotten."

Getting the Information

The Supply Chain Working Group, the Brand Integrity Committee, the Gray Market Study Committee—these are all names of groups within companies whose responsibility is to collect information, evaluate programs, and develop solutions for brand integrity concerns. These groups often develop solid loss information and make recommendations for organizational changes to better manage BI issues. Unfortunately, except in some organizations that have this type of group at the enterprise level, information and solutions tend to remain in a single business unit.

Hire a Consultant

Several consultant firms have expertise in assessing brand integrity and brand integrity and product attack problems. Using the information they collect from managing a product-related crisis, conducting an investigation, or gathering internally generated but previously uncirculated data, the consultants can provide you with a valuable report.

Interview Process

Several techniques, such as the Six Sigma voice-of-the-customer process for issue identification, can be effectively used for developing baseline data on brand and product problems that exist in the company. An initial assessment survey followed by a root cause analysis often will produce a comprehensive report.

☑ *Question 2. Are the lessons learned from BI incidents being applied?* All too often, corporate "memory" of incidents and how they were handled is lost as executives move on to other positions or other companies. The experience in one business is often not passed on to other parts of the company. A "good crisis" should not be wasted, but shared.

Every company should have a process for the collection, evaluation, and use of BI lessons learned. Yet very few large organizations have a process for sharing this type of experience, as it is localized within a business, security, legal, or audit department.

Establish a Process

Capturing lessons learned from product attacks can be accomplished by the corporate brand integrity department, security department, legal department, operations executives, or brand management. What is needed is an incident reporting system that specifically asks for product-related losses and attacks to be reported to a central place in the company. We have found that many organizations collect information about product attacks in the business where they occur, but nobody ever asks for the data outside of that business, or the business does not want to share its problems for fear of looking bad.

Get an incident reporting system in place. Issue a statement that it's OK to have the problem . . . the first time. After that, the lessons learned should be applied and the losses prevented. Several incident reporting and data collecting systems are available for BI. Choose one, and have it used throughout the company.

FIGURE 11.2   Dashboard Questions

	Region			
	Latin America	North America	Asia-Pacific	European Union
Number of counterfeit products identified				
Number of counterfeit investigations				
Percent of compliance audits completed				
Percent of distributors' compliance audits completed				

Roll Up the Data

Establishing a reporting and analytical process is the next step. Selecting the criteria for what, when, and how to report depends on what you decide is important to know. At a minimum, the information in Figure 11.2 should be included in the list.

☑ *Question 3. How much risk do products and brands have in the market?*   There are different risks associated with products as they move from R&D to maturity in the market. At the various stages of managing the products, the risks change and need to be measured so that cost-effective protection can be used. These tools include:

- Product risk analysis
- Product arbitrage risk
- Supply chain risk analysis
- New-product launch analysis

FIGURE 11.3   Life Cycle and Exposure Chart

Tool/Stage	R&D	Manufacturing	Distribution	Marketplace
Product risk	X	X		
Product arbitrage			X	X
Supply chain risk		X	X	X
New-product launch	X	X	X	X

Figure 11.3 shows how each is used in a specific stage of the product life cycle and market exposure.

Product Risk Analysis

Each product has an intrinsic risk associated with it in various stages of development and manufacturing. In R&D the risk of intellectual property theft before, during, and after development and introduction is high and the potential losses catastrophic. The risk of these types of losses declines as the product moves into manufacturing and then into the marketplace. While counterfeit and copy risks are always present and potentially significant, their potential dollar losses drop over time as revenues are received from product sales. Product risk can be measured if appropriate values can be determined for sales and losses caused by copy products entering the market soon after the real product is introduced. These losses can be ever more damaging if copy products are introduced in key markets before or simultaneously with the release of the real product. Once these financial measures can be determined, the risk of loss can be assessed against the intrinsic and variable features of the product. Changes can then be made to the way the product is designed or controlled during the critical stages of development and manufacturing. For products with significant IP or where trade secrets are to be employed over the life of the product, these changes in controls may extend forever.

Product Arbitrage Risk

Pricing products for different markets is a fact of global product management. Being able to monitor sales and leakage of products from low-cost to high-cost markets is increasingly important to maintain the stability of pricing around the world. The susceptibility of products to price arbitrage is a function of pricing, availability, distribution systems, and marketing. If marketing executives know market capacities and are selling more than expected, there may well be an arbitrage problem developing in another part of the world. Tracking products into and out of markets is important. What is happening with arbitrage in a specific market affects global pricing. Products flow from low- to high-price markets.

Products flow from low-price special orders to any market, but mainly to high-price ones. If an analysis can be done to show which countries pose the highest risk for arbitrage, special controls can be used to lower the risk for these products (see Figure 11.4).

An arbitrage opportunity for a single product can be defined in several ways: "buy low . . . sell high"; find cheap prices in Hong Kong and sell for a profit in California; find an opportunity to buy in volume and sell smaller amounts for a profit after all associated expenses, taxes, customs duties, transportation, and the like are deducted. In other words, product arbitrage is a function of an expected revenue opportunity net of associated fixed costs and associated potential risks, such as violation of criminal laws, exchange-rate fluctuations, and unexpected costs for the deal.

FIGURE 11.4 Product Protection Chart

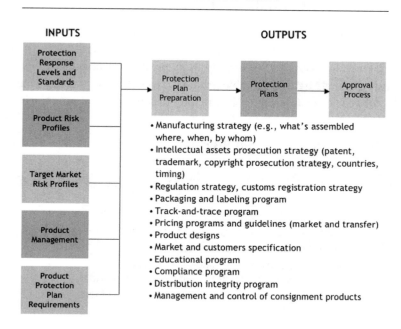

There needs to be a potential payoff between countries or regions for the product to flow from low-cost to high-cost areas. This difference can be as little as a few percentage points to make it worthwhile.

Supply Chain Risk Analysis

Who is touching your products before they get to the customer? Controlling the supply chain is essential to product integrity. Managing customer and marketplace expectations is a function of product movement. Since every product is global, managing it must be the same. Controlling the flow of products within the company from manufacturing to customer prevents counterfeit goods from being sold as legitimate through company channels. It also lowers the risk of gray market products being sold and counterfeit products being introduced into gray channels. Control over third-party manufacturers, subcontractors, and material suppliers, as well as plant locations, lowers political, criminal, and environmental risks. Several case studies of supply chain risk analysis have been presented in this book. Any of them can be used to begin collecting information to assess these product risks. Figure 11.5 describes the various points of risk along the manufacturing supply chain.

New-Product Launch Analysis

Knowing where and when to launch a new product is essential to successful market penetration and acceptance. Several of the risk tools already presented should be used to develop basic profiles on financial value and intrinsic product risk. If a valuable product is to be introduced in a country with high risk for counterfeit or gray market products, how should the intro-

FIGURE 11.5   Supply Chain Risk

Secure Supply Chain Looks Like

- Legitimate product traceability from sourcing through sale
- Information transparency across supply chain
- Verified trade-partner performance
- Market awareness that promotes early detection of counterfeits, counterfeiters, and contract violations
- Data to drive additional regulatory and enforcement actions

duction be handled? Should the product be introduced there first, or should it be introduced after successful introduction elsewhere?

Some countries require that manufacturing of localized products take place internally. Is this something that should be considered a product risk? What happens if a new product is counterfeited immediately after introduction and is sold in other global markets? Is this a risk that is acceptable? Can special controls be established and maintained before, during, and immediately after the launch of a new product in a high-risk country? Establishing a process for analyzing risk using the various tools presented is essential.

New-Facility Preparedness

Another key risk for product integrity is the location of and control over manufacturing facilities. Several examples of manufacturing plant problems have been presented in this book. It is important to establish a process for ensuring that new facilities can protect the IP, processes, and know-how wherever the plants are located at a level of at least that required to maintain the integrity of the products to be produced there. Locating a plant to produce a new high-value product in a high-risk country may not be the best decision even if labor costs are low (see Figure 11.6). The only way to tell for sure is to conduct an analysis using one of the various case study tools previously presented.

FIGURE 11.6   Sourcing Cannot Be Overlooked

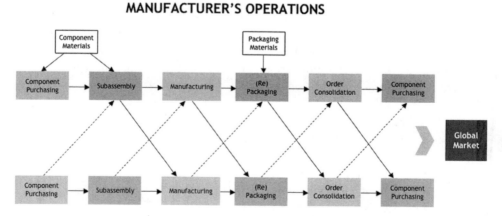

☑ *Question 4. Can we identify our own products?* There have been several case studies presented in which companies could not take legal action against counterfeiters because they could not properly identify or authenticate their own products. One of the most basic protective things that a company can do is establish a process for positive identification of each key product. There are two basic ways to do this:

- Use a legal filing index.
- Use forensic identification tools.

Legal Filing Index

As discussed previously, establishing legal ownership rights is a critical first step in any brand integrity program. This is building the fence around what you own, and it displays your right of ownership to everyone in the world. Additionally, ownership is often commercialized by licensing technology that can be transferred to joint ventures, third-party manufacturers, and so on. Patents, trademarks, and copyrights are also registered in foreign jurisdictions to increase global protection over intellectual property rights. Decisions about when, where, and how to make these filings are the subject of numerous texts and articles. For brand integrity purposes however, it is essential for risk planning and product management to know what is filed and where. Without owning a key trademark in a key country, a market can be lost or a patent infringement cannot be pursued. As the commercial says, "What's in your wallet?©"

Forensic Identification

Can every key product be identified, or does a standard exist to prove that a counterfeit product is really counterfeit? Multiple case studies have been presented throughout this book in which products could not be adequately identified as either real or not genuine. Let's look at the minimum types of identification tools that are essential:

- Size and shape
- Manufacturing techniques and processes
- Materials
- Colors and pigments
- Chemical composition
- Source codes
- Electrical designs

Each product should have a standard against which suspected counterfeit and nongenuine products can be evaluated in a timely manner. Counterfeit cases often demand that forensic examination of the suspected products be conducted by third-party laboratories or by company laboratories using standardized procedures. If a suspected product uses the same materials and processes and has the same chemical composition and colors as the original, how do you positively determine that it is not genuine? If you can only test the chemical components of a product in the plant in which it was produced and only when that product is in a production cycle, how can you take effective legal actions against a counterfeiter? In short, you cannot.

It is essential that for both quality control and product integrity purposes a comprehensive standardized process be established for product identification. If product compositions vary because of third-party manufacturers or the supply chain inconsistence of suppliers, these variations need to be a part of product identification standards or the supply chain needs to be cleaned up to eliminate these variances. If materials are changed for low-cost manufacturing that vary from the standard product, this needs to be noted. In short, everything in every product you manufacture and sell should be identifiable by you and be the same anywhere in the world. If it is not, you may not own it!

Quality control, manufacturing, R&D, and the returns department may have the product descriptions used to verify authentic products and any hidden markers, identification marks, etc., used on your products. A single point of contact, information collection, and final verification is essential for crisis management and the day-to-day separation of good from bad products.

The same issues hold true for packaging and shipping containers. Various security measures, such as holograms, specialized inks, and packaging materials, are used to differentiate products and make counterfeiting more difficult. While useful, they all can be copied at the expense of your products and your customers. Having identification procedures such as those used by Pfizer and Johnson & Johnson on Web sites for quick, positive authentication is essential for high-risk products with patient safety concerns. A system tailored to specific company requirements is crucial.

☑ *Question 5. Can we respond effectively to product or brand attacks?* Remember, a brand is a promise to the customer. Making sure that the promise is fulfilled is a key component of responding quickly to attacks against products. Exxon and Johnson & Johnson are often considered the two ends of a spectrum in how to respond to a crisis. In the Tylenol case, J&J responded quickly and took decisive action to recall the affected product. In the *Valdez* oil spill in Alaska, Exxon was reportedly slow to respond. Tylenol regained its customers, while Exxon is still remembered for the ecological problems resulting from the spill.

Identifying the Important Things to Protect

The first and most important thing to determine is a brand's exposure to various corporate and operating risks. Once you begin, you can then develop an index to brand risk based on the various categories within the company. A self-inspection report for senior executives can be provided (an audit committee of the board?) that will give them some sense of risk or opportunities to get ahead of potential problems and possibly change organizational approaches.

In order to get a baseline of known or reported risks to your products in the global marketplace, research is required. It is necessary to collect all information related to brand integrity issues during the past two years. This will involve some comprehensive research using all sources available, including, but not limited to, the following:

- All databases
- All legal actions, citations, filings, decisions, new legislation (background to the act, etc.)
- All newspaper articles in the United States, Asia, and Europe
- Magazine stories
- Internal incident and case files
- Other company information, use of other sources, and so on

You will need to collect information about the frequency of incidents, number of incidents, types of incidents, losses in dollar amounts and units taken, and the like, in the following categories of losses:

- Trade secrets
- Patent pending
- Infringements
- Counterfeiting
- Clones
- Unauthorized production
- Gray market
- Distribution theft
- Product extortion

- Abuse of discounts and rebate programs
- Social awareness problems (child labor, sweatshop conditions, etc.)
- Brand reputation problems (channel problems causing contamination, etc.)

The purpose of this project will be to produce an initial report and possibly yearly updates to collect information about attacks against brands and products in the global marketplace. The report also should identify the various groups, associations, coalitions, and so on, providing services to deal with each category of risk. Once the baseline data are identified and analyzed, the current risk profile in each category of product or brand can be established. The research approach will provide you with objective data that can be used to calculate various risk formulas and that can be applied to program development criteria. Once this "identification and analysis of the problem" is completed, the actual work of structuring the program begins.

Several techniques can be used for risk identification. The three most common are objective risk evaluation, subjective evaluation, and calculated evaluation. Product and brand risks are often cast in terms of their operational, fiscal, reputation, and strategic characteristics and are analyzed using this set of factors. Subjective risks such as patterns and profiles, intuition, statistical measures, and group consensus are distinguished from objective risks that include such things as trends and historical and calculated statistical data.

A very common method of developing a BI program and structuring implementation is the use of a task force or working group. The activities of such a group normally consist of the following:

- Developing assumptions regarding the business environment, product developments, evolving problems, and the need for and value of brand and assets controls
- Describing the organizational assets to be safeguarded
- Identifying potential sources of danger and risk
- Determining the types of losses that are possible and the expected likelihood of each
- Assessing the impact of losses upon brand and product lines
- Devising alternative prevention, detection, and recovery mechanisms for each significant exposure area
- Providing an overview of relevant control practices utilized by comparable organizations (benchmarking)

- Identifying special control problems faced by the product in its various business exposures
- Making a valuation of the strengths and weaknesses of existing control systems within the company
- Recommending actions, policies, control objectives, and expected costs and benefits

Crisis Management Plans Developed and Tested

An incident management process is essential to handle all types of product-related problems. From a Bhopal-type disaster to a product safety recall, a developed and tested process is required to marshal the necessary resources. What is the company policy for handling a crisis, who needs to be involved, and how should it be handled? These are the key elements of a plan. There are literally hundreds of variations of approaches, but all have a common theme. Manage the crisis quickly, collect good information about what has happened, determine what needs to be done, manage this specific incident, correct the problem underlying the incident, resume operations quickly, communicate openly and quickly with the public, and take responsibility for managing the problem. Basically, admit the problem, fix it, and move on. The "deny everything, admit nothing, make counterallegations" approach is to be avoided.

A procedure for testing the process by conducting simulation exercises with key crisis team members is essential. Crisis plans need to be updated as new products, operations, or facilities are added to company operations and responsibilities. A sample crisis management plan may look something like the following, previously addressed in Chapter 9.

Dealing with Product Extortion

1. Respond to the specific situation, assess the damage, and contain the problem.
2. Establish a crisis center and staff.
3. Contact the K&R insurance carrier immediately.
4. Activate the crisis management committee.
5. Establish contact with the appropriate governmental agencies.
6. Manage the incident following established internal policies.
7. Use an active PR program as the situation dictates.
8. Communicate with the public as required for public safety and image enhancement.

Cloned Products

1. Start a market surveillance program.
2. Perform audits on computer systems to determine if information has been compromised.
3. File and enforce patents.
4. Conduct test buys of competitor products for reverse engineering.
5. Perform awareness education and training.
6. Review policies and procedures.
7. Perform compliance reviews.
8. Conduct manufacturing site inspections.
9. Require signed contracts with all contract manufacturers and subcontractors.

☑ *Question 6. Do we have reliable loss information?*   How bad are the problems with our products? Which ones are under attack? Why do these problems exist? Do we have a system that collects data about everything that is happening related to our products and brands? These are the key questions that a loss information system should provide answers to for the CEO.

Product incident handling on a day-to-day basis requires a robust system for collecting information and managing it. Such systems have several common elements: what incidents are covered, how to report them and to whom, what actions to take, what to say about the incidents, when to call in law enforcement, and so on.

It should be noted that incident management involves numerous parts of the organization and possibly multiple outside vendors or public agencies.

☑ *Question 7. Do we have anyone responsible for brand integrity?*   Whom do I go to for BI information? Who is responsible for managing BI issues in the company? These are the key questions to ask. If you cannot think of the person charged with this responsibility or if there is no one, you have a problem. There are probably one or two people in the company who know the organizational history of brand- and product-related problems or who are the ones that executives go to when these problems arise. It may be an auditor, lawyer, security manager, or brand manager who gets this call. The person may or may not have the files and statistics about what has been happening in the company or in your industry.

☑ *Question 8. Do we have brand integrity policies and procedures?*   Policies and procedures are a function of executive leadership related to an area of management concern. "No concern" equates to no policy, standards, guidelines, or procedures. How the CEO views brand integrity is understood by all senior management. If it is a matter of personal concern and integrated into management reviews, it will become a part of the organization's approach to brand and product management. If not, BI issues will be considered either a necessary evil to be handled on a case-by-case basis or an occasional problem to be solved.

Assuming that BI is viewed as a brand-enhancing opportunity, policies will be developed to incorporate it into daily management of the business. The dashboard questions for the CEO will come from the following information sources:

- Incident tracking
- Brand and product assets tracking
- Risk and threat analysis
- Monitoring reports
- Audit reports
- Response protocols
- Best-practices manual

☑ *Question 9. Are brand integrity costs justified by risks?*   If brand integrity is built into the everyday operations of the company, then minimal additional costs will be present. Clearly, the start-up of an organizational analysis, an internal committee initiative, additional staff to manage the process, and so on, will all have costs. They should be treated as any other management restructuring that will yield a financial return to the company. Remember that all companies have current fixed BI costs within their operating systems at the present time. These costs include:

- New-product introductions
- Supply chain controls
- Legal defenses
- Product design and security
- Marketing strategies
- Distribution strategies
- Market surveillance
- Consumer education

A BI program may shift some of these costs, eliminate some of them, and add others, depending on what a comprehensive program might look like for your company. Most likely, after start-up costs, day-to-day operating costs will be offset by BI revenues.

Develop a cost-benefit analysis that conforms to others used in the company, and apply it to the anticipated margin recoveries and loss avoidance that will result from BI risk-reduction and anticounterfeiting programs. The net result of the changes implemented should result in an increase in the sales of real products. There is always an opportunity for recovery and loss avoidance if creative BI planning and programs are employed. The real question is how much can you recover or how much risk can you avoid by applying various approaches to BI.

Case Study

One major company that recently established a BI department analyzed its BI exposure situation and estimated that making the investment in BI would yield the same return as building an additional manufacturing facility that would generate $1 billion in revenue. While not all businesses could expect this type of revenue or margin recovery from BI activities, a significant return is probable.

Margin Improvement

Margin rates are determined using different factors in each company. The actual rate is usually a function of the anticipated or required revenue to be derived from the sale of a particular product during a specific period of time. Anything that adversely affects this rate needs to be reviewed and rectified. The use of audits to measure margins over time is important, and the application of BI concepts to factors surrounding "making the deal" and the fate of products in the market can dramatically impact margins.

What metrics should be used to monitor and analyze worldwide markets? It really depends on the current pricing systems and policies in place. How are they set and monitored for compliance? Who influences them, and are they consistently applied across all operations? Furthermore, are all transactions reported and all data captured, and are the data shared by all affected parties in the company?

If you know the products that are at risk, specific metrics can be established that may include:

- Current company metrics
- Best practices from your industry
- External data
- Internal data
- Price-volume analysis, both econometric and probabilistic

These data can then be used to establish policies to control how deals are made and how pricing is established in specific markets. The dashboard questions for margin maintenance will evolve from this process.

☑ *Question 10. How do we compare to other companies?* "When you're trying something new, the fewer people who know about it, the better" is an old cowboy philosophy. Some executives feel that establishing a BI function sends the wrong message to their customers—the message being "We have a problem with our products" rather than a positive response of "We want to make sure that you get our products in the highest of quality." Johnson & Johnson's Medical Devices & Diagnostics Company, in setting up its World Wide Brand Integrity Department, addressed this concern head-on by the tone it used in its mission statement: "The right product to the right customer at the right price, at the right time, over time." No other companies in its industry had a dedicated BI function, but other companies in other industries did. J&J's Medical Devices & Diagnostics compared the issues and the organizational solutions and determined that a dedicated corporate function was right for its needs and those of its customers.

So how do you compare to other companies? Do your homework and assess your needs, the internal resources available to manage them, and the way you deal with them going forward. Your baseline may be different from that of other companies. Your vision of risk, threat, safety improvements, supply chain security, and revenue enhancement should set the benchmarks to be measured against, not what others might be doing.

INDEX

ABOUT THE AUTHORS

Since 1965, Rich and Penny Post have lived and worked together around the world. This collaboration began at Michigan State University and took them to the CIA and then back to academia at the University of Wisconsin, where Rich chaired the Criminal Justice Program. They moved on to consulting and industry, with Rich serving as Director of Security and Political Risk for BF Goodrich and American Can. Rich participated in the restructuring of the American Can Company and received an early retirement in 1985. Rich and Penny then started a consulting business and moved to Hong Kong with Kroll Associates to start up and manage a joint venture with Jardine Matheson & Co. that provided security and investigative services in Asia.

Choosing to stay in Asia rather than transfer to Europe in 1990, Penny and Rich started Post & Associates and opened offices across Asia. They moved the headquarters of the company to Phoenix at the time of the turnover to China and subsequently sold the company, then called Brand Protection Associates, LLC, to Ernst & Young in 2004.

Over the years they have worked on hundreds of sensitive investigations, crisis management situations, and trade secret thefts around the world, concentrating on problem solving in Asia. The majority of their clients are Fortune 100 companies and major E.U. clients, as well as law firms and governments. Since 1999, they have dealt exclusively with brand, product, and information theft problems for high-tech clients.

This is their first coauthored text, but Penny has edited all of Rich's previous ten books on security management and two books for the *Economist* on strategic design for Asia-Pacific business.

Rich has a B.S., M.S., and Ph.D. and attended the Cornell Executive Development Program. He is a Certified Protection Professional (CPP). Penny holds a B.A. in International Affairs and studied Cantonese at the Yale in Asia intensive language program at Chinese University, Hong Kong. She is fluent in Cantonese. Rich and Penny live in Paradise Valley, Arizona. They can be reached at info@globalbrandintegrity.com.